SAGGISTICA 21

After Identity

After Identity
Migration, Critique, Italian American Culture

Peter Carravetta

BORDIGHERA PRESS

Library of Congress Control Number: 2016960636

COVER ART:
"GEOGRAPHY" BY CONSTANTINO BRUMIDI,
PHOTOGRAPHIC CREDIT ARCHITECT OF THE CAPITOL

ILLUSTRATIONS:
COPYRIGHT BY ROBERT CIMBALO, USED WITH PERMISSION

THIS BOOK HAS BEEN MADE POSSIBLE THANKS TO A CONTRIBUTION BY THE
ALFONSE M. D'AMATO CHAIR IN ITALIAN AND ITALIAN AMERICAN STUDIES
AT STONY BROOK UNIVERSITY, NY.

© 2017 by Peter Carravetta

All rights reserved. Parts of this book may be reprinted only by written permission from the author, and may not be reproduced for publication in book, magazine, or electronic media of any kind, except for purposes of literary reviews by critics.

Printed in the United States.

Published by
BORDIGHERA PRESS
John D. Calandra Italian American Institute
25 West 43rd Street, 17th Floor
New York, NY 10036

SAGGISTICA 21
ISBN 978-1-59954-072-6

TABLE OF CONTENTS

Preface (ix)

Acknowledgements (xv)

INTRODUCTION
Existence, Migration, History (3)

PART ONE
Theoretical and Historical Contexts

One: Con/Texts Before the Journeys: Migration, Narration, and Historical Identities (41)

Two: Dabblers, Small Fry, Canon Fodder: Problems and Perspectives in Italian American Literary History (79)

Three: The Silence of the Subalterns: Contact, Conflict, Consolidation during the First Wave (1880s-1913) (107)

PART TWO
Geography of Identity through Literature

Four: Places, Processes, Positions in Italian American Poetry and Poetics (143)

Five: Anthony Valerio and the Refashioning of an American Idol (167)

Six: Naming Identity in the Poetry of Maria Mazziotti Gillan (177)

Seven: The Historical Poetics of Robert Viscusi (195)

CONCLUSIONS
For a Topological Critique of Italian American Culture (223)

Bibliography (245)

Index of Names (271)

For Robert Viscusi, Anthony Tamburri, John Paul Russo
critics, teachers, friends

Quando la nova gente alzò la fronte
Vèr noi, dicendo a noi: "Se voi sapete,
Mostratene la via di gire al monte."

Purg. II, 58-60

Preface

The allegory of Geography on the cover painted by Italian exile Constantino Brumidi in the Capitol in 1858 (a lunette in the Lyndon B. Johnson room, formerly the Senate Library) suggests that even pictorial representations of social history are basically palimpsests marked for location, temporality, and inevitably by re-interpretation. Geography is looking to her right at a map featuring "the new world," as if invited to reconsider whether it confirms what was already on the globe to her left, a gesture that would fit in with an early XVI century iconography, when the likes of Amerigo Vespucci and Giovanni da Verrazzano were drawing new coastlines and soon made globes unusable for navigation purposes. However, though trained in classical painting in Rome and having worked at the Vatican before fleeing the failed 1848 revolution to the United States, Brumidi adds to his glorification of the Americas not just the by then over three-century-old myth of origin of his adopted country, but the actuality of time and place in which he was painting, the spirit that, notwithstanding the drums of impending civil war, would inform the great Westward expansion. Notice in fact that the angel on her left is holding a steam locomotive, the iron horse whose tracks at the time were furrowing the land on the backs of immigrants and minorities, becoming the glory of transportation, commerce, and banking moguls who amassed great wealth with these vital arteries that soon linked coast to coast. In the contested terrain of social and cultural interpretation, whether we are dealing with a painting, a performance, or a written text, there needs be a convergence of methodologies and ideologies in order better to focus upon and probe an elusive construct, a layered product that embodies instances of languages, memories, emotions, and politics.

The studies and essays gathered within these covers have been written over a period of twenty years, nearly always prompted by a conference, a book project, or an invited lecture. The links they try to establish between academic disciplines and cultural domains required continued effort to review and rethink the very assumptions of what we consider a stable cultural marker, as well as impose revision of the tools of analysis deployed. The chapters are thus meant to be read at least on two levels at the same time. First, they bear textual witness to an uneven, often conflicted personal journey into an amorphous field called Italian American Studies. And, second, and perhaps as a consequence of the first level, they are typically, and technically, of an *exploratory nature,* and turn out to ask more critical questions than they can possibly answer. For in analyzing different nooks and sites of Italian American culture, these writings seek and attempt to enlarge the scope of a criticism which must perforce question canons, mainstream cultural politics and, most importantly, go beyond the standard knee-jerk denunciation of cultural stereotypes or the iteration of a long denied cultural credibility.

Among the aims of this collection there is the attempt at a critical reconfiguration of the rhetoric of identity, and the first attempt slowly to construct a conceptual map which would characterize Italian American culture in terms of newer, multilayered and broader categories. Some of the key terms/concepts discussed in these pages that the reader will encounter are: *belonging and membership, polycentric consciousness, mediascapes, forms of translation, hybridity, strategic marginality, inventions of the past* and *the defusing of nationalistic mythologies.* Permeating these perspectives is the question of the *migrant* and the relevance of *migration* in general in shaping cultural identities or specific communities. Indeed, it will be argued that migration is the starting point, but by definition an unstable entity, not quite an axiom. The overall organization of this book will of necessity have a rhyzomatic nature, as themes and events appear and reappear at different junctures in the chapters, and some questions asked earlier will elicit a response pages or chapters later, or recur in a different key.

Italian American studies has grown into a full-fledged academic discipline in the past quarter of a century, and has drawn on the expertise of dedicated scholars from a number of different disciplines, from demography to folklore, from semiotics to cultural history, from gender and race studies to political analysis, from cinema to poetics to music and sports. In the papers that follow, I have touched upon several of these fields but mainly in the guise of an introduction, a problematic reference, or as *exempla*; other times the topics serve to link other and not necessarily Italian American issues, once again signaling possible paths for me and hopefully for younger scholars to pursue in depth in the future.

Of the three areas of investigation contained in the subtitle, the second, the question of interpretation, also looms large as well. Critique is also metacritique, an unceasing conscious retooling and refashioning of the means and methods of inquiry, crucial insofar as topics such as migration, identity and cultural politics constantly challenge any assertion or conclusion. In this sense the reader will find that I draw on theories and vocabularies of varied provenance, from hermeneutics proper to literary analysis, from sociology to anthropology, always essaying to elucidate a question with phenomenological clarity.

Nevertheless, in general, and retrospectively, a few hypotheses have guided me during these years. The critical task has periodically but persistently returned to one cluster of problems that go under the aegis of *cultural identity*. I believe it is high time we stop looking at Italian American culture in terms of a no longer tenable notion of identity when its very designation signals an embedded and tearing duality that is time and place bound and, as such, subject to specific dynamics that emerge, assert themselves, and then must change in some guise as newer or alternative and broader palimpsests are set in motion. As some of the earlier chapters make patent, not enough reflection has been focused on the question of how someone – especially if an artist, or a writer, or a public persona — can identify as being *both*, an American *and* an Italian, without confronting the thus revealed possibility that identity is a construct of multiple elements, all critically slippery, all historically contingent and multipronged, and perhaps constituting, deploying a post-modern moniker, *a plurality of discourses in constant conflict and exchange*. Identity has no contours, it is fluid, amoebic, viscous.

Which idea of identity one accepts and parleys in a heterological social reality betrays from the start a political stance, and the assumptions it rests upon. The title *After Identity* wants to foreground this double movement: an attempt to draw up some maps of identity, chasing it, as it were, first, in literary texts – which make up the second part of the book; and then in the historic continuum, which connotes the chapters of the first part. At the same time there are clear attempts to go beyond its monolithic presence in recent scholarship, leave behind its holistic, centering, neatly defined semiotic, and the façades that get tossed about without a more complex, problematic and timely content. As we will see, each horn of the dilemma is itself a palimpsest rolled into a maneuverable token for immanent validation but with little transcendent or trans-cultural usefulness. In brief, ethnic identity is found to be constituted by a cluster of different and not always coherent (sub)identities, some of which have little to do with nations and languages and much with politics and power.

Among the claims advanced in this book the reader will find: 1. That we opt for a *critique of margins* and of interrelations *across* identity-markers; this means situating the critical act in a locus where it can see both sides of any given question but can never make a claim to totality or comprehensiveness. 2. That we essay to interpret the Italian American experience as eminently suited to serve as a herm at the interstice where conflicting rhetorics of class, power, aggression and cultural distortion can be analyzed in their constitutive even if at times not so reassuring elements. Finally, 3., as a critique of margins is implicitly a questioning of boundaries, of limits, of disciplines, then we should devise a topology (sketched in the Conclusion) that allows us to explore and chart sites of negotiation and power as manifested in the experience of the transit, of the crossing, and the entering and exiting from situations which are eminently political. Here ethnic studies in general, and Italian American studies in particular, ought to spend a great deal more energy in revisiting and re-contextualizing for the 21st century the issue of migration, once again, *across* states, classes, professions, forms of knowledge, genders, ideologies, styles of expression. Migration is the *de facto* enabling trope of all Americans, hyphenated or not, stirring that "being on the road" perturbation that pricks at the reassurances of rootedness and unitary identity and, ultimately, gnaws at the very core of all three master discourses, that of America, that of Italy/Europe, and most pointedly that of the offspring squashed in-between, Italian America.

ACKNOWLEDGEMENTS

Almost all of the chapters have appeared in some form as articles or reviews in journals, or as contributions to anthologies. I have made only minimal revisions, mostly stylistic improvements, and often adding in square brackets necessary references to more recent materials.

Introduction, originally titled "Migration, History and Existence," appeared first in Vangelis Kyriakopoulos, ed., *Migrants and Refugees* (Olympia IV: Human Rights in the 21st Century), (Athens: Komotini, 2004): 19-50. [Shorter Italian version, "Migrazione, storia, esistenza, " *Nuova Prosa* (Milano), No. 50, 2009:69-104]. Slightly modified here.

Chapter One, "Con/Texts Before the Journeys: Migration, Narration, Historical Identities," in *L'Esilio come Certezza*, ed. by Andrea Ciccarelli and Paolo A. Giordano. West Lafayette, IN: Bordighera, 1998: 246-283;

Chapter Two, "Dabblers, Small Fry, Canon Fodder: Problems and Perspectives in Italian American Literary History," in *RLA Romance Languages Annual*, Purdue University, vol. VII (1997): 37-55.

Chapter Three, Previously unpublished, slightly modified version appears in the critical anthology edited by Stan Pugliese and William Connelly, *The Routledge History of Italian Americans* (New York: Routledge, forthcoming).

Chapter Four, "Places, Processes, Perspectives in Italian American Poetry and Poetics," in *Through the Looking Glass: Italian and Italian American Images in the Media*, ed. by Mary Jo Bona and Anthony Tamburri, Staten Island: AIHA, 1996: 149-73.

Chapter Five, Review article of Anthony Valerio, *Valentino and the Great Italians* (Guernica, 1994) in DIFFERENTIA No. 6/7 (Spring/Autumn 1994): 347-54.

Chapter Six, "Naming Identity in the Poetry of Maria Mazziotti Gillan," in *Estudios de la mujer*, III (Universidad Complutense), 1998: 1-23.

Chapter Seven, made up of two separate articles: "Figuras of Cultural Recognition: A Reading of Robert Viscusi's *Astoria*," *MELUS*, 23, 3 (Fall 1999): 141-154; and "The Other Columbiad" in *DIFFERENTIA*, No. 6/7 (Spring/Autumn 1994): 311-20.

Conclusion, Presented first as a paper titled: "Theory-Work: Dialogizing Italian American Studies," at conference *For a Dangerous Pedagogy*, Hofstra/Columbia/NYU, April 14-17, 2010, and greatly expanded.

I would like to thank the editors and publishers of the journals and books in which these chapters first appeared for their permission to reprint. In particular, I would also like to thank the editors of Bordighera Press, Fred Gardaphé, Paolo Giordano, and Anthony Julian Tamburri, for accepting to publish my work. A note of appreciation goes to Lisa Cicchetti for preparing the cover, Nicholas Grosso for the copy-editing, and Soren Whited for the Index of Names.

ILLUSTRATIONS. The black and white drawings are by Robert Cimbalo; published here with his written permission. Copyright of the artist. I would like to thank Cimbalo for allowing me to reproduce them. No further reproduction in any media is permitted without written authorization by the artist.

Pg. 38: "You the other one" (9 ½" h, 7 ¾" w)
Pg. 140: "Playing the part" (9 ½" h, 6 5/8" w)
Pg. 176: "Beast of Burden" (9 1/8" h, 6 ½" w)
Pg. 194: "Uniform makes the man (9 ½" h, 6 ¾" w)
Pg. 244: "Tumblers" (8 ½"h, 7" w)

For further information about Cimbalo's work, see robertcimbalo.net

After Identity

Migration, Critique, Italian American Culture

Introduction

Migration, Existence, History[*]

> *Le migrant, loin d'être l'image archaïque d'une phase révolu d'accumulation capitaliste, loin d'être cette entrave à la souveraineté des États-nations, est l'avenir du monde.*[1]
>
> — Bertrand Badie

1. The Field

This intervention focuses on the nature, history, and politics of migration. I will of necessity move from the broadest philosophical and historical perspective, to concrete and particular examples drawn from our present situation at the beginning of the twenty-first century, and only parenthetically refer to more detailed studies from the history of European and American migration. Schematically, and introducing my keywords, I intend to address the meaning of the word/concept migration, from the Latin *migrare*, literally "to move (on),"[2] which concerns the relocation of people at some time or other from one specific place on the globe to an-

---

[*] This lecture was first read in Nafplion, Greece, on September 5, 2003, with the title "Migration, History, Existence," at the international conference *Migrants and Refugees*, sponsored by the Human Rights Defense Centre, Athens, Greece. It was followed by the projection of 40 historical maps on migration. It was also read at the University of Rome, La Sapienza, Scienze della Comunicazione, on January 15, 2004. As an article it appeared in *Migrants and Refugees*, Ed. Vangelis Kyriakopoulos (Athens: Komotini, 2004): 19-50. The text has been modified in part, though the basic thesis still holds.

[1] *Les Migrants, Citoyens du Monde ou Meteques Planetaires?*, No. 1206, Paris, Mars-Avril (1997). This issue deals with the thorny issue of citizenship in Europe, which cannot be solely tied to nationhood or to social-juridical practices of legitimation. The author notes how the fear of dissolution risks changing all immigrants into "second degree citizens."

[2] But before Latin, the Indo-European root has the sense of "to change," and, later, "to depart." The semantic envelope broaches the sense also of "going off," "to wander," as in the Latin *errare*. For a broader discussion, see Carravetta (1995a).

other, and typically not under the most propitious conditions. This requires that I pay attention to at least three things:

First, the drama of leaving or *departing*, which compels reflection on the connected issue of uprooting, or the meaning of roots. In short, we must address the sense of provenance, and in the background the philosophy of *origins*.

Secondly, the complex reality of existence and survival "along the way," that is, we have to thematize the *passage* or *travel* itself, asking what happens, and what does it mean to someone, often to a family, a group or an entire people, to change geophysical dwelling and the sociohistorical world they know. I will attempt a typology of travelers in order to bring out how complex the issue can get, entreating policy-makers not to generalize extensively.

From that, critical thought shifts to the other end of the spectrum, that is, where the relocating, the *migrare* ends up: we have to account for the incertitude and anxiety of *arrival*, or destination, the existential and political realities that confront the traveler, the migrant, entering a different world. Among the themes that will surface, we need to consider the layered complexities of *culture shock*.

Taking a step back, momentarily, studying and thinking about migration requires that we consider issues relating to *identity*, to the sense of *belonging*, and therefore connect between geography and history or, better said, *historical memory*, which is *always localized and culturally marked*. My working hermeneutic premise is that I feel that all absolutes are *historically contingent*. Therefore, in order to not fall into the seductive traps of Theological Unity, Platonic Universals, Kantian Transcendentals or Hegelians Absolutes, we will also have to keep in mind the *actual concrete interpretations of these phenomena*, that is to say, the very fact that the reasons people migrate, the social role placed on people's life by demographic shifts, and their political relevance change continuously through *time and space*. Consequently, an exploration of and discussion on emigration goes hand in hand with an awareness of historical process *and* social and political transformations, while generating, metacritically, a hermeneutic geography. This may sound both sweeping and simple enough, but it is astounding how many researchers and experts speak about migration employing methodologies and concepts that are over one century old,[3] and suffer from the limitations of certain assumptions that are no longer tenable. Hence the relevance I attribute to geographical understanding, and its cruciality in academic research, politics and education, at all levels.

2. MIGRATION TODAY

There has been, in the last decades of the twentieth century, a world-wide resurgence of demographic shifts[4]; according to some estimates as many as 250 million people are abandoning their domicile.[5] The numbers have only increased, ten years later. This is like the entire population of Italy, France, England, and Germany combined! It corresponds to just under 5% of the estimated world population, which gives rise to the statistical possibility of affecting the rest of the ultimately finite set of inhabitants.[6] This global criss-crossing of paths, this traversing of/into territories, inevitably bumps into the social, political and urban dynamics of host countries, raising fears in the Euroamerican ethno-centric political and social mythologies, which are visibly under stress, and with real challenges for their social fiber, let alone their traditions.[7]

---

3 See, for instance, Immanuel Wallerstein's *Unthinking Social Science* (1991).
4 See among others the rich documentation in Klaus Bade, *Europa in Bewegung*; King and Pinder, *The New Europe*; and various issues of *International Migration Review*.
5 See *The Economist*, March 31st-April 6th, 2001. A recent (2015) visit to the United Nations website reveals that, especially since 2008, there is a world-wide surge in emigrations. The peak however hovers around 5%. See the following site:
http://unstats.un.org/UNSD/statcom/statcom_2015/seminars/migration/docs/UNPD.pdf.
6 With reference to the laws of mechanics, once we attain syntony, or reinforce resonances between the oscillations of a structure or system, the entire set risks shattering.
7 See among others K. Bade, *Europa en movimiento*, 253 et infra, where he recalls the case of Enoch Powell's "Rivers of Blood" discourse of 1968 concerning the feared loss of national

"Introduction: Migration, Existence, History"

America and the European Union have a migration issue: there are foreigners moving into our neighborhoods, and that creates feelings on anxiety. And although Americans and Europeans have developed sophisticated techniques of production, reproduction, distribution, and consumption of goods and services in the face of change, the migration question often appears to be off the radar screen, as there is a perennial slippage or chaotic element present in migration, and no model of analysis can deal with the problem as a whole. Demographic shifts are asynchronous, differentiated, conflicting, and certainly do not respond to any old fashioned idea of Unity, or Totality, or Universal Law. Or even Nation.[8] Migration challenges us to think about what is the sense of Nation today, what it means for one to have a "nationality" as more and more people live and work in more than one place at a time. Moreover, migration requires we focus on crossing borders, the problem of traversing a frontier, a barrier, going beyond some *limit* of sort. For other questions now surge to rock the Enlightenment and nineteenth century models of analysis we are accustomed to: can one not have several nationalities? Can one not learn to inhabit the space-in-between, the border itself?[9] Can one not have Multiple Identities?[10] Or differentiated historical memories, not always consistent with familiar or regional habits, practices, habitats? Can one not make a case for a new, and perhaps "planetary," type of identity, such as suggested by the condition of the *mestizo*,[11] a

---

cultural identity through the excessive increase of foreign, in this case black, immigration. Although in an era of de-colonisation, many Europeans spoke against the construction of the European Union precisely on these grounds.

8 Beyond the classics on nationalism, from Gellner to Smith, pertinent to our discussion is Murphy, "The Seven Pillars of Nationalism."

9 See the articles by N. Alarcón and E. Bruner in Lavie and Swedenburg, *Displacement, Diaspora, and Geographies of Identity*; Pries, *Migration and Transnational Social Space*; Bade, *Europa en Movimiento*, 323 et infra.

10 See on this Klusmeyer and Pirie's *Membership, Migration and Identity*; Pries, *Migration and Transnational Social Space*.

11 Cf. Gruzinski, *La pensée métisse*: "Que l'"hybride" et le métis puissent coexister en même temps que l'ethnique dans nos quotidiens comme sur les écrans de nos télévision n'est pas

complex identitarian, anthropological, and institutional dilemma? (Think of how it impacts on census data, for instance.)

Today's emigration is other than it was yesteryear, and new critical maps are required. On a world scale, migration cannot be summed up in one word or process any longer, as migration is made up in great numbers of a variety of constituents, from skilled labor to partly educated workers, from middle class or aristocratic highly educated fascias of society that seem not too troubled by national borders — many are the people who believe that there exists an amorphous economic oligarchy running or steering world capitalism[12] — to socially and politically connected interest groups, to intra-national relocations and military deportations, as well as by torrents of political refugees and victims of "ethnic" wars. All these groups are also marked by a growing number of extra-ethnic marriages, better educated than emigrants in the past, and by "feminization," insofar as more women cross borders independently of males than ever before in history.[13]

Considered from a broader perspective, however, no matter what type of migrant we deal with, and no matter what country we choose to serve as our exemplary field, we must convene that a great many factors in our social lives will be affected by the arrival and interrelating of these "foreigners," these "others." Predictably, ethnocentrisms and racisms are exploding everywhere. This has been the case in Italy, Germany, France and England; most recently, in Greece and Spain.[14] Although as an automatic reflex action,

---

qu'un indice de la confusion qui regne dans les esprits. Le phénomène aussi a l'aparition d'un "idiome planètaire" (34). In tune with similar positions by Armando Gnisci, Homi Bhabha and Gonzalo Aguirre Beltràn, Gruzinski is countering other more traditional views on hybrid identity, such as Laplantine and Nouss, *Le Métissages*, who believe that "Le métissage n'est pas la fusion, la cohésion, l'osmose, mais le confrontation et le dialogue," on the grounds it is "une composition dont le composants gardent leur intégrité," (10) which philosophically relies on an unshakeable idea of essential identity.
12 See for instance Joxe's *Empire of Disorder*; Castles and Miller, *The Age of Migration*, ch 10.
13 A good starting point here is Castles and Miller, *op. cit.*, 8-9 et infra.
14 [The list of states that manifest xenophobic and anti-immigrant policies and popular opinion has grown since this paper was written; recently Hungary, Poland, Denmark start-

"Introduction: Migration, Existence, History"

humans have always been wary of "strangers," it can be argued that as a socially concrete force in interpersonal relationships, *xenophobia* acquired a political dimension with the rise of nationalism, the "birth of nations," and with the foregrounded acceptance of a broader ideological formation called the nation-state Italy. This in concert with analogous movements going on in many other countries in post-Congress of Vienna decades.

To be sure, scholars and thinkers — the majority of the Post-Modern theoreticians[15] — have noted and expounded upon the pervasive social crises brought about by the decline of the humanist, European, and liberal ethos, and the necessity to reframe the problem, to seek alternative solutions. And yet, many of these critics went unheard, for their message has not slowed down the often paranoiac public rhetoric of the universal validity of theological or Enlightenment-derived legitimizing policies, has not prevented that international treaties be broken when convenient, and has not tempered economic plans that design underdevelopment and fiscal slavery right off the drawing board.[16] We have too many sad instances in which people (government, citizens), at the social-political level, have not lived up to their own convictions, making discussion of ethics a deconstructive parlor game of words. Yet the hard reality remains: we still don't know how to deal with the arrival of strangers.[17]

---

ed discussing whether to erect walls to prevent passage of people to where they can live as decent human beings!]

15 The list is long but not too long: without mentioning any specific work, I am thinking of critics of Eurologocentrism from *within* the Euroamerican *oecumene*: Nietzsche to Foucault, Lyotard to Serres, and so on.

16 See for example Franz Hinkelammert, *El nihilismo al desnudo*.

17 And then we have what in the United States we call the *nimby*s, those who preach that everyone is free or ought to be free to do as they please, as long as they stay far away from me: Not In My Backyard.

3. EXISTENCE AND THE POLITICS OF OTHERNESS

Against the platitudes, the indifference and the suspicion, I strongly feel that Migration, and its philosophical difference, its historical differences, and cultural heterogeneity, can point to new conceptual and therefore socio-political horizons. If we would stop considering it as *exclusively* a legal or economic problem, and think instead of *migration as a fundamental conceptual and defining force, primordially connected to our very existence, to being-human*, our understanding could change, and perhaps would prompt more viable solutions. As I have argued elsewhere,[18] the emigrant can be conceived as the *archetypal* stranger, the proverbial foreigner, every country's barbarian, the entry point to an understanding of alterity, and the *necessary other* for any definition of self or social-political identity. A man or a woman's cultural, better, anthropological self is intrinsically at play in the maelstrom of European constructs of identity and nationality. For it is when a foreigner moves next door with his/her different ways of speaking, dressing, cooking, praying, and playing that we almost instinctively become conscious of our own very difference, of how we are who we are. Therefore, it is absolutely normal at first impact to retreat, reassess and take stock of *our own* values. It is almost a biological response, an instinct. My point, however, is that we ought not react instinctively to the presence of foreigners, not at least in terms of acquired and automated *prejudices*, but, rather, act in a *conscious* manner, after a minute or two of reflection, in order to make a correct or adequate *judgment*. And I believe it is this very experience which ought to make us aware that, not being alone in the world, not being the only ones who eat, drink, work, and wish to live peacefully, a minimum *effort* is needed to construe a flexible social identity, and therefore a policy, or a set of principles that can accommodate both of us, me and my funny-looking neighbor. Even

---

18 See my "Viaggio," in *Segnalibro*, 1995, 205-56.

when you factually know very little about them.[19] And this will impact on how we even look at the problem. For instance, we have to revisit the by now abundant literature on the reasons people migrate.

4. LEAVING HOME

Why do people migrate? Summing up excellent studies on the subject,[20] and relying as well on my experience as an educator on a campus in which more than 50% of the students are born outside the United States, we can come up with a substantial list: epidemics and natural disasters such as floods and earthquakes need no explanation. Unemployment, Under-employment, Oppressions of various types, Invasions, War, Financial shocks that bring bankruptcy, Professional relocations, Possibility or Need to complete or pursue higher education degrees, may be placed under the umbrella of economic, and political forces. Then there are personal or family motivated reasons, such as the desire to join family members who emigrated at an earlier time, psychological pressure

---

19 In a World Studies class I team-taught at Queens College with my colleague Jack Zevin, we distributed about ten different photographs taken from the Ellis Island archive and asked students to identify or characterize the people. After initial resistance that ranged from their not being experts in anthropology, or photography, or history, or folklore, we suggested that they still attempt a description as if each were a photograph of a new neighbour, clearly from another country, who might have moved next door, and they wanted to tell their friends about it over the phone. Within minutes they described, using everyday language, the probable origins of the immigrants based on hairstyles, dress, facial expressions, posture, and other details. Finally we prompted them to take a chance and attribute a provenance, social class, attitude, years in which the photos might have been taken and reasons for their ending up on a ship directed to New York. Although their characterisation was not exact, they were not too far off. But the most important aspect is that at the end of the lesson they felt less challenged, or alienated, by these "strange" people, and empowered by the fact that they had, in their cultural unconscious, enough signs and indices to be able to look at the "other" with a reflective and to all accounts positive disposition. The aim was to shift from knee-jerk prejudice to reasoned evaluation, from instinctive distrust or fear to calm assessment. It was a first step, we thought.

20 I will make references only to a few, such as Portes and Rumbaut, *Immigrant America*; Keridis et al, *New Approaches to Balkan Studies*; Reimers, *Still the Golden Door*, and once again Klaus Bade.

to simply "get out," and personal ambition to make a better life elsewhere. There are countless tales of family dramas involving someone having to abandon family, friends, and native town to embark toward unknown lands.[21] What is most interesting at a social and historical level, however, is how over the centuries, at strategic moments emigration was considered both a boon and a disgrace for the sending country (or province, or town), at other times it was criminalized, yet at other moments it was promoted and advertised by agents from the receiving country. But in the last twenty or thirty years, it has increasingly coincided with bad economic policies in the sending country, political or military oppression, ethnic conflict, loss of traditional, microeconomic, or small scale production and commerce under the onslaught of globalization. All in all, we have before us a variety of reasons, which impact people whose identities, potential for negotiating the journey, and prospects of success once at their destination vary considerably.

5. IN-BETWEEN: TYPOLOGIES OF THE TRAVELERS

But now let us go back for a moment and rethink something else. If migration is to be understood in terms of movement, of crossings, of journeying, but with specific determinations, as we saw above, which require we look again at what happens *between* origins and destination we might learn something by focusing on the different kinds of travelers there are, strong in the belief that if we know what characteristics to attribute to the traveler, we might be in a better position to deal with them both in terms of ethics and politics, and in terms of attitude and policy, when they arrive in the host territory. One study from many years ago listed fifteen types (see Chart 1).[22]

---

21 This is especially true of migration narratives from the Mediterranean basin, the southeastern countries of Europe, Eastern Europe and the Balkans in the second half of the nineteenth and first decades of the twentieth centuries.
22 Chart 1 is from *The Social Psychology of Tourist Behavior* (1982).

"Introduction: Migration, Existence, History"

Let's reflect on this chart for a moment. Today we cannot but disagree and critique these characterizations, especially when it includes as an index how much given travelers "understand the local people," as if that is not in itself a huge problem. There is yet no indication of foregrounding the subjectivity of the ethnographer, the *participant observer*. Also, as the literature on the subject makes abundantly clear, the category of "migrant" itself has generated and validated several subsets, from the more classic one of *labor migrants*, to *professional immigrants, entrepreneurial immigrants,* and finally to *seasonal migrants*, distinctions that play a key role in historical and economic research,[23] and therefore in the everyday encounters that validate both ethics and politics.

However, these categories are still too broad. Today, to this catalogue I would add (see Chart 3) such pragmatically distinct categories as

> *merchants,*
> *ambassadors,*
> *attachés,*
> *spies,*
> *sailors,*
> *scientists,*
> *high profile intellectuals,* and even
> *couples eloping.*

Utilizing the same descriptive approach, it becomes clear that a merchant, for instance, would primarily seek to understand the commercial codes, marketing patterns, and even lifestyles of the host country, a sailor may be interested primarily in places to rest, have fun or meet people, and an intellectual would almost predictably

---

23 In the social sciences, the push-pull theory of migration, based almost exclusively on the dynamics of economic factors, on labor needs in one country and surplus of "hands" in another, has been a main tenet for interpretation since the late nineteenth century. However, as we will have occasion to mention further down, this is too simplistic and in need of serious revision.

seek the universities, the museums, the foundations, the publishers, the music venues, the bookstores or other "cultural" aspects beyond the mere surfaces and rhythms of the new city or country.

A discussion focused on the journeying itself must take into account the fact that the motivations for traveling, the choice of destination, the means deployed to achieve the passage, and the expectations upon arrival are hardly comparable, as spies, intellectuals and merchants typically inhabit radically different social contexts. Although the role-related behavior descriptions of the above set turn out to be very useful in making us zero in on specific potential problems that anyone might encounter when on foreign soil — starting with passports, visas, transportation and a suitable abode — we cannot help but notice they all can illuminate us in an understanding of the *self* of the traveler as it was *before* the journey and as it remains *after its return*, that is, these categories concern people who do leave to go abroad, in a different elsewhere, but also implicitly return home, for they are *viators* who do not leave for good. Upon embarking, they would more likely say *arrivederci*, than *addio*.

It is evident that from the perspective of a positivistic, statistics-driven, "objectifying" social science, the migrant is simply one among many other types, an analogue or parallel to the other travelers. But in our view, *the migrant is the greater category of which these types of travelers and border crossers are specific instances*. In fact Pearce did not consider those people whose traveling is informed and triggered by social unrest, economic straits, legal difficulty and political and military aggression, as we saw when considering the reasons why people embark upon the journey. Thus there are other types of travelers, and to flesh out the list, we have:

> *runaways,*
> *fugitives,*
> *evacuees,*
> *deportees,*

"Introduction: Migration, Existence, History"

> *hobos,*
> *vagabonds,*
> *gypsies,*
> *Romas,*
> *slaves,*
> *pirates,*
> *nomads,*
> *adventurers,*
> *conquerors,*
> *pioneers,*
> *exiles,*
> *refugees,*
> *asylees,*
> *expatriates,*
> *virtual/digital workers,* and various
> *ethnic diasporas.*[24]

all of which have this in common: they are more *relevant to the country of destination* than the country of origin.

This fundamental aspect has not been studied enough. These travelers are going somewhere for good, they will carry the baggage of cultural habits and memories, no doubt, but they typically have no intention of returning (or not for a long time). Taking each category up briefly, we can sketch some basic semiotic traits.

Runaways, fugitives (and *escapees*), whether from a tyrannical family, or strict laws and inevitably therefore prisons and jails, will challenge any established order or imposition on their freedom, but their journeying will occur under cover, in constant hiding, in constant fear of being apprehended.

---

[24] See for instance Challiand and Rageau, *The Penguin Atlas of Diasporas*, which graphically and dramatically illustrates twelve different group relocations on the globe (Jewish, Armenian, Gypsy, Black, Chinese, Indian, Irish, Greek, Lebanese, Palestinian, Vietnamese, and Korean [under the same heading!]) but somehow failed to include the greatest peacetime exodus of one ethnic-national group in modern European history, that of the Italians to the Americas, between 1880-1913 (and which resumed after World War II): I suppose it is a question of how we define "diaspora." [See now Robin Cohen].

Evacuees are made travelers either when natural disaster strikes, or when government, the military usually, impose mass relocations in view of some terrible conflict that has happened or is about to happen.

Situation is different for a *deportee*, who on the basis of not meeting some protocol, or having broken the law while not yet a legal citizen, is sent back to a "home country" from which probably he had escaped or emigrated.

Hobos and *vagabonds* are not to be confused with *gypsies* and *Romas*, who have a more layered social and genealogical identity, and who travel as (small) groups, have families, and oral traditions; hobos and vagabonds are more likely to be dissatisfied loners who hang their hat wherever they can find a place to eat or sleep, and whose social bonds or sense of belonging to any strata of society are tenuous at best.

Nomads can be understood anthropologically, especially in pre-industrial revolution contexts, who move with their food source, cyclically. The arrival of national or regional boundaries and civil codes and policies usually cuts or limits their range of movement, and in Euroamerica they are slowly vanishing (except as metaphors for artistic vagrancies and existential alienation).

To speak of *slaves* and therefore of slavery can quickly turn into a wholesale condemnation of how political and economic powers have historically betrayed religious and ethical principles, and permanently blemished plain human dignity. It has existed since time immemorial, and been legitimated by all sorts of exceptionalisms and absolutisms. Though mass slavery has been outlawed at different times in the known world, it is still practiced under the radar by individuals and criminal organizations that know no country or principles beyond profit. To the chagrin of enlightened ethicists and of decent people everywhere, the latest manifestation, even in Europe and the United States, is a scourge hitting children, women, and once again the "wretched" of the earth.

"Introduction: Migration, Existence, History"

These travelers, objectified and vilified and abused to no end, do nevertheless transfer ideas, beliefs, and values from place to place, and certainly contribute to the differentiation of the human gene pool.

Pirates are also travelers, not particularly bound to any territory or political configuration, and motivated by plunder. To the degree that they have been nearly eliminated, they can be considered the forerunners of more "acceptable" types, at least historically, such as *adventurers*, and those driven by the will or need to learn and control the territory or the waterway to some future advantage.

Explorers managed to earn respectability once they put their journeying to the service of special interest groups and governments. Much like *missionaries*, explorers historically have been (in general, against their intentions) the avant-garde of their country's later unfolding of occupation and colonization.

Conquerors, boundary breakers by definition, occupiers and typically destroyers or subjugators of the social life of the saunter or burst upon, manifest well-hewn traits. However, they can also be understood as key forces in shaping the birth of empires and nations.

Pioneers have become mythic, for their adventures in search of greener pastures have been made synonymous with a positive aspect of the civilizing compulsion, and legitimation, to occupy new lands and deal in the most acceptable way with the people encountered in the new lands. It is also an ambivalent category, like that of explorers, insofar as what is a pioneer to one group, is an invader, or conqueror, to another.

Much more press has been allotted to the *exile*, which Edward Said says is "strangely compelling to think about but terrible to experience. It is the unhealable rift forced between a human being and a native place, between the self and its true home: its essential sadness can never be surmounted." Of course, the exile is generally not to be confused with the wretched of the earth (though he may sympathize with and fight for them), and they certainly can pen down "in elegant prose" their plight. Its origins go back to the ancient Greek practice of banishment of a *persona non grata* from the *polis*, which symbolically was worse punishment than prison or death. In fact exile makes sense only in a political realm. The mythology goes that the achievements of exiles are permanently undermined by the loss of something left behind forever. But that's only partially true, because they continue to live with their body in one place and their minds in their *patria*, and most of the time do manage to "return."[25]

Refugees are also a very special kind of traveler, and it has been argued they are a creation of the twentieth-century state. Next to slavery, it is the most disgraceful condition humans are subjected to and should make all lofty moralizing and politically-correct speeches about universal human values shut up with shame for a while. I know of no religious or ethical principle that has advocated or legitimated it. But certainly political and military power of various denominations are behind it. In fact the word "refugee" has become almost exclusively a political one, and it conjures up spectacles of large herds of innocent and bewildered people requiring urgent local and international assistance. In the United States, after 1960, with fewer restrictions on immigration, the tide of immigrants from southern Europe slowly yielded to those from

---

25 Unlike what takes place with the travellers we saw above, the exile's isolation and displacement often produce, Said writes, "the kind of narcissistic masochism that resists all efforts at amelioration, acculturation and community," but in the case of the exile it may also ignite spontaneous "defensive nationalism" and in extreme cases lead to the construction of a nation, of the "native place," but from the outside, as it were. While we recall the many exiles in the nineteenth and twentieth century who laboured to influence the liberation of their native countries, there exist particular cases that demand finer analyses, such as with the ayatollah Khomeini's Iran, which is an exile's re-construction of a caste and political theocracy, *not* of a nation as such. In other cases, exiles even work to protect or salvage the language, as is the case of the Greek poet Seferis. As the majority have always been of a higher social class, and have had access to the press, it became a *topos* for exiles to be "romanticised" in the various national literatures.

"Introduction: Migration, Existence, History"

Asia and the Latin American countries. The latter quickly became "unwanted refugees."[26] As they changed their legal status and worked out their own sense of identity, or perhaps we should say of double-identity, many of the Latinos still felt they were object of culture bias and silent discrimination. It got worse in Europe, which having been made up of sender countries for several centuries, in a few decades found itself receiving millions of new people. Through the 1990s and up to this morning, if you check the newspapers you will learn that somewhere on the globe, from the South China seas to the Caribbean, from the Mediterranean sea to the Indian ocean, there are constant reports of boatfuls of straggled people running away from political and military abuse and threats of death, searching for landfall where they might at least *survive*. And too often die in the attempt. It is a complex problem for the modern, mostly Western nations, and it is a major concern at the United Nations; we cannot be thankful enough for the work conducted by the United Nations High Commissioner for Refugees[27] and the UN Office for the Coordination of Humanitarian Affairs, as well as from a variety of similar agencies in most countries.

Expatriates are a strange breed, but in general do not exact sympathy from the host society, as they voluntarily live in an alien country, usually for personal reasons or in view of a particular idea of social status. "Hemingway and Fitzgerald were not forced to live in France," writes Said. Similarly, and to give another ex-

---

26 See Reimers, *Still the Golden Door*, ch. 6. Today we have the explosive situation in the Middle East that fuels debate and prompts hard political solutions.

27 In 2004, there were 20,556,000 Persons of Concern for the UNHCR, which is more than the entire population of sovereign nations such as Australia, Greece, Israel, Norway, Portugal, Chile. The term more widely used is now Global Forced Displacement, which includes internally displaced persons. From the infographics posted on the UN website, one can see that the combined number of refugees went from 38 million in 2000 to 59 million in 2014. And that's of course assuming we have data on *all* refugees, which typically are trying not to be seen and counted. For the year 2013, 800,000 had crossed the Mediterranean alone northbound to various European states.

ample, in post-WWII Italy, many intellectuals who sought to improve their chances at a university post, or to scope and climb the social ladder out of personal ambition, commercial interests, and occasionally class pressures, or political tensions, left their "patria" and sailed on to the Americas, constituting what has been appropriately called "migrazione di lusso."

And the *emigrants*?

Even Edward Said is silent on this one!

6. REFLECTION

It is crucial that we are clear at both the level of sociological definition, as well as of existential-personal characterization, that *not all travelers are the same, not all migrants are the same, because not all individuals are the same*. This signals fundamental differences, which scholars and policy-makers ought to take into account in their evaluations. We must reconsider again whether often the contemporary migrant might not seek a sense of reality, discover a meaningful value or sense of self, or chance upon a deeper truth, in the passages themselves. I think it can impact upon their predisposition upon arrival. Because the experience of the passages, the borders crossed, and the social classes visited while trampling through well-hewn and oiled categories of labor are themselves indexes and turning points of history as well as shifting symbols of existence. What the entrenched, mediatized, investment-capital driven and technology-dependent corporate ideology shoving globalization relentlessly down our throat really cannot accept (and will tacitly sabotage) is this: that these very people, the migrants themselves, can teach us a thing or two about human needs and about social covenants, tolerance and freedom.

Because *migration is borne out of necessity, of the need of both survival and living. It is the primary force in the aggregation of human groups, it establishes the us and the them.*

Perhaps that is why they have not been allowed to speak for such a long time:[28] their literature, in fact, is only now being taught in some schools. On the other hand, the accounts written by exiles and expatriates, and the practitioners of the Grand Tour — as well as that of traditional travelers such as the explorer, the conqueror and the pioneer — have become a staple in journalism and humanities departments in American and European universities. Their experiences have become metaphors, even cognitive symbols, as implied by stock expressions such as: the journey to enlightenment, the path to truth, the difficulty of crossing an obstacle in life, and so on.[29]

7. ARRIVAL

Let us now turn our attention to how difficult and anxiety-filled life must be for someone to have to learn new languages, customs, social institutions and so on upon arrival in your neighborhood. Once again, scholars have attacked this problem strictly from the sociological and legal side, and no doubt this furnishes hard evidence of a demographic issue, one which touches upon various components of the lives of both the new arrivals and the local populations. But rather than dwelling on the modalities, which vary from country to country,[30] of how the newcomer engages the

---

[28] In the archival research I am conducting on Italian migration in the post-Unification decades, one of the main problems is precisely the fact that the vast majority of emigrants at the time were practically illiterate, making it impossible to recover what they had to say about the experience. This raises the hermeneutic dilemma of representation and the political issue of what it means "speaking for others." As it turns out, it was relatively easy to downplay their relevance in the romance of unification, and to consider, for over half a century, about a fourth of the nation's population "a people without history," to borrow from Eric Wolf.

[29] See my 1996 essay "Viaggio" for an exposition of how these travel metaphors complement the very fiber of our Western logomachia. Indeed, for the Christians life itself is but a journey (cf. Tabori, *The Anatomy of Exile*).

[30] Portes and Rumbaut in *Immigrant America*, 286-87, have a chart in which there are only three types of immigrants: Manual Labour Migrants, Professionals and Entrepreneurs, and Refugees/Asylees, and for each there are descriptions concerning Mode of Entry, Legal Status, Next Legal Step, Representative Nationalities. For the situation in Greece, which has

host society, I would like to gloss over the less technical but in reality more complex problem of the stages the individual goes through after his/her journey. This is the classic problem of *culture shock*, which sociologists and psychologists have studied rather intensively. Let us take a quick look at some of these dynamics (See Chart 2[31]).

As can be seen at a glance, when dealing with immigrants, one must be alert to the passage not only of space, but of time, personal-social time, in the sense in which an immigrant that has just entered the host country, compared to one who has already resided there for three years, or ten years, and so on, may be susceptible to different stimuli, react in markedly different ways, and may consequently act and think in not always decipherable ways.[32] The range is broad and covers areas that go from the merely personal/psychological to the cultural, from the cognitive to the political. A pondered adaptation of these stages, not always predictable not even within the same family or group, would be extremely useful to policy makers and legislators alike, who ought to shy away from one-formula-for-all-immigrants (thus flattening out their very distinct provenance and differentiated needs and desires). And this applies as well to immigration law, as one set of legal,

---

changed dramatically over the past twenty years, see Katerina Linos, "Understanding Greek Immigration Policy," in Keridis et al, *New Approaches to Balkan Studies,* 309-344, and Anastasia Christou, "Geographies of place..."
31 Chart 2 is from "The Transitional Experience View of Culture Shock," in the *Journal of Humanist Psychology* (1975).
32 This is particularly noticeable in children, where a couple of years already mark a substantial difference in cognition, perception and socialisation. Consider the added problem of language, family mythologies, and "mainstreaming" in the host society. Though Portes and Rumbaut do acknowledge the psychological complexity of entering a "foreign world," (ch 5), they consider these stages only with regard to the "second generation," and dwell on the dynamics of assimilation. In this model, the immigrant *lui-même* literally vanishes, becomes merely a silent unrepresented worker. Today, however, as the case of the Latinos in the US and the Africans in Italy makes clear, even before their own children, the migrants themselves take the mike, or the pen, and speak, and being educated can rightly and legitimately stake a claim to what is equality, empowerment, and justice under the local laws.

labor and education requirements that do not include provisions for the time frame in which the person requests access to social structures and services, and does not consider age, language, religion and gender, is bound to create unnecessary and often dramatic problems.[33]

8. RETHINKING THE MEANING OF MIGRATION

Migration is a one way trip,
there is no "home" to go back to.
— Stuart Hall

The migrant's journey is of a special kind. As we said at the beginning, it goes to the very bottom of the human condition. Because it is not simply a question of relocation in space: *geography is also and perhaps primarily a question of place, of domains and dwellings* upon and around which humans inter-act and institutions are created and develop. Migration scours, scrapes and rips at unseen depths of our constitution, both psychic and cultural. Too many take refuge in their own class, or bloodline, or power lineages when confronted with these unpleasant others who seek social asylum, want to work, practice strange rituals and speak undecipherable languages. The "rejection" derives from many concerns, some concrete and some not so much. To all effects, however, the immigrant can be read as *the uncanny other*, an unsettling reminder of how either we used to be, at some point in our past, or what we can become if through some act of violence, or by edict or legislation by governments, or corporate abuse (or God, always a safe choice to justify anything), the tables are turned, and find ourselves literally, not metaphorically, "out there," better, in the

---

[33] A comparative analysis of present-day Immigration policies in the major European countries would be a very useful critical exercise. See for example Klaus Bade, *Europa in movimiento* (2002) and A. Messina and G. Lahav, eds., *The Migration Reader. Exploring Politics and Policies* (2006).

street. The migrant reminds us of the shadow, the dark otherness we all conceal so well and society glosses over with reassuring panaceas or exorcizes by criminalizing or demonizing these different "others."

Much like *errare*, *migrare* is a profound component of the human psyche, it responds to the needs of the real, flesh and bones person (let's leave the soul out of this for the moment). Behind the concrete evidence that people more and more are willing to request and adopt dual citizenship, there lurks the possibility, at a more abstract level, that *it is feasible to theorize a dual, co-enabling ontological-political structure: I have a right to be rooted, but I am also free to move about and onward as I please, or, more dramatically, as I need to*. We must be aware of the fact that philosophical, psychological and political solutions to the question of rootedness, which has historically yielded claims to primacy and privileges of all sorts, slide quickly into identity issues (of self, of nation, of class) and spawn self-fulfilling prophecies and often bizarre social habits. Indeed the discourse of roots and genealogies has time and again proved to be arbitrary, insidious, and exclusivist. It has also proved to be tragic when a certain idea of the State supplants, subjugates or informs in various guises all other human bonds, civil structures, spaces for interpersonal realization in the name of saving, bolstering, defending one's supposedly self-evident legitimacy for occupying a given territory, or staying planted in one place.

9. *MIGRARE* AS CONSTITUTIVE OF HUMAN HISTORY

The anthropological and historical record does show that humanity is forever on the move:[34] there has always been a need to

---

[34] See the article by Kingsley Davis, "The Migrations of Human Population," where we read: "Human beings have always been migratory...Excluding Antarctica, Paleolithic man made his way to every major part of the globe. Except for species dependant on him, he achieved a wider distribution than any other terrestrial animal. Since this propensity to migrate has persisted in every epoch, its explanation requires a theory independent of any particular epoch." This complements the recent study by geneticist Luca Cavalli-Sforza, *The Great Human Diasporas*, and confirms historian William McNeill, *Plagues and Peoples*. [A

search for safer or bigger and better pastures. It was when walls were erected, and territories had to be divided and adjudicated, that people lost their freedom to travel, and their capacity to cross the seas, rivers, mountains, in order to try to be better off elsewhere on the planet. These boundaries or definitions set up the premises that allowed groups of individuals to identify themselves against the other's difference. At the earliest stages of aggregation into clans or regional groups, there is a boundary drawn between what the group thinks of itself and whatever else is outside of it (possibly arriving from some other foreign location). The origin of (group)identity begins with differentiation, but not necessarily with exclusion. The philosophical "question of the migrant" is a relatively recent phenomenon, arising with the Enlightenment first and nationalism later. But against the background of other types of migration, such as we listed above, including conquests, banishment of specific groups and forced relocations, people have always continued to move about.

Historian William McNeill makes it clear that polyethnicity — and by extension, I shall argue, hybridization and *Métissage* — have really been the rule in history, not the exception. Speaking to a Canadian audience, he says:

> My fundamental thesis is that the Canadian public experience of polyethnicity on the one hand and of ambivalence towards a richer and more powerful neighbor on the other is shared with most of the rest of the world throughout recorded history. *Marginality and pluralism were and are the norm of civilized existence.* Metropolitan centers were and are necessarily exceptional, though they do command more than their share of attention in surviving records. And ethnic and political unity, even among barbarians, was often illusory and always fragile, because mili-

---

discussion today would have to include two recently published important books, Gregory Feldman, *We are all migrants*, and Thomas Nail, *The figure of the migrant.*]

tary conquests and other encounters perennially resulted in mixing one sort of people to others (14-15, my emphasis).³⁵

The argument he makes is that at the origin of the nation-state there is the paradigm of the city-state, where historically it was possible — numerically, economically, practically — to have a rather homogeneous group of people sharing in the rights, privileges and cultural identities of the *polis*. But *modern nations have nothing to do with ancient city-states*. The Romans, in order to control a large sprawling empire, developed the concept of *citizenship* (for certain classes, to be sure), allowed freedom of religion (as long as the state was not threatened), and demanded adherence to their institutions, but individual freedom of speech, creed and mobility were pretty much left alone. Pluralism and multiculturalism are not our recent invention.³⁶ Moreover, and a key observation to bear in mind, the main social characteristics developed by and representing Modern Europe — freedom to contest the ruler, Christian values, secularization, capitalism, individualism³⁷ —

---

35 See William McNeill, *Polyethnicity and National Unity in World History*, 6. Further down the historian writes: "it is my contention that civilised societies have nearly always subordinated some human groups to others of a different ethnic background, thereby creating a laminated polyethnic structure. The idea that a government rightfully should rule only over citizens of a single ethnos took root haltingly in western Europe, beginning in the late middle ages; it got into high gear and became fully conscious in the late eighteenth century and flourished vigorously until 1920, since which time the ideal has unquestionably begun to weaken in western Europe, where it began, but in other parts of the world, especially in the ex-colonial lands of Africa and Asia, it has continued to find fertile ground" (6-7).
36 I am generalizing out of necessity. As expression of diversity and plural cultural discourse, the identities of subgroups in ancient times and through the Renaissance were always marginal, disempowered and necessarily abstract, having to be first legitimated by ruling elites. It is only in the last two hundred years that specific claims (or "discursive formations") of personal, ethnic, linguistic and cultural identity entered the arena of social discourse at large and claimed relevance. But this could only happen in democratic states, where the claims of recognition and empowerment — typically fought against residual racisms and xenophobias — go hand in hand with the possibility of redistribution of goods, services and access to previously closed sectors of the commonwealth. See S. Benhabib, "The Liberal Imagination and the Four Dogmas of Multiculturalism."
37 See Henri Mendras, *L'Europe des Européens*, 12-13; and Carravetta, *La questione dell'identità nella formazione dell'Europa*.

were unknown in ancient Greek and Roman times. From another perspective, on another wave-length, if we integrate McNeill's insights into the diachronic population dynamics (and the variety of social arrangements it can lead into), first with the work of geneticist Luca Cavalli-Sforza and then with the insights of cultural anthropologist Clifford Geertz on the constantly changing nature of the very idea of what makes a culture (and therefore Italian or Greek or Armenian or Palestinian culture), then we may come away with an understanding that *change, movement, and heterogeneity are more intrinsic and fundamental than stability and homogeneity*. If globalization and post-Modern capitalism are dismantling the certitudes and guarantees of the democratic Welfare State, which includes stability of domicile and labor and equal representation before the law, then we ought to look at how people managed before the Enlightenment and the French Revolution, on the one hand, and at the lives of all these different transnational travelers, on the other, in order to grasp what it means to negotiate reality, to *survive* first and then manage to *live* with constantly shifting sets of social, linguistic, and economic forces. In a way, *we should attempt to think as if we all were migrants*, even when we reside stable for several years at the same domicile.

10. BEYOND ROOTS

Whether emigrants, refugees, exiles, or expatriates, these border-crossers, boundary-breaking individuals, these intercultural violators are constantly moving "according to a different calendar." Their lives are generally "nomadic, decentered, contrapuntal," marked by periodic bouts against authority, or limits, or what will now prevent the passage. Not to mention another aspect which we have not addressed but which plays a key role in orienting policy makers, the situation of return migration.[38] Neverthe-

---

38 See R. King, "Generalisations from the history of return migration," and K. Bade, *Europa en movimiento*.

less, being that there really is never a true "going back," even the notions of being *deraciné*, uprooted, begins to lose its exemplary value, spun as it is on the metaphor of being "ejected" from one's Home, or "fatherland." This is a difficult idea to subject to a radical hermeneutic in a brief space, but some points can be made by seeing how the notion of "origin" or "own" is contingent to sociohistoric conjunctures and never fully ironclad. Hiding in occupied France in the middle of World War II, Simone Weil wrote: "To be rooted is perhaps the most important and least recognized need of the human soul."[39] I think we ought to modify that by asking: can one not have several roots? In fact, in the same chapter, elaborating what she means by rootedness, Weil cannot but come up with the same conclusion:

> A human being has roots by virtue of his real, active and natural participation in the life of a community which preserves in living shape certain particular treasures of the past and certain particular expectations for the future. This participation is a natural one, in the sense that it is automatically brought about by place, conditions of birth, profession and social surroundings. **Every human being needs to have multiple roots.** It is necessary for him to draw well-nigh the whole of his moral, intellectual and spiritual life by way of the environment of which he forms a natural part (41, my emphasis).

Weil's notion that uprootedness is "the modern version of tragedy" must be read in the context of an imposed or violent extirpation from one's "natural" – which may mean "habitual," it does not necessarily mean "eternal" – environment. In line with what we observed above concerning the traits of certain types of forced immigrations, uprootedness is closer in meaning to the condition of the refugee, or the hostage in one's land:

---

[39] Simone Weil, *The Need for Roots*, 41.

"Introduction: Migration, Existence, History"

> Uprootedness occurs whenever there is a military conquest, and in this sense conquest is nearly always an evil. There is the minimum of uprootedness when the conquerors are migrants who settle down in the conquered country, intermarry with the inhabitants and take root themselves. Such was the case with the Hellenes in Greece, the Celts in Gaul and the Moors in Spain. But when the conqueror remains a stranger in the land of which he has taken possession, uprootedness becomes an almost mortal disease among the subdued population. It reaches its most acute stage when there are deportations on a massive scale, as in Europe under the German occupation, or along the upper loop of the Niger, or where there is any brutal suppression of all local traditions, as in the French possessions in the Pacific. (42)[40]

Although throughout recorded history there have always been struggles, or wars, whose primary motivation was possession of land and the wealth it contained above and below ground, the legitimizing ideologies have consistently been anchored upon notions of primacy, national or cultural superiority, some well-construed myth of belonging, or divine right, or manifest destiny. In more recent Euroamerican history, there arose the notion of "rights" and "fairness" or "justice," but this did not compel the enlightened people of the more civilized nation-states to avert the ravages of laissez-faire capitalism, colonization and two monstrous world wars. When some philosophers in the earlier part of the twentieth century said that the same logic and the same absolute (indeed: totalizing) convictions that gave us the steam engine and electricity and nuclear power is the same logic *and* rhetoric that justified genocides and unparalleled deportations, politologists, ethicists and the educated upper classes gave a smirk and

---

[40] There are therefore different kinds of migrations or relocations, at both the social and ethical level. Some do cause havoc and humiliate the inhabitants of the host region or country, others do not or go about it in more tolerant, integrative, positive way. The literature on post-colonial critique of the past twenty years ought to take that into account, before generalizing about the meaning of colonialism. This will be developed in another paper.

confined such hypotheses to the back shelves of deserted libraries, together with the mutterings of poets, visionaries, and crackpots.[41] To make it clear against the skeptics, the thesis submitted can thus be rephrased this way: that *migrations*, and all the subcategories glossed above, *are not something epiphenomenal, or an aberration, or an "exception," or a threat*; and that *change, metamorphosis, and variations in ethical approaches and economic perspectives are "acceptable, viable,"* often *"normal,"* inexorably intertwined and ultimately something positive, whether one leans to the right or to the left.

11. BEYOND IDENTITY

Developing these topics at the philosophical level, one first consequence would be to address the notion of a unitary identity. It may work in formal logic or mathematics, but may not apply in psychology or in political theory. Contradiction as a principle of determining what is right or wrong, and what is coherent or not, in any absolute way, is really not useful anymore. Does this necessarily render the notion of identity irrelevant? less compelling? less "strong?" Yes, in part, but if we want to live with our newly arrived neighbor — or if we want to be accepted by others when it is we who travel elsewhere — what is desirable, what is in order, is a weakening of the idea of Subject, a less rigid idea of Self, a more flexible conception of origins and destinations, and of course a more tolerant and accepting social system of values. Embracing this world-view would result in lessening the "need" to resort to weapons, or walls, or exclusivist foreign policies,[42] or discriminatory immigration policies.

---

41 One is reminded of Michael Moore's film *Bowling for Columbine* (2002), when he interviewed an executive of the rocket and weapons facility just miles away from where the high school shooting spree occurred. Asked whether he saw a possible connection between the existence of a large weapons plant and the obsessions with guns in the nearby community, the executive said he did not.

42 We have all heard, in the wake of growing distrust of immigrants and diffuse xenophobia, of a growing "fortress mentality" in Europe. For an analysis, see Saskia Sassen, *Guests and Aliens*, and Kristen Hill Maher's review in *SAIS Review*. The idea of "walls," or "fenc-

"Introduction: Migration, Existence, History"

If we want to look at this from an anthropological or even biological perspective, existential changes such as are entailed in readapting religious and ethical patterns when relocating to different environments, inter-ethnic marriages, and a variety of boundary-crossing are ways in which humanity regenerates itself, and keeps its vitality and creativity. The fact that neoliberalism, globalization and superpower politics are utilizing a worn out set of stylemes, a dualistic logic, a disemboweled pseudo-religious Platonism, plainly unsustainable myths of nationality and security,[43] and, at the same time, capitalizing (!) on the fragmentation, dissemination, and uprootedness of people, does not invalidate my argument; rather, it points precisely to where the problem lies. Migration is persistent through recorded world time, and at times it has had some ugly effects when the "encounter" was fraught with fear and greed (such as during explorations and conquests and other forms of colonization). Today, however, migration is at the mercy of practically centre-less and widely distributed power mechanisms. Still, the aim is to control it, not to change it. But metamorphoses has consistently ruled the day in the end. Empires have fallen, and power has again and again devised configurations appropriate to the situation. To explore the pattern, perhaps we ought to revisit and readapt a cyclical theory of history to the XXI century. People have moved, have transited, through the cycles, and will continue to do so. Semper.

The primordial shiftless hunter-gatherer has undergone incredible changes from the Neolithic age to today, and at an increasing rate of speed. Today we call this eon the Anthropocene. It is crucial we recall that human nature itself cannot be defined

---

es," is another disgraceful reaction to the inevitable if not necessary porosity of borders that warrants freedom of movement. I suppose the fall of the Berlin Wall was not enough of a major epochal symbolic event, as some Republicans in the US have actually suggested building a wall along the Rio Grande to keep illegal aliens out.
43 See among many voices on this subject, B. Anderson, *Imagined Communities*, J. Pilger, *The New Rulers of the World*, A. Roy, *Power Politics*.

"Introduction: Migration, Existence, History"

without reference to a *where* and a *when* it is we are talking about. And what *place* (Bhabha) or *situation* (Sartre) the persons involved are in. As anthropologist Clifford Geertz puts it:

> There is no such thing as a human nature independent of culture...we are, in sum, incomplete or unfinished animals who complete or finish ourselves through culture — and not through culture in general but through highly particular forms of it: Dobuan and Javanese, Hopi and Italian, upper-class and lower class, academic and commercial.[44]

Vicariously readapted to the age of full blown technocracy, virtual capitalism, shrunken distances, a greater array of interstices, strange new crossroads and bridges, highways, connectors of various styles and substance, the question of dealing with migration flows is much more complex than statistical analyses of labor and market dynamics can yield.[45] Yet I hold that we must begin by concentrating first on the travelling itself, on the destination much more than the origins, on the experiences of the bridging, and on the modalities (dangers, resolutions, accounts) of the crossing of the various borders, and the metamorphoses of character, in the psyche itself: for that is what ought to inform our readings and reflections, our social policies, our attitudes toward strangers.[46]

---

44 Clifford Geertz, *The Interpretation of Cultures*, 49.
45 See for example Brettell and Hollifield, eds., *Migration Theory*.
46 Migration *within* a country also ought not be studied as something separate or different from the more obvious trans-national, inter-national movements. It is said that the average American relocates every five to six years. Indeed, as a book by Vance Packard from my college days put it, right in the title, we are *"A nation of strangers."* Given that the laws of the land, the language, and the social infrastructure are more or less the same from state to state or region to region within the national territory, one would think that no major problems exist in the case of intra-national inter-state demographic shifts. But much like what takes place when Italian Southerners migrate to northern Italy, and American Northeasterns migrate to the South and Southwest, other elements surface which are not that different from those encountered by a Vietnamese in Florida or a Senegalese in Lombardy: distrust, racism, exclusion, alienation, resistance to social-communal integration, scapegoat-

"Introduction: Migration, Existence, History"

And as a result question and re-write the home-spun universalistic mythologies we live by, beginning with unconscious or unquestioned theories of homogenization, of generalized identity, in short, continue unwittingly to believe in the melting pot theory of assimilation. It is high time we abandon such ideologhemes.

12. PROVISIONAL CONCLUSIONS

Immigrants make poor nationalists, it is well known, but that's because they dispose of a stereoscopic vision,[47] a multilayered cultural unconscious, a cognitive flexibility that is automatically not restrictive and exclusive, but which is existentially primed to allow for the reception of differences and otherness. I argue that this may actually be the sole ontogenetic precondition, the primordial drive through the ages: *change, travel* and *metamorphoses*, not repetition, predictability and therefore manipulation and abuse by those who wield power and legitimize it to their taste and needs. And this entails, for us listeners to the stories of the migrants,[48] that we develop a more tolerant, self-aware and gen-

---

ing, and so on. The chart on culture shock above ought to be complemented with one reflecting the various Stages of How Locals Receive the Strangers (or Foreigners).

47 Writes Henry Grunwald in his autobiography, *One Man's America*, 43: "Every immigrant leads a double life. Every immigrant has a double identity and a double vision, suspended between an old and a new home, an old and a new self. The very notion of a new home is absurd, as impossible as the notion of new parents. One's parents *are* who they are: one's home *is* what it is. It is one's birthplace, ratified by memory. It is the nursery wallpaper, the family dining room, the stories and songs that surround one's growing up yet home, like parentage, must be legitimised through love; otherwise it is only an accident of geography or biology. Most immigrants to America received little love in their homelands or saw it betrayed; whether they starved in Ireland, or were persecuted in czarist Russia and Nazi Germany, or, later, were driven into the sea in Vietnam, they did not abandon their countries – their countries abandoned them. In America they sought not only a new life, but a new love."

48 The experience of the new immigrants toward "advanced" Western countries should give us a renewed interest in re-reading the tales of a former generation, despite the uncanny sense of *déjà-vù* which may color the reading. As we observed above, with today's greater access to education, immigrants can now speak on their own behalf. As Bharati Mukherjee put it in a *NYTimes* article: "They're bursting with stories, too many to begin telling. They've lived through centuries of history in a single lifetime — village-born, colo-

erous interpretation of other people's "strangeness," that we renew an ethical sense of co-participation — to counter or even just subdue the excesses of competition — in the social project, and teach greater sensitivity when listening to the allegories of silence, the transfigurations of the unsayable, or the experiences of rebirth.

Thought of in this fashion, migration can provide us with a philosophical notion from which — or with respect to which — we can continue to demolish the Great Metaphysical Absolutes of the pre-Moderns which still linger in post-Enlightenment times, those that continue to harbor crude and tragic contradictions and which recent media history has shown to be entirely vacuous, public lies. This includes the dogmas of the contending religious faiths: after all, the obsessive preoccupation with Origins and Primacy and Election would here be subjected to a powerful critique, because realistically speaking the origins of these theologemes are buried in obscurity, the conditions of today's societies and the migrations that inform them are not comparable to those of a thousand, or even of a hundred years ago, the self-legitimizing mythologies are no longer or are only partly relevant and inevitably distorted, and whether one believes in progress or not, modern science has made *some* strides in attenuating self-serving universalistic convictions predicated on some Supernatural being. In short, living according to time-worn and hazy beliefs, and seeking a justification in the literal reading of ancient texts, is truly untenable, undemocratic, definitely not conducive to peaceful civil inter-national co-existence. Tolerance is perhaps one of the few notions developed in the early modern era that ought to be protected and fine-tuned according to place and time, on the basis of specific needs and dynamics in individual territories, in the twenty-first century.

---

nised, traditionally raised, educated. What they've assimilated in 30 years has taken the West 10 times that number of years to create. Time travel is a reality."

"Introduction: Migration, Existence, History"

Migration teaches that history changes, that values are never supra-historical, that what applied once in time (say: antiquity) or space (say: the home country), perhaps no longer applies, or would actually gain from being modified, from being brought up to date to confront problems that were unthought-of, unimaginable a generation, a century ago.[49] Migrating on the other hand is the best image for an existence profoundly informed by change, transit, uncertainty, fear at times, but also freedom, dreams, excitement, fuelling a need to discover, stimulating the necessity to stay forever on the alert, aiding the capacity for renewal, developing scenario for possible worlds, new or more useful theories of representation and participation, and for many groups, even begin to reconfigure their disappeared past. This is a condition which, beyond economic fears and personal hardships, is marked by a profound inner rift, an unnarratable experience...but one which somehow must be told.

Again. And again.

---

[49] See discussion in Portes and Rumbaut, *Immigrant America*, 8-14 et infra, on how comparing today's migration to that of a century ago requires entirely different explanations. An entreat to do so came also from D. Massey, "To Study Migration Today, Look to a Parallel Era," which begins by pointing out how international migration has been considered marginal by the majority of experts: "Out of about 2,500 demographers in the United States, only about 120, including students, express an interest in immigration" (84). [It must now be added that the situation is dramatically changed, and immigration is a daily concern world-wide, and is being studied carefully].

"Introduction: Migration, Existence, History"

CHART 1

| **FIFTEEN TYPES OF TRAVELERS** |
| Philip L. Pearce |

Traveler Category	The Fifteen Clearest Role-Related Behaviours (in order of relative importance)
Tourist	Takes photos, buys souvenirs, goes to famous places, stays briefly in one place, does not understand the local people.
Traveler	Stays briefly in one place, experiments with local food, goes to famous places, takes photos, explores places privately.
Holidaymaker	Takes photos, goes to famous places, is alienated from the local society, buys souvenirs, contributes to the visited economy.
Jet-setter	Lives a life of luxury, concerned with social status, seeks sensual pleasures, prefers interacting with people of his/her own kind, goes to famous places.
Businessperson	Concerned with social status, contributes to the economy, does not take photos, prefers interacting with people of his/her own kind, lives a life of luxury.
Migrant	Has language problems, prefers interacting with people of his/her own kind, does not understand the local people, does not live a life of luxury, does not exploit the local people
Conservationist	Interest in the environment, does not buy souvenirs, does not exploit the local people, explores places privately, takes photos.
Explorer	Explores places privately, interested in the environment, takes physical risks, does not buy souvenirs, keenly observes the visited society.
Missionary	Does not buy souvenirs, searches for the meaning of life, does not live in luxury, does not seek sensual pleasures, keenly observes the visited society.
Overseas Student	Experiments with local food, does not exploit the people, takes photos, keenly observes the visited society, takes physical risks.
Anthropologist	Keenly observes the visited society, explores places privately, interested in the environment, does not buy souvenirs, takes photos.
Hippie	Does not buy souvenirs, does not live a life of luxury, is not concerned with social status, does not take photos, does not contribute to the economy.
International Athlete	Is not alienated from own society, does not exploit the local people, does not understand the local people, explores places privately, searches for the meaning of life.
Overseas Journalist	Takes photos, keenly observes the visited society, goes to famous places, takes physical risks, explores places privately.
Religious Pilgrim	Searches for the meaning of life, does not live a life of luxury, is not concerned with social status, does not exploit the local people, does not buy souvenirs.

"Introduction: Migration, Existence, History"

CHART 2 - THE STAGES OF CULTURE SHOCK

STAGE	PERCEPTION	EMOTIONAL RANGE	BEHAVIOR	INTERPRETATION
Contact	Differences are intriguing. Perceptions are screened and selected.	Excitement Stimulation Euphoria Playfulness Discovery	Curiosity Interested Assured Impressionistic	The individual is insulated in his or her own. Differences as well as similarities provide rationalization for continuing confirmation of status, role, and identity.
Disintegration	Differences are impactful. Contrasted cultural reality cannot be screened out.	Confusion Disorientation Loss Apathy Isolation Loneliness Inadequacy	Depression Withdrawal	Cultural differences begin to intrude. Growing awareness of being different leads to loss of self-esteem. Individual experiences loss of cultural support, lies, and misreads new cultural cues.
Reintegration	Differences are rejected.	Anger Rage Nervousness Anxiety Frustration	Rebellion Suspicion Rejection Hostility Exclusive Opinionated	Rejection of second culture causes preoccupation with likes and dislikes; differences are projected. Negative behavior, however, is a form of self-assertion and growing self-esteem.
Autonomy	Differences and similarities are legitimized.	Self-assured Relaxed Warm Empathic	Assured Controlled Independent "Old hand" Confident	The individual is socially and linguistically capable of negotiating most new and different situations; he or she is assured of ability to survive new experiences.
Independence	Differences and similarities are valued and significant.	Trust Humor Love Full range of previous emotions.	Expressive Creative Actualizing	Social, psychological and cultural differences are accepted and enjoyed. The individual is capable of exercising choice and responsibility and able to create meaning for situations.

"Introduction: Migration, Existence, History"

Chart 3

THE MIGRANT AS TRAVELER: A CONTEMPORARY TYPOLOGY		
Type	Domains of Experience, Dynamics	Approximate Social Class
A. TRAVELERS WHOSE "RETURN" IS PRESUMED		
Tourists	Varies considerably, a major economics engine for nations	middle, high
Merchants	Business exchanges, urban, peripheries, capillary dislocations	middle, high
Ambassadors	Diplomatic corps, political elites, proximity to power centers	middle, high
Attachés	Cultural, political circles, and educational institutions	mostly middle
Spies	Business, politics, military, finance	unknown
Scientists	Government, academic, corporate research institutes	mostly middle
Intellectuals	Universities, publishing, media, politics, art projects	varies: low, middle, high
Lovers	Romantic or familial, communities, all trades & professions	varies: low, middle, high
Military personnel	Restricted range to known localities, periodic stays	low, middle, high
B. TRAVELERS WHOSE JOURNEY IS "ONE-WAY"		
Runaways/escapees	Unpredictable, emigrated, undocumented	low, middle
Fugitives	Unskilled, blue or white collar, mainly outlaws	low, middle, high
Evacuees	Rural or urban, victims of natural or political disaster areas	varies: low, middle, high
Deportees	Rural or urban, subject to politicized migration laws	low, middle
Refugees	Rural or urban, subject to socio-economic instability, undocumented	mostly lower classes
Slaves	Rural, peripheries, urban, variety of trades, subject to abuse	mostly low
C. TRAVELERS WHOSE JOURNEY IS CIRCULAR OR REGIONAL		
Hobos	Regional & folkloric (modern era)	low, "disaffected" middle
Nomads	Rural archaic, urban ("existential") variants	low, middle, "high brow"
Vagabonds	Urban, periphery, unemployed, often undocumented	low, disaffected middle
Gypsies	Urban, periphery, tradition dependent, unattached to states	low, lower middle
Romas	Urban, periphery, culturally autonomous, transnational	low, lower middle
Pirates	Extra-urban, transnational spaces, illegal circuits	varies: low, middle, high
Adventurers	Unpredictable, most any suitable site, "romantic" explorers	middle, high
Seasonal migrants	Rural (& mechanized urban), impacts local economies	low, lower middle
Virtual/digital migrants	Body at home but work elsewhere, global networks	low, emerging middle
D. TRAVELERS WHO CONSTITUTE DIASPORAS		
Conquerors	Historically everywhere on the globe; colonial relations	middle, high, elites
Pioneers	Rural (with urban variants); romanticized settlers, innovators	low, middle
Missionaries	Everywhere proselytizing, converting, spreading values	restricted, varies
Exiles	Urban (with premodern variants); politically banned	middle, high, elites
Expatriates	Urban, suburban, free to leave native country	middle, high
Emigrants	Rural, periphery, urban: economically forced to leave native country/region; Often constitute labor, trade, and business diasporas across international spaces; colonial aspects	low, middle

PART ONE

Theoretical and Historical Contexts

CHAPTER ONE

CONTEXTS BEFORE THE JOURNEYS:
MIGRATION, NARRATION, HISTORICAL IDENTITIES

> *The questions which the historian puts to the past are, as a general rule, intimately related to the questions he puts to himself and to his contemporaries.*
>
> — Bronislaw Backzo, "La responsabilité morale de l'historien" (1969)

1. PRELUDES

Discussion in Italy on the consequences of certain ideas about history, and national history specifically, has grown considerably during the past twenty years.[1] From both left and right, center and periphery, and years before the fall of the Berlin Wall, radical critique and self-critique dismantled many Modern myths, splintered many exclusivist ideologies.[2] We recall the "burying" of the

---

1 See, for instance, works by Enzo Biagi, Giuseppe Galasso, and Norberto Bobbio, and vaguely resonating with our approach the probing if not provoking book by Virgilio Ilari, which asks the fatidic question in the subtitle: does a national identity exist? Giulio Bollati, who echoes him with the following subtitle: "the national character as history and as invention," is openly polemical of Ernesto Galli Della Loggia's melodramatic *La morte della patria* ["the death of the fatherland"]. These discussions on national identity should be juxtaposed to the more traditional take by historian Massimo Salvadori (1994), the self-critique of the left by Giuseppe Vacca, and the debates surrounding the "death of ideology," the advent of "post-political politics," and the decline of the "revolutionary imagination." Some of these discussions can be found in the pages of *DIFFERENTIA review of Italian thought*, 1986-1999, now retrievable at www.petercarravetta.com.
2 To get the broader, philosophical, picture, one might bear in mind various writings by authors (not dealt with in this book, and not listed in the Bibliography) such as Giacomo Marramao, Remo Bodei, Salvatore Veca, Massimo Cacciari, Lucio Colletti, Emanuele Sev-

mito del '68, the flash of political terrorism (such as the Red Brigades), a mellowed and controversial retelling of the experience of Fascism, the flourishing of scientific methodologies, and a surge in national economic well-being unprecedented in absolute terms. A new discursive formation enters the scene near the end of the 1980s and occupies a place of relevance in the 1990s: how Italy's cultural and philosophical heritage is really part and parcel of the emergence of a "new" Europe.[3] Last but not least, considerations of the magnitude of (post-Cold War) Euro-American economic, social and cultural hegemony in an ever more problematic international arena are marked by increased connectivity, dissolution or fragmentation of some states and reorganization of new social subjects across a wide spectrum. As many studies in various disciplines have pointed out, soon even the very vocabulary required to deal with all these changes appears wanting.[4]

It is in this uncertain horizon, in the last decade of the millennium, that *the issue of migration entered the Italian national consciousness*: forcefully, disturbingly, and with perplexing consequences. Migration may effect how the whole (or parts) of the complex discussion on Italian history and identify turn. In fact we will argue that it cuts deep and obliquely across all of the above sectors and fields of exchange.

Migration signals a primeval physical shift between socio-economic realities and therefore also cultural worlds. It involves *travel*. Before we take a closer look at this in a later chapter, let me

---

erino, Antonio Negri, and others, all of whom in very different ways had lodged massive critiques against universalizing and self-affirming myths about Italian history, politics and, more broadly, about other metaphysical assumptions about special or peculiar traits of Italian public consciousness. These reflections make books like *The Italians* by Luigi Barzini (1965) woefully outdated.

[3] Very lively, probing, and worthy of further study is the flurry of books that engage the issue of the relationship, culturally and economically above all, of Italy with/in Europe. See, for instance, the pamphlets by Alberto Asor Rosa, Armando Gnisci, and Patrizia Calefato. Let us not forget that the Maastricht Treaty was signed in 1993, and that Italy committed to entering the Eurozone in 2001.

[4] On this issue, see my Italian book *Del postmoderno*, 2009.

quickly say here that the notion, or metaphor, or image of travel has been a magmatic and profoundly influential one in the memory of the Western cultures. And if among the Italians' collective mythology people variously refer to, and have in fact used as a critical *figura*, an Aeneas, a Dante, a Columbus, a Vespucci, an Umberto Nobile, in brief, "a people of explorers and travelers," (cf. Mangione and Morreale), we might consider whether contemporary critique should not train its sights on the depth and range of meaning of *travel* in Italian history in the wealth of its articulations and renditions, from travelogues to newspaper fodder, from scientific explorations to geographical mapping, from postcards to military plans to fantasy trips and fairy tales. This may help in drawing more nuanced contours of the archetypal traveler, the proto nomad itself, the *emigrant*. But now, stepping back into meta-critique, we notice how, through a conceptual short circuit, we find that the question of migration in general suddenly discloses the gaping absence, in particular, in Italian public discourse, of the Great Exodus of Italians to the Americas, and at the center of the debate on the identity of Italy on the threshold of the third millennium.

This chapter revolves around three highly problematic and timely issues for literary and philosophical study, namely, Migration, History, and Narration. Specifically, the project intends to study the interconnections between the problem of *origins* in Italian (and Italian American) culture, the role (im)*migration* has had on the early attempts at a *self-definition* (or socio-cultural ethnonational preferred identity), at how the migrants experienced the process, the "what" of their very journey, and finally at how their (hi)story was constructed, that is, written, or better yet, told, narrated, circulated through generations.

Therefore, I look at various, not necessarily isomorphic or immediately analogous, *topics* or themes embedded in records that deal with what is arguably the greatest peacetime exodus in mod-

43

ern history, the emigration of Italians to the United States (and the Americas in general) from the time of Italian Unification in 1861 to the break of World War I. Though I have already begun looking at the issue in philosophical and sociological terms, it is the combined historical and (socio)linguistic dimensions that I feel must now be addressed: who was speaking/writing when this story was told? How did they speak? Who, and where, were the listeners? In this spirit, the following remarks are really pursuing a question, the en/framing of the topos or topoi that will allow us to locate the speaking, and from there who the listeners were, or might have been.[5]

American historians and Italian American scholars have of course studied many aspects of the great Italian exodus to North America, but the focus has been, predictably yet understandably, on how the immigrants adapted to their new environment and experienced the various phases of integration, assimilation, and so on.[6] However, concerning how, why, and what happened before they sailed westward, very little has been done, and whatever we have is typically confined to an introduction or a predictable hagiographic chapter.[7]

Naturally, we would want to look at how emigration was handled by researchers and historians more familiar with conditions and perspectives on the Italian side. Many pages will be dedicated to this web. By and large, however, Italian historians have not accorded the phenomenon the relevant role it actually played in shaping modern Italian society, being more concerned with the coherence and continuity of a General History of Italy, the Great

---

5 In this vein, see now cited works by Fontanella, Marazzi 2012 and Serra 2007.
6 See the superb collection of papers exploring with complex and vigorous theories the growth of Italian American historiography and cultural critique, in Tomasi, Gastaldo, and Row, *The Columbus People*, and my review in Carravetta 1994a, as well as in many publications resulting from AIHA conferences. See also cited works by Cannistraro, Mormino, and Krase and De Sena.
7 For example, in J. Mangione and B. Morreale: *La Storia. Five Centuries of The Italian American Experience* (1992).

Narration scheme of the newly founded nation called Italy.[8] Moreover, Italian historians have been consistently and explicitly arguing their story within a precise scheme or set of beliefs in mind, such as the various schools of the left, or the right, or in accordance with Church politics, or playing to the tune of the Christian Democrats.

The story of Italian emigration has never been written by the agents themselves, by the very people who experienced it.

As I researched and developed my argument, I found that perhaps much more than discovering *new* materials or re-compacting well known facts, what was pressing at the doors of the critical mind were more compelling questions about contemporary frames of reference. I thus decided to organize my remarks into several blocks, each one mindful of delivering some emblematic or representative facts, reports on some authoritative accounts of these facts (i.e., by historians, political scientists, economists, or other specialized disciplines), and expand on some open-ended questions in the light of some broader theoretical and educational concerns.

Let's begin by staking the territory: The country is Italy, the chronology is roughly 1860-1914, the issue is migration, the problem is how to (re)interpret it today, at the beginning of the third millennium. And, again, we cannot even for a moment forget that we are looking at this cluster from the vantage point — I mean geographically, physically — of the United States. The critical I must think of the two possible genealogies of the notion of an Italy. One of them, Hesperia, was designed to name the lands to the West, where Hesperus, the evening star, sets (from the point of

---

[8] This can easily be argued on the basis of successful reconstructions which shaped millions of students, such as the herein often cited authorities on Italian history: Rosario Romeo, Valerio Castronovo, Raffaele Romanelli, Massimo Salvadori, Giorgio Candeloro, Giuliano Procacci, Renzo De Felice, even Denis Mack Smith and Indro Montanelli. In nearly all of them, the relevance of the Great Exodus is relegated to a footnote, a passing mention, maybe a page or two.

view of the Greeks). But borders are never stable; in fact they actually do not even exist in "real life" except through some (often self-) imposed agreement. Once the Greeks colonized Trinacria and Elea, Kroton and Metapontum, Hesperia as the site where the known world ended, was pushed further westward...so for a while Spain was Hesperia...and skipping through the Ulysses myth and Christopher Columbus, in modern times it turned out that the *Abenland* was "Amerika"...most recently, indeed, and without irony, we look to California, to Silicon Valley, to guestimate where the rest of the world is going.

Though this sort of opening may irk some, I believe it is intellectually reductive and ideologically untenable to pretend that we can broach our topic as if we could stand outside history and, as Galileans from the moon, scan, plot, and map the Italian immigrant experience without being involved, without relating to our present global, post-modern condition.

2. MIGRATION, I

The issue of migration — of immigration — is back on the front page of newspapers, and has been steadily influencing both national politics and local policy. It is estimated that by the end of the decade it may well reach the all-time high of 15%, a figure achieved only once before, just before World War I.[9] Migration has become a most pressing issue in social and political life, both here and in Europe. During the past twenty years, and in particular after the fall of the Berlin Wall, huge groups of people shifted across Europe. Germany and France were forced to look at their immigration policies, usually in view of tightening up border security. In Italy the phenomenon of an unprecedented wave of immigrants entering the country took everyone by surprise, and reactions especially in the big urban centers have been wildly in-

---

9 A most intelligent and useful volume is that by Castles and Miller, *The Age of Migration* (1993, but republished several times), which we shall refer to often.

"Contexts Before The Journeys"

coherent, often violent, fueling a previously hidden streak of racism.[10]

In the United States the problem has picked up enough momentum to play a substantial role in the recent presidential elections. It appears that a common-sensical, let's protect "us" before "them" type of ideologeme is going bankrupt (certainly it forced Pete Wilson out of the Republican slate). A nation of immigrants, as John F. Kennedy writes as late as 1957, cannot treat migration superficially, as a juridical and labor-related side issue not worth politicizing. There is much more at stake, to be sure, something perhaps as profound and complex as the very possibility of cultural identity, nationhood, and tradition. But is that why the issue becomes touchy, slippery, and unmanageable?[11]

On the other side of the Atlantic, and consistently with the great demographic shifts that have followed upon the fall of the Berlin Wall and the end of the Cold War, Western Europe in general and Italy in particular have witnessed the massive arrival of foreigners which has rocked them quite a bit and has already created a number of problems in internal politics. On the cultural

---

10 The growing xenophobia and related racism has already had a determining influence on government policies. When I first began researching this topic, I learned that the coalition holding up Dini's government was threatened by a disagreement over the Legge Martelli: the Polo della Libertà (Berlusconians) and Autonomia Nazionale (Fini) favor a smaller quota and suggested population control techniques such as magnetic ID cards for the immigrants...while the PDS, the Progressisti, the Cattolici Popolari favor solidarity over expulsion, integration instead of wanton rejection. Luckily, in August, 1997, Minister Giorgio Napolitano decided to face the question head on, prompt new social and legal reforms that protect the new immigrants, and declare that, ultimately, with less than two millions non-Italians on its soil, Italy is not facing an "immigration crisis." [As of end of 2015, ISTAT records 5,026,000 legal immigrants on Italian soil, representing 8.3% of the population.]

11 See the now very common articles dealing with migration-related issues in most dailies both here and in Europe. For example, *The New York Times*, Sunday, Jan. 7, 1996, writes: "Illegal Migrants Warned: Stay South of the Border." Concerning tightening border patrol for returning undocumented workers, following Clinton administration policy suggestions to Immigration and Naturalization Service (Congress voted $236 million "in additional funds for the Border Patrol last year ... allowing ... the number of agents deployed along the 2,000 mile frontier ... from less than 4,000 to about 5,000." Now there's a way to re-cycle all the workers laid off by the multinationals (IBM, GM, AT&T, Microsoft, etc.).

front, this has generated novel crossings and remixtures of styles and motifs, creating a peculiar literature and theatre. We will ponder time and again and try to understand how migration is being experienced or written about, explained, and if it is influencing (yet, or at all) how intellectuals look back at their own national history, and their cultural politics.

3. FROM LITERATURE

At the con-junction of history, migration, and narration, one finds literature, or an art form. I will submit a few examples, here to be read figuratively, iconographically, later on in this paper for their "content" or "referentiality" against a short empirical history of the political economics behind the Great Exodus of Italians to North America. Before tear-jerking Neapolitan popular/populistic songs on the melodrama of "parte nu bastimentu, ppe terre assai luntane," or "pp'e l'America", there existed highly individualized regional ballads, stornelli, nursery rhymes, *cantilene* linked to pre-Christian rituals. Perhaps poetry can disclose something for further reflection. A Calabrian saying at the turn of the century said:

> Cristofiru Culumbu, chi facisti?
> La megghia giuventu' tu ruvinasti[12]
> [Christopher Columbus, what have you done?
> You ruined the best of our youth]

Another provincial ballad from Tuscany from about the same period (1880-90s) said:

> Italia bella mostrati gentile
> ei figli tuoi non li abbandonare
> senno' se ne vanno tutti ni' Brasile
> non si ricordan piu' di ritornare
> [Beautiful Italy show your gentle side

---

[12] Degli Innocenti, *Un secolo*, 230.

"Contexts Before The Journeys"

> And do not abandon your own children
> Otherwise they will go away to Brazil
> And will forget to ever come back]

Likewise, in the hills of Lucca, the populace would rhyme to:

> Ancor qua ci sarebbe da lavorar
> senza sta' in America a migrar
> [Around here there would still be plenty of work
> Without having to emigrate to America]

Not very far down the peninsula, on the eastern flank abutting the Adriatic, in Abruzzo, one might have overheard the following ballad:

> Nebbi a le valle e nebbi' a le campagne
> ne le campagne nun ce sta nesciune
> [Fogs hover over valleys and fields
> But there is no one left in the fields]

This signals the possibility of "using" texts ("literary" as well as "popular") to gain access to a socio-political reality too often ignored in cultural analysis. Fact is, as no literature exists in a vacuum, no society no matter how "backward" or illiterate can exist without a repertoire of symbolic actions and values, of "habitudes," of rhetorical evidences. The ignorant farmer can express himself through ballads and simple songs and prayers. Attention to these forms of cultural production and the range and impact of communications along these terms have not been great, neither Italian American historians nor Italian historians have truly tackled this possibility. The problem is serious enough, methodologically speaking, since it would require the taking account simultaneously of specific semiotic spheres, of semi-autonomous language games, in short a variety of specializations, such as in art history, mythology, sociology of literacy, a theorem concerning the religious and philosophical depth of certain beliefs or rationalizations for one's actions. The interpretation of a people who never spoke or wrote is no weekend project.

Let us focus on a specific example. In 1894 Cesare Pescarella published a long poem of 50 sonnets, written in the Romanesque dialect, titled *La scoperta de l'America*, The Discovery of America, where we read, in my prosaic approximation of the metric original:

> [II] In those days there reigned in Spain a Portuguese King, from whom Columbus requested a fifteen minute audience. He talked to him somewhat vaguely at first, then said: "I have in mind, if you would kindly help me, to discover America!" "Well," said the King, who was a smart man, "Yes, I will help you...but, without meaning to contradict you, this America, does it exist? Are you sure about it?"
>
> "Ah, said he (Columbus), I am surprised that a man such as yourself would even doubt it. Or do you think I am here to make a fool of you?"

He then proceeds by stating that, if the King were to consider the situation seriously he would soon realize that the world is, after all, shaped like an orange (with a play on "portogallo" which means an orange, but also the country Portugal), indeed like a human head. There follows a brief interruption by the presumed audience of the poem, which is that of an *osteria*, or saloon of sorts, and the narrator is made to answer the question:

> "How do you know such nonsense?"

Whereupon the narrator retorts:

> "I know because I read it in a history book."

"Contexts Before The Journeys"

Someone from the gaia brigata interjects:

"In Roman history?"

To which follows:

[IV] "Obviously, in the greatest and most magnificent history, which is the great universal book."

What clinches the hermeneutical short-circuit mentioned above is the conclusion of this first scene, which sounds eerily proleptic, almost prophetic if we consider the tone of some recent cultural criticism:

[V] "Of all other books, I don't mean to speak ill of them, I have nothing against them, there are probably good things, but in the end they are all alike: you read and read, and what is that you read? A made up story.

The original text is of course brilliant:

"Legghi legghi, e che legghi? un'invenzione!"

Is history an "invention?" In what ways is a documented, "empirical" history, but a *story* nevertheless? And if so, what rhetorical strategies does it deploy, and what does it re-present?

4. THROUGH HISTORY

Let us develop this *topos*. History is an "invention," a linguistic, rhetorical construct, no less than any other written text, *pace* my professional historian friends, as the social sciences during the past quarter of a century have amply demonstrated.[13] However,

---

13 I am thinking of a body of work which comprises cited works by Michel Foucault, Gilles Deleuze, Friedrich Nietzsche, Edward Said, the American "Neohistoricists," Benedict Anderson, Jean-François Lyotard, Hayden White, Paul Ricoeur, and Ali Ahmed.

this does not mean that any story is fine, or equally valid. The narrowing of the boundary between the true and the likely or possible — if we wish to rely on the ancient Aristotelian distinction — does not in any manner disengage us from the responsibility of seeking the coherence, intentions, and effects of the accounts we inevitably spin, stitch and weave. Not to speak, of course, of the formal constraints of discourse. Historians base their arguments on examples, writes Braudel, but which examples are chosen, and their positioning within a rhetorical construct *does* have a crucial effect on the overall meaning of the narration, or, in the language of yesteryear, on the angle or ideology of a particular *theory of history*.[14]

Coming out of the debates on deconstruction, but fortunately sane enough not to throw up their arms in vexing self-referentiality and undecidability, social and cultural historians have turned the tables on Euro-logocentric discourse (whether of the left, or the right) and revealed the hidden strategies of legitimation of key concepts, such as progress, empire, colonization, civilization, even of identity, rationality, or human rights. In the wake of studies and theoretical suggestions by Michel Foucault, Edward Said, Hayden White, Daniel Bell, Eric Wolf, and Benedict Anderson, critics have explored the possibility of, for lack of a better word, "revising" the standard accounts of any given national history (especially when that history was being narrated by an outsider). I am thinking here specifically of the work of Edward Said, *Orien-*

---

14 Leonard Markowitz observes that "[Abdi] Kusow (author of "The Somali Origin: Myth or Reality", in Ahmed, 81-106) has not only demonstrated the historical context within which identities are formed; he has also revealed how *theorizing* about identity formation is also historically conditioned" (Ahmed, 64). In that particular context, the reference was to the accounts of Somalian ethnic and social stratification given to Westerners by – no surprise there! – an endless series of Western observers, company agents, even anthropologists, who described, categorized, and ultimately acted on the basis of European conceptions of language use, social organization, and codes. When, with the end of the Cold War in 1991, the government of M. S. Barre fell and violence erupted in Somalia, Westerners were first caught by surprise, and then proceeded to unfurl a litany of predictably negative common places about Somali instability, origins, habits, cultural traits and so on.

talism, and of Eric Hobsbawn and Terence Ranger, *The Invention of Tradition*, but we may keep in the foreground as well works such as Mudimbe's *The Invention of Africa*, Ali Jimale Ahmed's *The Invention of Somalia*,[15] Martin Bernal's *Black Athena* (about the "invention" of Classical Greece), which has raised a veritable storm among classicists of all stripes and nationalities.

A plethora of stereotype ideas about southern Italian immigrants to the Americas have undergone a similar process of mystification, denial, and suppression. And, vice versa, many of the received ideas about America were no less the result of misinformed constructs about what America was really like, and to which both the Italians and the Americans contributed. In this game of inventing and sticking historical traits on the body, both physical and political, of the non-Western countries, in fact, it is less a question of what the real facts are, and more an issue of who tells the story, when, and why (cf. Ahmed, 224). Along these same lines, historian Terence Ranger introduces another deeply relevant and connected cluster (whether foregrounded or operating in the background, as we will see): "the concept of *empire* was central to the process of inventing traditions within Europe itself" (Hobsbawn and Ranger, 211). He holds that empire – what it means, how to expand it, etc. – was a driving force which would shape the evolution of capitalism in Europe through the second half of the nineteenth century, and is behind the European powers' cutting up of Africa. As Italy participated in the Berlin conference of 1884-85, the seduction and destructiveness of empire impacted the Italian ruling class well before the end of the century.

The relationship between emigration, colonization, and imperialism[16] is a profoundly complex knot, one that must be analyzed

---

15 The trope of "invention" has had growing success in academic publishing. See titles by Dieckhoff on Israel, Martucci on Italy, and Wulf on the concept of nature and so on.
16 For Schumpeter, at the origins of imperialism there is the warrior myth of the ruling élites, whereas for Lenin imperialism springs from a crisis of overproduction. See, *Theories of Imperialism*,

in a broader, multilayered, and dialectical context than that of national history. This is especially pertinent inasmuch as the notion of Nationalism itself, and the rise of the nation-state as a juridical set of constraining and legitimizing forces, reveal themselves to be no more — but also no less — than cultural artifacts set in motion by specific centers of power, vested interests, and powerful single individuals with a broad agenda.[17]

But calling something an *artifact* is not to imply that it is merely fabrication or falsity. It may also be, and indeed represents, creation, an imagining (Anderson, 15), an articulation of sorts. Therefore, we can hypothesize it will wield a lexicon, cut a syntax, exhibit a style, possess a rhetoric. And rhetoric, as demonstrated elsewhere (cf. Carravetta 2012), is never *just* words: *rhetoric is discourse pronounced at a particular time and place, with a circumscribed audience in mind, with a specific intention to get a particular result.* This may cast light on the paradoxical and infuriating fact that often, too often, the same words and discursive strategies seem to be employed by opposing parties and contenting ideologies. They are saying the Same Thing. So where is the difference? What's missing?

The invention of a country is possible because "the members of even the smallest nation will never know most of their members, meet them, or even hear of them, yet in the minds of each lives the image of their communion" (Anderson 15). Throughout the eighteenth and nineteenth century, Nations are construed and imagined as limited and circumscribed, with elastic if porous boundaries, sovereign even against divinely-ordained and hierarchical dynastic realms. They are imagined as a community because despite the inequality and pluralism they presuppose a horizontal comradeship, a "fraternity" of sorts that binds localized differ-

---

[17] I have relied on well-known works by Anthony Smith, William Pfaff, and Benedict Anderson (cf. Bibliography). For a contextual discussion, see, now, my *Del Postmoderno*, 2009: 372-80 et infra.

ences (Anderson 16). It is almost ironical that nearly a century earlier, in 1882, Ernest Renan had penned similar observations on the ambiguous origins of "classes" and the bloody "births of a nation":

> Forgetting, I would even go so far as to say historical error, is a crucial factor in the creation of a nation, which is why progress in historical studies often constitutes a danger for [the principle of] nationality. In deed historical enquiry brings to light deeds of violence which took place at the origin of all political formations, even of those whose consequences have been altogether beneficial. Unity is always effected by means of brutality. (Renan, 11)

But today we know that the notion, status, possibility of "nation" has changed drastically. Will this have an effect on how we interpret "backwards," on how we (re)tell the story of possible origins, of justifiable cause, of worthwhile preservation.[18]

5. RE-VIEWING HISTORY

In view of the critique of historical accounts that will follow, and bearing in mind some representative documentation referred to in the notes, here's a convenient micro-synthesis of what took place between Unification in March, 1861, and the crushing defeat the Italians suffered at Adwa in Africa, in 1896. For the benefit of historiographic clarity, and readapting a scheme by the historically acute and nearly clairvoyant Robert Foerster (1919, 474), we will parse the three phases or periods of Italian Migration to North America.

---

18 See, for example, the highly discussed books by Francis Fukuyama, Kenichi Ohmae, and the already cited Pfaff. While there exists a surge in nationalistic ideologies throughout the globe, there is present at the same time a flurry of theories about the "end" of the nation-state, at least if we rely on its nineteenth century formulas. At some level, in other words, nations today seem to be headed toward borderlessness, being highly porous, with unstable geopolitical coherence; this fuels a crisis in the construction of national, ethnic or cultural identity. Question to ask now is: does this apply only to Western nations?

But in order to do so, let us recall momentarily some key dates or events from Italian history, and bear in mind the complex knot unraveling itself at the time of the Birth of the Nation Italy from where so many were eventually to emigrate into the Americas, Englishdom in particular. There is the atmosphere of post-Congress of Vienna industrializing Europe. There are Romanticisms and the growing wildfires of nationalisms. Mazzini promotes a unification in light of the Mission of the Third Rome, a utopist who saw in the Young Italy the germ of a supranational world order. He came close in 1848-49 with the short-lived Roman Republic, but ultimately lost to the Piedmontese, who had a different agenda. Then there is Vincenzo Gioberti, *Del primato morale e civile degli italiani* (1843), who writes of a different Manifest Destiny for Italy, one which demonstrates past and present superiority of the Italians, their inhabiting the geographic center of the earth and boasting an endless variety of talents and geniuses. Beneath that, an invented continuity, a necessary trans-historical set of references. Gioberti argued that through all the social upheavals and the recurrent foreign subjugations, Italy had retained a form of unity and cohesion thanks to Christianity and the Church establishment. The Church, "a spiritual monarchy," like the Roman Empire, the Comuni, the Renaissance-style city-republics, was another institution quintessentially Italian (cit. in Cunsolo, 19). But "Neo-Guelphism was historically late," and his dreamed confederacy of a tripartite Italy with the Pope as titular president was not to win out, either. Like Mazzini's evangelism, Gioberti's universalism has permeated Italian culture, and it was to be reappropriated at will by subsequent generations of historians and politicians. The specific variations it took later in justifying sending troops and laborers to Libya, seem delirious in retrospect, but were compelling forms of discourse, information-cum-demagoguery nonetheless, and cannot be dismissed as merely rhetorical against some platitude of the post-World War II period.

"Contexts Before The Journeys"

But in terms of how Italy came into being, politically and economically the peninsula simply was not on par with the rest of Europe, or at least with the three or four major nations it aspired to join. The vehement opposition of the Church to any political configuration which contemplated unification was also weakened by its internecine struggles, the polarization between Jesuits and Jansenists, Freemasons against papists and anti-clericals. And then there was that cumbersome hero, Giuseppe Garibaldi. The stage was set for a new leading character to enter the historical scene, namely Count Camillo Cavour.

The principal architect of Italian unification was a master schemer. Yet Cavour was still caught between nationalism and statism. By 1870, however, it appeared that Italian politics was to be dominated by a statalist conception of the public and social domain, and nationalism was to adapt itself to it. Having achieved nation-hood, Italians still could not quite agree on national identity, on the right or best or most representative idea of oneself, of one's culture.

This confirms that Italy, apart from raucous retrojected stories that enlisted Dante and Petrarch and Machiavelli up to Foscolo and Leopardi, was imagined from the top down, *fatta a tavolino*, as the Italians would say. It took a key event, the Plombières Agreement in 1859, for Cavour to see how all the competing forces could be brought together into a plan to unify the country. Immediately after Unification, a new problem arose — we cannot cite this phrase often enough: that there was a need "to make the Italians." This is important because in order to understand how Italians viewed and mis-constructed America, we should first look at how they forged a preliminary idea of themselves. And there was no general agreement among the masses as there did not exist harmony among the fractious elites, and the populace speaking hundreds of different dialects.

"Contexts Before The Journeys"

Of course a dominant role in the shaping of the socio-cultural context of post-Unification Italy was played by the Crown. With a poorly educated, secluded, arrogant King who dreamed of military victories and matching the greatness of all previous and contemporary world leaders, thousands of innocent youths lost their lives "for the sake of the Monarchy." Denis Mack Smith's reconstruction of the lives and political misconceptions of the House of Savoy gives us a sad and infuriating picture of a social force that was eons removed from what was happening right under their noses in a wildly heterogeneous and fragmented "country." After the disaster of 1866 at Custoza and Lissa (where the King did not listen to his otherwise uncertain and unwilling generals), the national debt ran high. Industrialization was in its infancy and agriculture did not supply enough revenues. Commerce and shipping were outdone by the more powerful and modern fleets of England and France. The solution? a grist tax (*tassa sul macinato*) in 1868. Coupled to increased property taxes, administrative fees, and the reluctance to develop a concerted politics of domestic investments, this was the first dramatic signal that the largely poor Italian farmers, which made up nearly 80% of the population, were going to have a hard time in years to follow.

Historians have argued about the meaning and consequences of this under-researched, unwarranted legislation: in an attempt to justify the unfolding of a liberal agenda, Rosario Romeo viewed it as a necessary move, at the time, to raise some badly needed capital to re-launch the economy (especially to sponsor the building of railroads and ships) and put Italy on par with the other European countries (cf. also Romanelli, 86), while others interpreted it as an ill-advised motion by the Crown and an alienated parliament that would have repercussions on the distribution of wealth and therefore on the productive potential of the economy, as well as in exacerbating social and regional differences. No one can argue with certain geographical and geophysical circumstances, so the

Northerners, who had already a more layered middle class and were successfully wedding technological innovation to their more extensive farming potential, did not shudder as much, but it began to stress and crack the feudal organizations in the South. Not that in the North they were enjoying the easy life.[19]

But it was the beginning of what was to be known as the *crisi agraria*. The dissatisfaction created moreover followed upon the sale of ecclesiastical properties and government holdings to the landed gentry, which created a decrease in the number of proprietors. In addition, absentee landlordism required contract cultivation, and a free-for-all search for the lowest possible wages. This phenomenon is well known, as it applied also to the receiving developing countries, for instance in Brazil when slavery was finally abolished, and in Africa when the Europeans deployed local manpower for their colonies. In all, strapped tenants and small landowners saw themselves shut out of a viable route to develop the harsh agricultural terrains of the hinterlands. These were the prodromes of the Italian exodus.

6. MIGRATION, II

Here are some figures, reminders really, that tell a stark story.

Between 1900 and 1910, more than two million arrived to the US; in 1913, 872,600 "expatriated," of which 376,700 came to the US. From 1891 to 1921, some four million entered the US. Then after World War One, there followed immigration laws of 1921 and 1924.[20]

In short, it has been estimated that no fewer than 25 million Italians have emigrated between 1876 and 1976 (Cordasco, 499). If we consider that Italian population at the founding of the nation-state was anywhere between 26 and 30 million people (cf. Romanelli, Romano) and that today's population is just under 60

---

19 I subsequently researched this topic further. See, now, Carravetta 2007.
20 See, below, Ch. 3.

million, then what we have is an Italian presence in the world of which fully a third (and probably more) lives outside its national geopolitical borders. If we extend this Italian identity to second and third generation Italian-Americans (including both continents), and reasonably bring this figure to over 50-60 million people, we can speak of an *Italia dell'altrove*, or, and more significantly, as in the title of the Agnelli Foundation's distinguished contribution to these studies, *AltreItalie*, literally, the *Other Italies*.

In 1868 half of the Italian emigration was from Liguria, Piemonte, and Veneto. Genova was the leading port and transportation companies were favoring the flow of labor out of the country: it was good business, extending to the Swiss and the Germans. But it was thought of as a scandal, a blow to national pride: how could Italy not take care of its own![21] Sample gestures: Ercole Lualdi pressed government to look into the matter and consider ways to send these workers back to the farms. In January 1868 the government issued a decree barring emigration, and required prefects, mayors, and security forces to stem the (at that time still nominal) tide of migrants to the Americas by denying passports and take the first step toward what later became a full-fledged criminalization of emigration. On the other hand, shipbuilders, travel agencies, merchants, and other peripheral businesses appealed to the Minister of the Interiors against this action. Economist Jacopo Virgilio read a memoir explaining that spontaneous migration was good to siphon off the unemployed as well as to foster commercial exchanges with other countries. It should be remembered that at this time the destination was primarily South America, the Plata region and later Brazil. The notion that emigration contributed to the national economy by the revenues sent back to families left behind appears for the first time — a topic that will assume greater relevance in years to come.

---

[21] See the excellent reconstructions complemented with a wealth of philological data by Grazia Dore and the statistics collected by Ciuffoletti and Degl'Innocenti.

"Contexts Before The Journeys"

This is a sign that the "State" is intervening in the future of the country, and marks the embarrassment of the ruling elite. In 1875, Pasquale Villari publishes his *Lettere meridionali*, and the new nation "discovers" the underclass (Romanelli, 147), a situation that would bring the Right — *la destra storica* — to its downfall in 1876. In the 1870s among the major issues on the Italian panorama there was the *Questione Romana*, the tariff war with France, the consolidation of the bourgeoisie, the first organized workers movements (1874), the scandals behind the building of the railroads, and the debates over industrialization. But agriculture, from Lombardy to Sicily, lay waste among contending theories and interests. In 1877, Francesco Zanelli published an article that points to the grave situation the country was in:

> People migrate because needs have grown and earnings either remained stable or have diminished; people migrate because the farmer works six days and one day alone is for the tax on milling his product, which means that fifty days a year of labor are going to the State, whereas a high functionary or a councilman works a few hours to cover that same tax. Italy is buried in debt in order to build an army, create a navy, lay thousands of miles of railroad. But from all this the contadini have to date drawn no advantage: It shouldn't surprise anyone if they choose not to remain home and foot the bill. (Ciuffoletti-Degl'Innocenti, 36 sgg)

An important area of research is here flagging to be recognized: The debate around the legal, moral, and economic explanation, or justification, of the "story" of migration *after* the Italian peoples became the nation-state Italy. And the key role played by the Genovese shipping companies in determining toward "where" the migrants would go ought to be retold as well. Moreover, through which rhetorical strategies, on the basis of what presuppositions were articulated the role and function of public discourse were the reasons of the right (the *Destra storica*) and those of the Catholics (especially as they were losing their hold on the "Papal States"), as well as the wildly speculative theorems on the complementary dynamics of emigration and expanding mercantile venues (J. Virgilio in Ciuffoletti and Degl'Innocenti, 27), and the need for new and fast growing foreign markets. All traditional historians concur on the pervasive role played by basic economic dynamics, of course. What we are interested in here is how this tale was framed, who came up with it and for whom, who was the *destinataire* of these ideological mystifactions. And how specific types of travelers, or travelers who assigned themselves an identity (or social/bureaucratic "position") refer to these amorphous clusters of meaning, these unforeseen inexplicable social problems. The Crown and the Prime Ministers never got along on much of anything, except when it was useful to channel the King's expansionist military programmes toward the lobbying parliamentarians who first thought, in the 1870s, that perhaps Italy should secure colonies south, on that immense sleeping giant called Africa. Angelo Del Boca's *Gli Italiani in Africa Orientale* is still a necessary starting point to begin to grasp the complex interrelated forces behind the Italian presence in Africa. Many, in short, are the archives that need to be dusted off and thrown back around in circulation.[22]

---

[22] Politics, Costume, Literature: of course, a chapter here should be dedicated to *Trasformismo*, that peculiarly Italian invention of doing politics specifically aimed at gaining advantage and retaining power while meeting the demands of the most powerful capital interests. The "blocco agrario" against which Gramsci wrote compelling pages is one of the results of a confused politics, one that saw diverging forces pull in different directions but which sanctioned what today might be called "structured underdevelopment" of some parts of the country. Ironically, it began with the advent of the government of Agostino Depretis, fueled by the *sinistra storica* (recall that the Socialist Party was founded in 1892, so don't confuse the two), and it had to appease the Crown's dream of waging fantastical European wars and conquests beyond the seas. *Trasformismo* has lived many lives, from Crispi to Berlusconi, and it has marked the "national character" in some not so noble ways. A stimulating proposal concerning its effects on literature comes from the book by the late Giulio Bollati.

"Contexts Before The Journeys"

7. THE OTHER SHORE

The Other Shore in this subtitle is willingly ambiguous. The phrase "La Quarta Sponda" comes from the nationalistic prose of the beginning of the twentieth century, when pre-fascist elements were coagulating to justify the occupation of Libya. Although in the 1860s the interest in the Horn of Africa was primarily scientific and exploratory, the opening of the Suez Canal was very much in the mind of the first generation of Italian leaders (Del Boca, Dore, and Mack Smith). By the 1870s the need to secure a port on the Red Sea justified the taking of Massawa in Eritrea. Coupled with the hemorrhage of unskilled labor and the agrarian crisis, the seduction to find, in the words of Francesco De Renziz, "our place in the Sun," gained momentum. The Southern liberals actually had considered a rather dubious occupation of Somalia, and Northern interests backed the idea (cf. Romanelli, Hess, Ciuffoletti and Degli'Innocenti). But the King's incompetent armies, and Crispi's intemperate politicking would not allow for a peaceful settlement of the region, complex and literally unknown as the Horn of Africa was to Italian leaders, and jostled among contending European powers (Germany, France, and England) (cf. Pakenham). The result was a crushing defeat in 1887 at Dogali. Nevertheless, this was turned into a victory of sorts, and wounded national pride, together with the need to find a solution to the *questione migratoria*, only raised the ante, so that colonization turned into full-fledged imperialism by the 1880s. Fact is, with the waning of the Brazilian option, falling prices of coffee, a general economic crisis in Argentina, and growing pressure on the government to legalize migration, by the early 1880s the fork in the road became: Africa or America? (cf. Ciuffoletti and Degl'Innocenti, 126 et infra).

8. REFLECTION

According to Castronovo, the history of Italian journalism tells us how big business influenced what and *how* news was reported.

"Contexts Before The Journeys"

Not that there was no opposition to the peaceful occupation of Africa: Sydney Sonnino first and Nicola Colajanni later criticized severely the politics of coupling emigration with colonial expansion, but Francesco Crispi would not be shaken (he was prime minister several times, and can be considered a prototypical Mussolini himself).[23] Some newspapers did in fact report:

> Neither water nor commerce nor vegetation nor roads towards the interior, but fiery unhealthy desert, peopled by barbaric tribes: this is what Assab and the Red Sea offer. Their strategic value is not much: a funnel whose extremities are in the hands of England. (Cit. in Castronovo, 104)

But when parliamentary discussion turned, a few years later, toward a necessary justification to send troops and colonists to the horn of Africa and indeed beyond, inland, it was necessary to invent a different context. The opportunity was offered ironically, tragically, after the defeat at Dogali in 1887, and then after the one at Adwa in 1896. A rhetoric of revenge started circulating among the populace. When the dead soldiers arrived from Adwa in 1896, the best writers were called upon to express their dismay, anger, blanketing the country with a sense of tragedy, loss, and shame. When the Italians, having failed in the Horn of Africa, finally took Lybia, years later, we read:

> The Arabs are extremely pleased at the arrivals of the Italians because the Turks treat them like beasts and hope the Italians help them kick the French from Tunisia. The Arabs travel only on our ships, speak our language, because in their eyes we are the best of Europeans. (ib., 103)

However, the defeat at Adwa caps a series of events which include the first organized strikes by the emerging *movimento operaio*,

---

23 See now the biography by Christopher Duggan in his *Francesco Crispi*, 2002.

the crude repression of the *Fasci siciliani*, the growing debt which Crispi had racked up and the fall of his government. Despite the bombastic prose of the likes of Scalabrini (*Il trionfo della civiltà sulle barbarie*), Di San Giuliano (*Estinguere sull'altopiano l'antica sete di terra*), by the 1890s the choice was clear: the Other Shore was going to be North America.

Colonialism. Very little has been written by Italians on Italian colonialism, and even less outside of Italy, which is especially unsettling if we remind ourselves that the most intriguing research and theoretical debates in Anglo-America (as well as France and Germany) have come out of cultural studies, neo-colonial studies, post-structuralist analyses of texts and monuments, post-political reconfigurations that replaced the classical eighteenth, nineteenth, and early twentieth century political thinking.

In short, the guiding critical question returns: what is the relationship between Italy's colonialism and the mass emigrations during this period. A number of takes are possible. Consider Angelo Del Boca's *Gli italiani in Africa orientale*, which

> si propone di dimostrare, essenzialmente, che il colonialismo italiano dell'ultimo quarto dell'800 e dei primi decenni del '900 non e' stato "diverso", cioe' piu' umano, piu' illuminato, piu' tollerante, degli altri colonialismi europei coevi e del tardo colonialismo fascista. Intende anche provare che lo stato liberale, che e' l'artefice dell'espansionismo italiano in Africa, ha trasmesso senza ombra di dubbio alcune pericolose eredità al fascismo: una grande carica aggressiva, non frustrata neppure dalle sconfitte, la pratica del genocidio, il disprezzo per i popoli di colore, gli uomini per ritentare le imprese una prima volte fallite. (*Avvertenza*)[24]

---

[24] "[The book] aims to show that, basically, Italian colonialism of the last quarter of the XIX Century and of the first decades of the XX Century was *not* "different," that is, more human, more enlightened, more tolerant than that of the other contemporary European colonialisms and the later Fascist colonialism. The book intends to prove that the Liberal State, the mainspring of Italian expansionism into Africa, has consigned without the shadow of

"Contexts Before The Journeys"

The experience, the lives and resources spent, the prophecies and the disillusionments of European Colonialism and the Italian versions of imperialism enmesh Italy in African social history, while lodging themselves also, uneasily, in the Italian cultural unconscious. The Italian presence in Africa was connected with "l'imperialismo della povera gente" by Robert F. Foerster, and "imperialismo straccione" by scores of Italian political theorists and critics.

In general, however, there has been precious little on these intellectual arenas during the past twenty years.[25] Much like the quick page or extended footnote the phenomenon of the greatest mass migration in modern times receives in Italian histories of Italy, so does colonialism disappear as if something to forget or not to take too seriously.

The topic is becoming more complex, yet its political relevance could not be timelier. The critical questions behind cultural identity, and the incredibly complicated and conflicted origin "in the old country," evoke and provoke unsettling, when not paradoxical, considerations. Critical reassessment: what would a history of migration be like? Who would, or could, attempt such a task? What rhetorical structure would it adopt? What ideological and, more broadly, philosophical ideas, or truths, or beliefs, would be represented, vis-à-vis the historical actors, the social and political agents themselves, the very subjects of the narration, the emigrants...[26]

Among the problems facing the researcher in establishing what the actual immigrants thought about when they left, and

---

doubt a dangerous legacy to fascism: a powerful aggressive charge, which survived the defeats, the practice of genocide, the contempt for people of color, and the men willing to retake what they had previously failed to conquer."
25 [This chapter was originally written in 1996. See now listed publications by Donna Gabaccia, Ruth Ben-Ghiat, Daniele Comberati.]
26 In this context, documentary histories are of crucial importance in order to have the materials from the period back in circulation and subjected to contemporary analyses.

what idea they had of the lands where they were going, is the fact that the vast majority was illiterate.

9. HISTORY REVIEWED

It was not a grassroots politics that brought *piemontesi e marchigiani e lucani* under the same administrative legal aegis. It was an army; it was a king...a foreign king!!! It was European capital and industrialization...precisely, European political economies (cf. Castronovo among others). Why was the Unification experience never "popular"? This is not easy to answer, as we have to consider what a "popular" Italian consciousness would be like, or could have been, in the 1850s through the 1880s, when the word/concept has scarred our memories with the Fascists' re-semantization, its harping (yet again) to mythical and by now utterly distorted Roman history and origins; as well as with the fact that in the Western countries the notion of a *popolo* (or, in the US, of a "people") has been rendered practically vacuous and replaced by words such as public, audience, the masses, constituencies, and even political affiliation.

In some belated though no less compelling ways, Gramsci is still a crucial site to visit and assimilate. Gramsci's thesis is well known, basically it holds that a sense of national identity in Italy was never fully explored or developed on account of some infrastructural imbalances and dubious alliances of industrial and landed capital, the infamous *blocco industriale-agrario* which locked out the majority of the Southerners from partaking in the industrialization/modernization/Europeanization of the baby nation/state. But in a more subtle way by the self-promoting, inter-national, noble or aristocratic aspirations of a cultural elite, one which Gramsci places squarely in the lap of a Modern Europe, re-integrating into the narrative byways of Italian identity the relevance of the big tectonic shifts of the sixteenth and seventeenth centuries. [27]

In the background, the nascent colonialism, the exploding industrialization, grandiose investment schemes, the growing debate over labor, over rights of workers, over the vote for women. As well as new political theories. The Italian socialists understood this, they played with it structurally. An Italian Socialist party that started organizing strikes, earns itself a ticket into parliament, did not mind being Socialist *and* Italian. Historical events between the first and Second International made Filippo Turati and Antonio Labriola both accept the Nation of Italy as a necessary route, a dealt hand to play strategically.

On the other hand, other forces were unleashed after Unification became a reality. This was the re-configuration of an identifiable, specific Italian tradition, or what we call the Canon. In 1870 the Minister of Education Francesco De Sanctis publishes his masterpiece, the *Storia della letteratura italiana*. It was difficult not to be Hegelian in the heroic age of nationalism. And so the national allegory was written in a language for heroes, leading characters, of

---

[27] In a non-Gramscian context, but still consistent with it, Italy could easily be read as a master trope, or as a dominant figura, of the Modern World System (banking, accounting, complex relations among the rich and powerful even amidst regional fragmentation). It is a metaphor of abstraction, of thinking oneself as the outer limit of the possibility of the world (Hesperia), when in fact reality and society have dislodged that image and cast it back East...or Out. These intellectuals, says Gramsci, have consistently ignored or refused to engage concretely the great number of unskilled uneducated new "citizens" of the brand new nation-state called the Italian Monarchy, March 17, 1861. Sovereignty was diplomatically acknowledged by England on March 21. The *Nazione*, the *"nation,"* and the *Popolo*, the "people," did not really mix and blend, as they represented two different conceptual worlds, two different classes, two or more different geographic realities. In this dynamic, Gramsci disentangles the paradoxical situation of the Southern Italian intellectual, who must leave behind if not betray his original cultural milieu and become or play the game of the cosmopolitan upper crust intellectual (one which, as many have shown from Agnes Heller to Alberto Asor Rosa, was never too far from power, courts, big capital, influential statesmen, prestigious institutions, exotic connections, and so on). In a sense, Gramsci was telling us that a Modern Italian identity or cultural consciousness is already ideologically industrialist, politically on the Center-Right, culturally internationalist, and religiously ambivalent. Theses readapted much later by Pasolini to interpret post-WWII society.

no easy access, requiring academic packaging, specialized exegetes. But for 80% of the population, it might as well have been written …in Latin! Both God and Literature really only existed…up there.

Looking back, socialism and communism both only *appeared* to give a true alternative to the *questione del mezzogiorno*.[28] The underlying logic of these influential political-philosophical currents are overly rationalistic, capitalistic, expressions of bourgeois logic, belying an essentialist theory predicated upon a dualistic epistemology (cf. Hodge, Deleuze and Guattari). Perhaps they effected a critique in terms of *borghesi* vs *cattolici* or the left against the right or the upper class versus the lower class…but any such clear-cut yardstick for the evaluation of these narratives is no longer useful.[29] The story of migration cannot be told, cannot be spoken in a language, a syntax which is constitutively grounded in a true/false dichotomy, in a utopic Good to guard against all varieties of Evil. The great many Scholars and Historians who have tried to make sense of Italian history have consistently not-seen the emigrants because by and large their very methods of inquiry prevented them from seeing beyond the truth or validity paradigm. Or otherwise said, the economist has one method of analysis, the folklorist a different one, the literary historian looks for entirely different things.[30]

If we recall how complex the panorama was at the origin of the modern Italian nation-state, and how only by taking into account the joint dynamics of several constituencies, can a certain

---

28 Consider, for example, the very different reconstructions of the *topos* itself by S. Vacca and N. Bobbio.
29 Despite Norberto Bobbio's elegant, profound defense of the notion of a left and a right and wherein equality is seen as relative and not absolute, with at least three variables: a) the increasing or decreasing interest in equality: the subjects among whom one attempts to divide up the goods; b) which goods to divide; and c) the criterion on the basis of which they get divided up. It is clear how the last variable plays the role of ethical anchor to dynamics of the first two.
30 For the variety of theories of migration currently being practiced and developed, see the anthology by Brettell and Hollifield, eds., *Migration Theory* (2000), though the literary and artistic approaches are not included.

meaningful political palimpsest emerge, then what are we to say of today's even more volatile, media driven, cynical, ideologically bankrupt, and philosophically vacuous political scene? What kind of yet unsketched critical field do we need to even frame the issue of migration properly. And can it then be "applied" to literature? Or, what about today's writings by immigrants in Italy?[31]

To recall the questions at the beginning of this essay: can recent developments in Italy yield anything in the way of broadening our knowledge, or critical awareness, of the national allegories the emigrated knew (albeit poorly), or had heard about, and which were subsequently to be disconnected, and become lodged deep into their amorphous, non-culture-specific memories that get retold through later technologies like cinema?

On the face of it, very little. Just think of the Bossi syndrome. The nation and the state are obviously at cross purposes. Consider some period writings by Massimo Salvadori, especially his *Storia d'Italia e crisi di regime*, and Costanzo Preve's *Ideologia italiana*. The passion for institutional legitimations for given styles of (self-) analysis compels Italian historians to adopt easily reversible dualistic systems of explanation. After the fall of fascism, any new political configuration is grounded on being fundamentally anti-fascist. It spawned quite a few schools of thought, and several often colorful political parties. Recently, however, even the "mito della resistenza" came under attack, one might say finally: a *topos* that dominated party affiliations and historiography for well over four decades is now suspect, and owing to uncomfortable revelations and allegations, its rabble-rouser force is declining. Social history according to "party orientation" is no longer acceptable either. One can now ask: Why not review the horizon under consideration with alternative lens, more global notions. How do we

---

[31] This field has come into its own since I first wrote this chapter. See, for example, the work of Mia Lecomte, Armando Gnisci, Graziella Parati, Franca Sinopoli, Fulvio Pezzarossa, Simone Brioni, Cristina Lombardi-Diop, Caterina Romeo, Teresa Fiore, Clarissa Cló, and others.

re-connect between the "Origins" of the Archetypal Journey itself now fragmented in social national history, and the deeper forces of a signal investment in something called Progress, Europe, Emancipation, Freedom?

In terms of a periodization halfway between Braudel and Wallerstein, the Modern Era begins with the printed page and the major transatlantic discoveries, which favored a number of concurrent developments, primarily the hemorrhage of the Mediterranean eco-system, and then the rise of mercantilism, colonialism, absolute monarchies, scientific discoveries, the troubled gestation of the industrial revolution, etc. We cannot forget these factors, they are a significant component of the genesis of a sense of identity. Italy actually continued to be the major point of reference for European culture for another three centuries, its intellectuals present at all courts and academies, Naples was the New York of the earlier XVIII century. This created a cosmopolitan culture, a transnational community long before there was even talk of a nation called Italy. Risorgimento Italy, on the other hand, was also the product of the nationalistic winds that swept through the West in the wake of the American and French Revolutions, Napoleon, and the Congress of Vienna. Progressive, anti-clerical, industrious middle class persons endorsed nationalism. The more enlightened monarchies favored it. Thus the Italian sense of identity is heir to two overlapping broad cultural currents or set of ideologhemes, it inherits over the course of two centuries a noble if self-legitimizing and influential participation in international culture, and at the same it manifests the dynamics of a more materially based and 'regional" (here the "nation" is taken as a "region" of Europe) discourse, driven by a combination of business (agricultural as well as industrial) and an expanding urban class. Nevertheless, the larger myth usually is more quickly cited. Noble aristocratic Italy prized art for its own sake, was used to conversing about its fabulous past, and is very literate, linguistically sophisticated and versatile (the tradition of rhetoric, ecclesiastical first and then legalistic, bureaucratic), which will articulate the ideas, the specific syntax, of those very authoritative powerful now-become-original Fathers of the tribe. You might even say, thinking of oneself as Italian entails placing oneself into the very *humus* of Modern Europe.[32] At the same time, though, millions of emigrants with little or no knowledge of any of this "History" kept on being proud of being Italian, descendants of Dante and Columbus and Michelangelo and Verdi…

10. NARRATING THE NATION

In a sense, a *popolo* as understood by Gramsci and described by Carlo Levi was not to be the major agent in the history of the modern nation-state called the Italian Monarchy. Or rather, it was a relevant indeed necessary participant, but as a political subject, or objectively an under-class, disempowered, systematically excluded, and abused.

It is easy to develop this line of argument, and fall within the well-debated abovementioned parameters of *meridionalismo*. The notion has received fresh attention upon the Northern Italian provinces having suddenly re-discovered their "*Identità etnica, morale, culturale, insomma, il Nord o settentrionalismo.*" Just when through the late seventies and the early eighties regionalism and racism had shown signs of abating in public discourse, a spate of books came out on the subject. Luciano Cafagna, for example, goes over once again the likely explanation for the origin and development of the North/South social and political dynamic, and condemns those who enlist old ghosts to fight radically different battles.[33] Critics and historians such as Hobsbawn, Benedict An-

---

[32] A case can be made that the key figure in the rise of Modern Europe was Machiavelli. See my article "On the Formation of European Identities" in Carravetta 2003.
[33] It is the critique of the disenfranchised old left, those whom elsewhere I called the neo-modernists (Jameson, Luperini, Habermas). Their premises cannot yield more than what their theoretical limitations prescribe, as analyzed in my *The Elusive Hermes*, 2013.

derson, and Henry Louis Gates, Jr. have warned us against the insidious logic of interpreting history as a reversed guilt trip against one's present and past *padroni*, or *prominenti*; or worse to conceive of history as the story of the growing democratic middle class which had somehow the divinely inspired right to be redressed, to have justice rendered at last. For nearly a century, in the throes of two post-World War reconstructions, Italian society had no time to think of its brethrens' fate. The danger that lurked beneath is that of silently loosening an anachronistic *resentment against emigrants*, which worked in tandem with the aggressive transition on the social scene from an *Italia straccione* prior to WWI to *un'Italia fortemente (piccolo-)borghese e provinciale*, especially from the 1950s to about 1990.[34]

11. MIGRATION, III

Migration, immigration if we look at this from the point of view of where we are standing when we write, though inescapably the *arche'* of Italian Americans, manifests itself as an historically changeable dynamic, with many faces, varying aspects. We have to be conscious of the fact that the American forefathers had entirely different experiences than what one can imagine today. If we compare migration movements around the world today, we can make out some general tendencies which, to all accounts, are likely to play a role during the next twenty years, and will therefore influence how we look back at all previous migratory phenomena. Historical reconstructions cannot but be grounded in the present, it's an unnegotiable required punctum for historians, hermeneuticians, psychoanalysts. What are some general characteristics of today's migrations that may or may not apply to the Italian Exodus? Here is a list:

---

34 The country has subsequently witnessed a growth of foreign nationals to close to 8% of the population, approaching the number of immigrants to France, Germany, Spain, and the UK.

"Contexts Before The Journeys"

1. The globalization of migration. More and more countries are experiencing some sort of relevant demographic shift.
2. Acceleration of migration, which is to say that people's movements are increasing not only in frequency and size but also in speed, in *tempo reale* (no more three-week to three-month treks across oceans and continental divides).
3. Third and most important is the differentiation of migration, which throws havoc in the older theories (sociological, political, historical) insofar as countries no longer have only a relatively homogeneous group of immigrants, typically labor migrations (either skilled or unskilled), or otherwise single-drift relocations (such as for refugees) which entail a single major settlement. There are now several different types going on at once, among which are varying levels of specializations, specific and not easily acceptable political motivations, a different consciousness on the part of the principals who will now not settle for anything offered them, but can speak loud and clearly through previously unavailable means of communication.
4. Another key tendency is the feminization of migration. In the past women were accounted for only insofar as the family reunion part had come into the migratory process. Today this is no longer the case: Turkish women precede the men in Germany, just as Capo Verde women land in Italy, Filipino women seek work in the Middle East, and Thai women migrate on their own to Japan.

And we cannot ignore the very concrete problems immigrants face. Increasing ethnic diversity can appear threatening, can suggest loss of control, dissolving of everyday habits, indeed proliferation of what is different, or other. Hysterical reactions generate xenophobia, which then have a negative effect on the social order and policy. It is a fact, however, that whatever the social and economic patterns and equilibria of a given society, or environment, might be, immigration complicates them and unwittingly forces radical re-thinking or renewed awareness of one's own values, priorities, indeed the very philosophy and history that a society writes for itself generation after generation. *Ethnic diversity, racism, and multiculturalism are all implicated and reshuffled the moment we bring into the critical field the migrant or the migratory experience.* And these topics, these issues inevitably represent a challenge to strong thought, to canonical values, to national and cultural identity. There ensues, in the end, a calling out the name of a particular class' imposed tropology:

> The nation-state, as it has developed since the 18th century, is premised on the idea of cultural as well as political unity. In many countries, ethnic homogeneity, defined in terms of common language, culture, traditions and history, has been seen as the basis of the nation-state. (Castles and Miller, 14)

But now we must ask? Whose common language? Which idea of culture? What version of history? Once again: "Migration can change demographic, economic and social structures, and bring a new cultural diversity, which often brings into question national identity" (Castles and Miller, 3). In the nineties, my effort was first to attempt to give a broad semantic valence to the idea of migration, to the migrant itself, and use it as a working hypothesis. Still, a history of Italian American migration must nevertheless be built on solid empirical evidence. As John Saggar makes clear, Italian American ethnicity will receive less and less support for its life blood from the immigration factor, owing primarily to Italy's recent decades of economic wellbeing. On the other hand, Italian American scholars are, as Vecoli puts it, "coming of age," commenting moreover on the surprise manifested by Stephan Hall, who remarked on how Italian Americans "swell the ranks of the middle class, amass power and wealth and help set the decade's social and political agenda as never before" (in Tomasi 1985, 89).

In the mid-nineties Samuel Baily, in his article "The Future of Italian American Studies: An Historian's Approach to Research in the Coming Decade" (Tomasi 1985, 192-210), lists at least five new assumptions about migration that inform recent research:

1. Italian migration is a complex and dynamic process; we must reject mono-casual explanations such as those focused solely on labor markets and the environment.
2. Italian migration is an open-ended process. There is no one outcome nor does the process necessarily terminate after any given period of time.
3. The Italian background is essential to an understanding of what happens to the migrant in the US as well as to why he/she migrated in the first place.
4. The immigrant is an active participant who has influenced the nature of the migration process and is not just a helpless, passive pawn whose fate has been determined exclusively by larger impersonal forces.
5. Both change and continuity are at the same time part of the migration process.

The suggestions for future researchers include trying not to focus on just one issue, item or assumption, as the more dogmatic strong rationalists of yesteryear did, but accept the co-existence of continuity and change and attempt to see the phenomenon with two or more perspectives in mind. He furthermore sketches his own fruitful approach to any future history of Italian migration, one which combines *micro-historical methods of inquiry* (already used by anthropologists and recently adopted by Cinel, Arlacchi, and Sturino), *a dialectical framework* (which brings into the narration the pre-migration cultural context, or if you wish the problem of the origin), *and a comparative approach* (see Donna Gabaccia in Tomasi, Gastaldo, Row, 391-405). Francesco Cordasco's guide to the "Chronicles of Italian American Mass Migration," focusing on the *Bollettino dell'Emigrazione 1902-1927;* (ibid., 499-508), reiterates the cruciality and the validity of these new tendencies. He writes: "the exodus of Italians is inextricably linked to the fortunes of other nations." Thus we can conclude that *Italian migration history appears to be linked to European history, to the rise of Modernity, to the very fiber of the rise of the middle class, as well as to totalizing forms of discourse (Enlightenment, Emancipation, unlimited production, and reproduction) and the technocratic worldview.*

We must now enrich, develop, and transform these interpretive strategies. The rhetoric of legitimation during the years 1861-1913 is equally important as the silent, untold, unheard stories of the players themselves, of the bedazzled travelers themselves.[35]

12. THE MIGRANT

In a first and necessarily broad conceptualization, the emigrant is poor, poorly educated when not altogether illiterate, a straggled fearful and humiliated individual, a *superstite* in search of a better dwelling, anywhere. The emigrant cannot write his/her own history. It will have to be written by others, as we saw, or by succeeding generations. An emigrant can be talked about, preferably by his/her direct descendants. This history will be constantly threatened by unforgiving, obtrusive autobiographical references. It cannot be otherwise.

But the emigrant *lui-même*, comes out of nowhere. And cannot dig beneath nationalism, great ideals of liberation and emancipation, or appeal to God or Church. Though they share much with the history of the Jews, Italian emigrants to the Americas did not possess a congealing and spiritually/ethnically identifiable cement for the community such as the Torah and the unchanging rituals it required and provided for the Jewish diaspora. This alone has dire consequences: for it will be others, and predictably from a socially, economically higher class or grouping of interests, who will write the rules of grammar, the accepted encyclopedia of that society,

---

[35] Subsequent to writing this paper, I began a decade-long period of actual archival research in the said period, and have read several papers on topics ranging from the geographical societies to the rise of the public press to the Berlin Treaty. These will go into a projected volume on Italian identity, colonialism and emigration. See also chapter 3 below.

their controlling symbolic system, in the end, the history of the emigrant. They will come to be written ... off the history book, off of the memory of descendants, out of circulation in the commerce of cultural ideas and symbols of validation and entitlement.

The notion of being an emigrant cannot be defined univocally: it is a condition of *ontological foreignness*, the ultimate (e)stranger, either severing ties and leaving, or moving in to alter those present at arrival, already situated, with perhaps different language customs etc. The migrant is spontaneously, primordially to be feared, to be put quickly in place (whatever that may be at any given point in history).

CHAPTER TWO

DABBLERS, SMALL FRY, CANON FODDER: PROBLEMS AND PERSPECTIVES IN ITALIAN/AMERICAN LITERARY HISTORY[1]

> *Literature in the making, as well perhaps as our conception of what literature ought in the future to be, plays an important part in our definition of what will become history.*
>
> — Jean Starobinski, "The Meaning of Literary History" (1975)

> *The rhetoric of the "post-" indicates a kind of mercurial, theoretical progression that is constantly marking out new thresholds, frontiers, and boundaries, and in this very marking keeps crossing, traversing, and transcending these frontiers through a momentum that is irrepressibly indeterminate, nameless, and anomic. But it also represents the discovery of a temporality that deconstructs the authority of such structures as "genre," "period," "epoch," "episteme," "canonicity," etc.*
>
> — R. Radhakrishnan, "Ethnic Identity and Post-Structuralist Difference" (1990)

> *Until the lions have their historians, tales of hunting will always glorify the hunter.*
>
> — African proverb

1. QUESTIONS

The following remarks bear upon a cluster of recent cultural events in Italian American studies whose very existence and significance stirs renewed attention to critical and ideological assumptions of a broader nature. We can begin by mentioning the poets,

---

[1] This title is borrowed from a statement made by Italian writer Emilio Tarchetti (see below).

writers, and translators who gather about once a month and in different locations throughout the city of New York who named themselves *IAWA: Italian American Writers Association*.[2] IAWA is a new creature in the New York cultural ecosystem, a budding spore, an amorphous poetic attempting to figure itself out.

In concrete terms IAWA has been constituted by a group varying from as few as six or seven to as many as twenty poets, writers, and translators with the sporadic participation of intellectuals of all stripes who manage to meet, discuss, read, rethink, prospect, and project anything related to their craft, identity, and presence as a cultural force in these here United States, in this here Northeast. The common denominator, the major issue being: what is an Italian/American Writer? Is there such a thing as an Italian/American literature? And if so, why has it not emerged earlier in history, and why did it just come to surface in the eighties and nineties, amidst confusion and contradictions, excitement and distrust?[3]

2. CONTEXTUAL BEARINGS

There have also been some institutionally endorsed cultural encounters whose very titles lend themselves to deconstructive upstagings. Limiting myself to a circumscribed period, I am referring

---

[2] IAWA came out of several discussions held in Spring of 1990 between Robert Viscusi, Peter Carravetta, and Theresa Aiello-Gerber, soon joined consistently by Vittoria Repetto, Adele La Barre, and Kathryn Nocerino. It started monthly encounters in Greenwich Village in the Spring of 1991, mostly at the Cornelia Street Café'. Among the more assiduous presences in the first few years I would like to mention Anthony Valerio, George Guida, Rosette Capotorto, Claudia Menza, Luciana Polney, Carmine Risi, Maria Mazziotti Gillan, and Daniela Gioseffi. Under the leadership of Robert Viscusi, the group has been organizing readings at the Cornelia Street Café, the Nuyorican Café and other locales, setting up book presentations at major bookstores, and has begun a Literary Canon Project which entails selecting one Italian American publication a month and have as many people as possible buy it and discuss it. The motto has become: *Write or Be Written*. [The Association has had since an incredibly successful run; for details go to www.iawa.net].

[3] Needless to add that a strong stimulus toward assembling these remarks was provided by Gay Talese's provocative "Where are the Italian American Writers" which appeared in the *New York Times Book Review* in March, 1993. For various responses see issues of *VIA* and *italian americana* dedicated to the topic.

to a poetry reading held at SUNY Stony Brook in April of 1992 titled "La Vita Nuova: Italian and American Poetry" (with the participation of D. Gioia, J. Tusiani, and others); one at Yale University on the symbolic October 12th, 1992, titled: "American & Italian Poetry: New Directions?" (with poets A. De Palchi, E. Paulicelli, C. Luisi, and M. Mazziotti Gillan). The following day, on the 13th, the Italian Cultural Institute in New York hosted a reading bearing the title: "Italian and American Poetry Today." Notice that the label "Italian/American" is nowhere present — whereas it was present at innumerable readings throughout the late eighties at various venues such as clubs and local or regional associations, picking up in the early nineties at colleges and universities, such as those held at Purdue University's annual Romance Languages Conference in October 1990, 1991, 1992, and others since, in addition to the group readings organized by Robert Viscusi and myself at Brooklyn and Queens College respectively, during the spring semester of 1992, and for many years after that.

The reader should bear in mind that all the intellectuals (shorthand for poets, critics, translators, professors, teachers, and so on) mentioned up to now generally know of one another, and in many cases some have worked together on common cultural projects in the past: we are, as they say in Italian, *quattro gatti.* Therefore, one might casually ask: is there a motivation behind this labeling of separate groups or identities, this subtle politics of naming? We must also ask ourselves why in some of these encounters the organizers chose to state in their official public announcement that they were *not* going to feature what is/has been called Italian/American poetry, especially as some of the poets invited can be, and have been, called precisely Italian/American poets.[4]

---

4 Let us ask more specifically: Why have the American poets Dana Gioia and at various times the Ferlinghettis, Sorrentinos, De Lillos and Ciardis been so bothered by their being associated with something called Italian/American poetry or literature, and why, conversely, are the Italian poets — who are longtime residents in America — such as Luigi Fontanella, Alfredo De Palchi, Paolo Valesio, and Giovanni Cecchetti so reticent and conflicted

3. METACRITICISM, I

Perhaps we should think about the politics of naming. If a group of intellectuals does not associate under a name, a title, a label of sorts, it practically does not exist. It will be invisible and inevitably considered irrelevant, as its namelessness (and therefore lack of "identity") will at best place it outside the legitimizing systems of signs that co-exist and communicate in various guises in a given society. This becomes more compelling if we think about the fact that such a grouping is unable to travel and transfer its symbols and ideas along the many media channels that make up the most pervasive aspects of our social lives: the press, TV, publishing, internet, universities, etc. On the other hand, the moment a group of poets or intellectuals comes together under a Name, a banner, a poetic, many peers feel compelled to decide whether to be included in or excluded from their midst or association, often manifesting complex yet explicit political diffidence, and/or stake out precise claims in the terrains of contemporary culture. A name brings something to light, makes it interact, but by virtue of acquiring *an* identity, it also acquires *one* identity amidst many other possible ones, whether actually existing or yet to be devised. Criticism and historiography will have to accept the risk of abstraction by speaking in categories and labels, or suggesting groupings. This act of critical intervention may actually be a semiotic and pedagogical precondition, and it does not necessarily subscribe to or impose a restrictive or definitive value. Like literature itself, criticism must constantly negotiate and revise when opportune its conceptual grid, its ideological claims.

---

about their association, inclusion, and therefore occasional identification with Italian/American poets? The fact that such diverse and highly individualistic writers in the two languages manifest a certain *disagio*, unease, warrants investigation into a cultural semantics, or discursive formation greater and more complex than any one of its specific articulations. [In more recent times, Helen Barolini as well claimed that she wishes to be identified as a writer, not as an Italian American writer. It appears the qualifier is deemed either too restrictive or…perhaps no longer necessary?].

4. RESPONSES

At first, I thought we could read and listen to the poetry at these events in relation to American literature, and then to Italian literature, separately, before considering possible future directions for an Italian American literature. This is as valid an approach as any, being acceptably grounded in our collective institutional memory. However, the fact stood out: hyphenated or not, Italian American literature had disappeared. The reasons for the exclusion from the title of these representative, "typical" academic encounters, the force of this silence, may be embedded in the empty space between the two words, Italian [ ] American.[5] It may also rest buried beneath the diacritical mark: Italian-American, even if turned sideways till it becomes a slash, Italian/American.[6] Or the ampersand, or better yet, in the conjunction "and." Whichever of the three paths chosen by literary criticism, one can still register an underlying discomfort or annoyance, and the energy of an unstable yet uncodified discursive formation. There is certainly some resistance to a more sympathetic and open-ended exchange. And there are many signs that equal opportunity is not desired.

I think we should explore this "border" that haunts the relationship between the Italian community in America (made up in great part by professionals who grew up and studied in Italian cities and came to the US as educators, or specialized labor) and the Italian American communities, which encompass, especially in cities like New York, Philadelphia, Toronto, San Francisco, and

---

5 This is a difficult path, mapped out most recently by Viscusi (1995), where the originary identity of the Italian American is evoked through Ignazio Silone's political allegory *Fontamara*, that is, by baring that sense of imposed/acquired "nothingness" vis à vis a more economically, politically, and linguistically empowered social class. For a couple generations of Italian immigrants to the United States, that "provenance" or "originary group identity" is precisely the environment depicted by Silone. We could just as easily evince a similar background, a deep unspeakable sense of existence out of Carlo Levi's *Christ Stopped at Eboli*.

6 On the complex implications of this minute detail, see Anthony Tamburri, *To Hyphenate or Not to Hyphenate* (1991), which among its merits totally circumvents deconstructive approaches!

Chicago, people of greatly differing social and economic status, with the simultaneous presence of aging immigrants and first, second, and third generation...Americans. For it is my contention that *the two cultures, the two worlds, cannot communicate unless they trespass into the conjoining tertium of Italian/American culture and literature*, and through that, reconfigure whatever the latter thinks it is.[7] Perhaps the *and* between "Italian and American culture and literature" should become an *is*....[8]

I feel it is an ethical imperative for an intellectual to explore the force of cultural legitimation of a certain group of writers who must willy-nilly find an identity of sorts. Moreoever, the focus must be directed to the persons and the realities whereof they speak, stand in as, and ultimately *re*present, inasmuch as there is present a struggle to survive and a desire to inscribe their (hi)stories in the shifty borderless quilt called America, and not become, to borrow from the title of Eric Wolf's illuminating book, *a people without history*.[9] This ushers us to a political domain and a diffuse cultural politics of empowerment and legitimacy. We must in short address specific ideologies and comportments, which can nonetheless be loosely understood: in the present case, as a postmodern version of the old class struggle, that is, not simplistically a contest of economic and managerial power, rather a trans-class

---

[7] See Robert Viscusi's illuminating 1991 essay on the birth pangs of a literature struggling to emerge from misrepresentation, chaos, and silence.

[8] Incidentally, in Italian what distinguishes one è (verb) from the other e (conjunction) is a mere *accent* which, by the way, is a cryptic way of understanding the entire *questione della lingua*. To assess the complexity of the problem of a founding literary language faced by Italian American writers, see Viscusi (1981).

[9] Besides Eric Wolf, my underlying approach to the issues dealt with in this chapter has profited also from the "global" interpretations of history provided by Immanuel Wallerstein, Benedict Anderson, and Janet Abu-Lughod. I have also gained crucial insights from the interventions contained in the listed anthologies by David Goldberg, Stuart Hirschberg, René Jara and Nicholas Spadaccini, and Abdul JanMohamed and David Llyod. See *References*.

struggle for symbolic cache and prestige.[10] The reason why I feel that any discussion focusing on Italian poetry and on American poetry *at the same time and place* without considering Italian/American literature as its hermeneutic fulcrum is untenable and misleading is that, if this were not case, then the intellectuals who organize such conferences and readings must presuppose the existence of and belief in a Hegelian Spirit of sorts, one that unites teleologically such concepts as La Letteratura, the Eternal Canon of this or that National Allegory,[11] and providentially speckles them with the Great Works of John Doe. Alternatively, the organizers and promoters of Italian Literature only, or of American literature only, who disallow the legitimate participation of a mixed category, or the hyphenated cousin, must perforce be trustees of a Standard or Unified History of the rise to power of *la bourgeoisie*, with all the trimmings thereunto appertaining. In either case one could reasonably sustain a class conspiracy theory of history. That would be overly conservative at this point! Most critics I know would not accept it: we are, *volens nolens*, in the Post-Modern Age, so we must fashion alternative instruments of inquiry, reclaim the faculty of *inventio* insofar as interpretive discourse is no longer "secondary" to the mythical Original Text, is not an "enemy" of

---

10 I am aware some of these terms and concepts are *unzeitgemassen*, untimely (as in the sense of unwanted even), as many, too many intellectuals have quickly tossed leftist critiques out the window after 1989. Nevertheless, has anyone listened closely to the "infomercials" concocted for and spewed by our presidential and gubernatorial candidates recently? The variety of cultural and political discourses are hardly ever synchronous, to be sure. But that is another story. Yet not mentioning the issue of class does not mean it is now gone away. [For an analysis of American culture in the nineties, see now Carravetta 2009,153-238; English translation forthcoming]

11 Interestingly enough, Italy's greatest nineteenth century critic (and to some of the twentieth as well) was Francesco De Sanctis, whose *Storia della letteratura italiana*, published ten years after Unification, strings in one spiraling paradigm seven centuries of literature in which the Italian "spirit" was forged, leading to its historical realization in the Piedmontese sovereign monarchy (De Sanctis had studied and translated Hegel's *Logic* while in prison after the 1848 war. After Unification, he became Minister of Education).

poetry, and its political import cannot be casually glossed over.¹²
We must rethink the capacity to effect a critique of history, primarily by weaving a different narrative strong of some peculiar or unique characteristics of "our times," our declining century. As Radhakrishnan writes:

> In its very relational and differential disposition, the "time of the post-" makes perennial pre-histories of grounded, authoritative time. The flow of the "post-" is hence the transformational and critical momentum of a certain way of knowing that is incompatible with knowledge as conservation. (1990, 70)

There is something polemic in this, attuned as it is to what we can call the microphysics of power, and the constantly shifting portrayals of society, of art, and indeed of ourselves. Interpretation must regain or return to the social, political, public *agora*. In short, there is need to re-write the Italian literary canon, looking for the reasons for certain exclusions, for certain taboo topics, and for certain stylistic prejudices.[13]

In the post-modern context, there are no overall unifying onto-theologies any longer, or at least any credible or overwhelmingly empowered versions of it. Therefore, Italian American literature doesn't have to be absorbed, integrated, or homogenized within the precincts of a (pre)dominant aesthetic or critical community — not that American literary history has been kind to it. Only in a

---

12 For extended explorations on these topics see my Carravetta (1991), (1995a), and (1995b), besides the well known though diverse works by Pier Paolo Pasolini, Edward Said, Homi Bhabha, Arjun Appadurai, Stuart Hall, and Jean Baudrillard.

13 Italian literary theory and history of the past twenty years, for example, shows an uneven map: strong and challenging writings in semiotics, political criticism, European history, and philology; a long-standing reductive judgment on *meridionalismo* (and its associated topics: poverty, pre-bourgeois rural life, fatalism, migration, superstition, and of course oppression) and the "sociological" literature it produced. But there is nearly nothing in feminism, third-world studies, minority literature. [We can now add the reticence to "accept" immigrant writing. See on this latter topic the work of Armando Gnisci, Franca Sinopoli, David Forgacs and Graziella Parati].

handful of books, and only in the past twenty years, has mention of Italian/American poetry been made.[14] The pioneers have passed away not long ago (I am thinking in particular of John Fante, Pietro Di Donato, and John Ciardi), while the grandchildren — fully certified "native" Americans — have only relatively recently taken to the streets to flag their existence. Yet this literature remains at the fringes, in the cracks, in the occasional encounters off- off- Broadway, so to speak, or *From the Margin*, as the 1991 milestone anthology edited by A. Tamburri, F. Gardaphé and P. Giordano explicitly states in the title.

5. BOUNDARIES, MARGINS

Nevertheless, it is preliminarily necessary to try to decipher this marginality. Some Italian American poetry can express itself in the not always visible or accessible folds of the "global city," or it can live a life that evokes ancient, medieval, and romantic traits. By and large, however, it sits comfortably in the high modernist arena,[15] or is impacted by the avant-gardes.[16] By the same token, when it is occasionally recognized, or even prominently displayed, we ought to ask how and why some have "made it" while others have not, and at what price.

What is wrong with a literature being called "ethnic?" And is that necessarily a negative association? Ethnicity today recalls or includes a class-dominating, colonizing, alienating dimension, something problematic, perhaps overblown, but no less a major social and political force. So in charting a hypothetical literary history, is the chapter on ethnicity something to be ignored, too restricted a theme, canon fodder at best? Or rather, is it not the case that the question of the *ethnos* may permit and disclose at once the inscrip-

---

14 See Helen Barolini's illuminating "Introduction" to *The Dream Book* (1985) and Mary Joe Bona's "Introduction" to *The Voices We Carry* (1994).
15 I am thinking of the fiction of Pietro di Donato, Nino Ricci, John Fante, and Helen Barolini.
16 I am thinking of course of specific artists such as Diane Di Prima, Gregory Corso, Lawrence Ferlinghetti, and Gilbert Sorrentino.

tion of this chapter into a larger network of problems? Why do so many poets need to express, at times in violent or rage-laced verse, that they are Italian?[17] It suddenly appears that the perfect, specular relation between self and society is disturbed, perhaps cracked. The need to assert an Identity which initially speaks its otherness or difference — now reflects, as if by default, as if a haunting shadow, the crises, uncertainties, and liabilities of the Society.

"My name is Maria,/ do not call me Marie." "My name is Vittoria, no 'c'." These lines, so powerfully launched out from the pages of Maria Mazziotti Gillan and Vittoria Repetto, quickly turn into synecdoches for an inexistent Italy, an apology and a lament, a revelation and a judgment. Something beyond myself, greater than me, compels me to state my public identity, my social identity, by uttering the name...of a foreign country!!! It is not much different when poets experience the compelling need to articulate in their otherwise high modernist and even experimental texts such disarmingly simple yet ever targeted (to the high brow intellectual) affirmations: Soy Chicana, hombre; I am Chinese American, I am a black American, I am an American Jew, I am a Native American.[18] This rhetoric immediately falls in step with other strong, often strident, claims for recognition and affirmation by other socio-political communities, such as by feminist and gay and lesbians groups, and begs the question of where the aesthetic ends and the political begins.

Perhaps we should look at when hyphenated America started circulating as a concept, a recursive discursive formation. Could it be that America can only speak through its otherness, its *others*, those who are from elsewhere? Or who do things differently? But

---

17 Especially when the great majority of these writers do not know the Italian language or its literature well or at all, and have at best a tourist's understanding of contemporary Italy.
18 Maria Mazziotti Gillan and Daniela Gioseffi in particular have done much work over many years in bridging gaps and weaving connections with other "ethnic" or "minority" or "hyphenated" poets and writers.

then, would this not cast some light, a new palette of vistas, on the rest of American literature, on the rest of all literary productions? Could it be that the ethnicity chapter makes Italian Americans aware of their historical exploitation, disempowerment, exclusion, devaluation? Rejected by both English and Italian departments and their critical infrastructure, an Italian American literary history would have to forge its theorems and methods out of the very experience of its travailed, long-standing, casually condescended to, and systematically boycotted history of its disturbing origins.

Yet the question can also be framed differently, for first and foremost, we would have to ask: what are they talking about? Because they *are* saying something, of that we can be sure. What are they elevating to aesthetic heights? What are they digging for beneath the humus? [19]

6. TRANSITION, I

Dana Gioia (1993) wrote that a distinctly Italian/American literature is necessarily another passing myth, "a transitional category." No doubt this triggers the parallel and broader question of whether "ethnicity" as a whole is not itself a passing category.[20] Deferring discussion on this paradoxical conundrum to a different chapter, the question we must still pursue is: But the poets and novelists who are identified by this category, their works, and thus what they spoke of, are those transitional also? If we abandon the category, and do not want to lose, in these times cruel to the

---

[19] Of course, these questions presuppose that poetry speaks about something. How could it not be so? The notion of an (ideal, or positable) autonomous work of art is ideologically deveined and philosophically no longer compelling, rendered harmless: the avant-gardes as resistance and rebellion are gone, make less sense, no sense. *Post-modern poetics entail preliminarily the heteronomous status of any cultural artifact or discourse.* For a more thorough articulation, see "The Wake of the Avant-gardes" in Carravetta (1991), as well as my 1994 article "Tuning in/to the Diaphora."

[20] See on this the influential articulations by Stephen Steinberg, *The Ethnic Myth* (1981), Rudolph Vecoli, "The Search for an Italian American Identity" (1985), and Richard Alba, *Italian Americans: Into the Twilight of Ethnicity* (1984 [2001]).

arts, the poets and narrators, how do we read the poetic? To phrase it differently: if the category or class is allegedly waning, does that mean that the individual families and species also vanish? If I do not name the rose, does the rose still exist? More than that: can I ever read them at all? I am not questioning their aesthetic validity, assuming as I must, provisionally at least, that they are all "good" and worthy of study. But I can still single them out by stylistic forms, by dominant metaphors, by the direction and force of their rhetoric, and compare them to fellow poets from the canon as well as from other marginalized territories. Echoing unforgettable lessons from graduate school, both phenomenology and philology taught us: go to the things themselves, return to the text! This, in fact, seems a rich path to explore.

7. CRITIQUE, I

Let us begin to approach Italian/American texts by theme, or dominant topic. For instance, we can perceive varying levels of expression of what the editors of *From the Margin* have called *italianità*, the "italianness" that exudes implicitly or explicitly from what is basically an American poem. Is this relevant to literary history? Of course. By electing to study the "Italianness" of a story or poem once again I am fishing in the larger sea called America:[21] Consider the following lines by Rose Romano:

> ...They seem to have come over
> accidentally. My aunt can't offer a satisfactory
> reason why they would leave a home of
> respect and riches — a count and a countess —
> to come so far to this classless
> society, where they were just two more

---

[21] For exemplary readings of how to retrieve the "Italian subtext" from writings which do not even appear to be dealing with the issue, see works by John Paul Russo on the poetics of Gilbert Sorrentino, Fred Gardaphé on Frank Lentricchia, and James Periconi on Don De Lillo.

> wops. I try to imagine the bay, the hills
> rising in green steps around it.
> Mt. Vesuvius smoking. But when my aunt
> explains that my grandparents owned a
> villa in Castellammare, which she describes
> as a suburb of Naples, all I can see
> is my cousin at his barbecue in his backyard
> in Staten Island. (1990, 10)

Suddenly the patent duality, the stereoscopic sense of existence, the double-life being lived/created splits the totalizing ontology of Self and Image, the Correspondence Theory of Truth, the very philosophy of Mimesis.

Let me make this clearer by citing a passage from the article "Interrogating Identity" by Homi Bhabha, in which he glosses Fanon: "What is often called the black soul is a white man's artifact." This transference speaks otherwise. It reveals the deep psychic uncertainty of the colonial relation itself: its split representations stage the division of body and soul that enacts the artifice of identity, a division that cuts across the fragile skin — black and white — of individual and social authority (1992, 44).

Translated into our current thematic, we shall emphasize a double locus from which to issue a different kind of discourse. Black and white can methodologically be substituted with Italian and American. It is clear that for the Italian American writer, a great deal of expressive tension and interpretive torsions occur right at inception as the text ventures to negotiate continuous reconfigurations of name and reality, in the inscription of a subaltern past or non-glorious (namely, not accepted, not wanted, not profitable!) background. And it is also evident that the imaging process that captures this tension between demand and desire fractures the logical (and) symbolic order(ing) of master tropes, textbook editing, and political correctness. One dominant, generating topos of this literature will be the question of an identity always predicated upon the state or status of being different:

> You're a doctor, a writer, a student, you're different, you're one of us. It is precisely in that ambivalent use of different — to be different from those that are different makes you the same — that the Unconscious speaks of the form of otherness, the tethered shadows of deferral and displacement. (ibid., 44-45)

In other words, what will surface time and again is not just the precarious and arbitrary complementarity between self and other, or the jeremiahs of individual hyphenated or foreign expressions against a deaf yet all encompassing, legitimizing American literary canon, but the "disturbing distance in-between" that constitutes the figure of hyphenated or binational otherness. Our subjects will be found translating themselves into an alternative life, a different name, stating an identity that immediately unravels the blanket lie of a self-defined and authoritative trope, the vacuous tokenism of a threatened constituency.

8. CRITIQUE, II

If we continue speaking of this hypothetical yet somehow relevant Italian "content" or "subtext" in the productions of some of the writers mentioned, we are setting ourselves up for the next major question, which rings thus: *which Italy*? Again, against some strong resistance from the academy, especially Departments of Italian in North American universities, we can draw inspiration from Antonio Gramsci's "Southern Question" and posit a yet unthematized *Italian American Question*. This route, however, requires that we take not an oppositional, dichotomous approach, but rather a two-pronged post-historicist, post-structuralist, and post-Marxist look at Italian historiography and indeed Italian history textbooks (basically from 1914 on) in order to start analyzing, first, how the exclusion, or omission, of some five million Italians from the National History, *la Storia Patria*, is or is not accounted for.[22] Second, on the other critical prong, we should begin to assess the dynamics, within the Italian American (self)narrative, of the degree and type of associations that actual agents and fictional characters alike make with *la Madre Patria*, what are the chosen icons, the recurring stylemes, whether this nostalgic yearning for the lost homeland changes in nature, adopts new metaphors, refers to specific political figures over time. Although this will turn out to be highly symptomatic of how multilayered and differentiated the Italian American psyche is and has been, what will prove most shocking is the incredible (and, to me, absurd) chasm that has existed and tenaciously persists between the sense of *italianità* of the Italian Americans (or, better yet, the Americans of Italian descent), and the sense of *italianità* of the Italians from Italy...the whys and wherefores of this paradoxical situation would require long interdisciplinary analyses, and must be taken up somewhere else, but I think it represents a field for future research.[23]

---

[22] I have done a preliminary incursion in this area in a paper read at the "Italian Migrations" conference held at Berkeley in September, 1996. [See now chapter One, above].

[23] Among the segments of greater New York City residents who are aware of this problematic yet somehow seem to contribute more to its falsification and misrepresentation than to its critical and creative possibilities, are the correspondents of some major Italian dailies or weeklies stationed here. With the rare exception of a Furio Colombo, the formulaic paucity of the modern Italian *politichese* combined with the facile yet supercilious reportage are not transmitting anything serious or worthwhile to an Italian American collective unconscious whose Italy is constantly threatened and simultaneously and forever *faraway*, *past*, an in/definite ancestor...and nothing more. In a recent special feature of the Sunday edition of *Il Corriere della Sera*, Vittorio Zucconi offers a cultural "anthropology" of the Italian Americans in Brooklyn, highlighting their uprooted and therefore unlikely hybrid town rituals within an American metropolis, with a rich predictable selection of photographs illustrating butchers, pizzaioli, and crazed soccer fans. Italians from Italy should try having that reportage done by one of the local informants, whereas those Italian intellectuals residing here and working in the universities ought to try to mediate and inform their compatriots "back home" directly. Given their years among the "natives," they are culturally better positioned to "understand" their Italian American counterparts, at least some of them are. But, theoretically, Italian America is much more complex than a superficial tour of Bensonhurst or Arthur Avenue can possibly disclose.

9. METACRITICISM, II

On what should a literary history of Italian/American writing be based on? Should it borrow the model from established American literary history?[24] or should it rather consider Italian literary history? The question is hardly moot as each has specific histories, asynchronous economies and peculiar ideologies. Or should it rather look into itself and forge the instruments of its own discourse, speak its own voice? But how can we determine "one's own voice" without reference to someone else's voice(s)? And how do we describe this voice if the very critical category which we employed to make it visible, has already been theorized out of historical continuity and relevance (as we saw above with Dana Gioia, and will see below with Werner Sollors). This problem has been already faced by Canadian/Italian writers, who had to consider the compound problem of a tri-lingual, tri-cultural interaction, wherein each single community at one time or another claimed the hegemonic role (Pivato 1991, 17-34). For example, should we adopt Fredrick Turner's "frontier hypothesis" with its attendant geographical determinism? or should we turn to a central theme, a master trope, say, that of "survival," as Margaret Atwood argues in her book *A Thematic Guide to Canadian Literature*, which begins with the question whether "Canada as a whole is a victim, or an oppressed minority or exploited"? (Pivato 1991, 23). On American literary territory, how does the Italian American "type" — whether it is Fante's Bandini or Puzo's Corleone — stack up against the deeply entrenched American hero tradition? the imperial self paradigm? the frontier loner category?

---

24 *The Harvard Guide to Contemporary American Writing* makes no reference to a supposed Italian American literature, while in the *Columbia Literary History of the United States*, only De Lillo and Sorrentino make the grade (Ahearn 206), and at that without any mention of the fact that they are...Italian. For historical background on the shifting mores of the American literary community vis à vis the representation of Italians see John Paul Russo's article "From Italophilia to Italophobia" in *DIFFERENTIA 6/7*, now in Russo and Casillo, 329-360.

10. GENERAL TOPICA

Italian American criticism stands to enrich its vocabulary and broaden its intellectual relevance by staying in tune with some of the revolutionary and inspiring work being done in Black studies, Latino American studies and colonial studies.[25] Topics explored in detail in these schools of criticism include the body in relation to place, which can most fittingly be studied through novels, from Garibaldi Lapolla's *The Grand Gennaro* to Helen Barolini's *Umbertina* to Robert Viscusi's *Astoria*, as well as in quasi-biographical works, such as Jerre Mangione's *Montallegro*, Josephine Gattuso Hendin's *The Right Thing to Do*, and the autobiographical-historical account by Richard Gambino, *Blood of my Blood*. Here equal relevance is automatically assigned to Italian American non-verbal communication, which can only be described through narration, by re-setting the body and its silent codes in motion in the given virtual space of the artistic expression, the narrative utterance.[26] Another area is religious life, and the ambivalent role the Church has played, historically, both in the country of origin and in the communities in North America. And then there is the issue of gender that started women studies, many fine poets and a growing body of criticism. Yet another, the relation between individual and place of work, or job, and the symbolic universes that sustain the questing and responding of the literary activity itself.[27]

---

25 See, for instance, the listed works by Henry Louis Gates, Jr. (1984) and (1988); Marta E. Sánchez (1985); *Yale French Studies*, 2 Vols., Nos. 82 & 83 (1993); Homi Bhabha (1992); and the rich collection in Jara and Spadaccini (1992).

26 Needless to say, the medium most appropriate for this recounting is film, and there exists already a substantive filmography. See Sautman's article in *DIFFERENTIA* 6/7 (1994). For a brief account of Hollywood's portrayal of Italian Americans, see Carlos Cortes, "The Hollywood Curriculum on Italian Americans" (1994). See now the anthologies edited by Camaiti Hostert and Tamburri (2001) and Muscio, Sciorra and Spagnoletti (2010).

27 On these last two areas also there is a growing body of criticism, often starting with rereadings of Di Donato's *Christ in Concrete* as paradigmatic case. See Gardaphé (1996), as well as the latter's Introduction to the reissue of *Christ in Concrete* in the Signet edition (1993, ix-xviii).

"Dabblers, Small Fry, Canon Fodder"

One debate in Italian American literary history focuses on the question of whether, where, and how an identification between stock characters and mythical figures such as Ulysses, Aeneas, Dante, Christopher Columbus, etc. constitute valid founding myths for Italian Americans, and a narrative for their long lost noble ancestors. This is an issue which more disciplined and conservative critics have decried as ill-placed, ideologically flawed, untenable, inapplicable to the not-so-glorious beginnings of the Italian American immigrants,[28] which at most succeeded only in suggesting a reprobate, low-life *res gestae*.[29] No one wants poor or uncouth cousins. Paradoxically, one great topos of Italian Americana is defined by its unmentionableness, birthing a question of silence. Partly though vigorously challenged by women writers, the Italian American critic will have to explore this unwritten, and perhaps unwriteable chapter, by going beyond the sociocultural common places typically associated with the Italian's reluctance to speak out,[30] and search if perhaps there is not something deeper, more elusive, more pervading that is locked up in silence. Closely connected is another dominant semantic cluster, that of "home life," especially in the early novels and histories of Italian American culture. This area foregrounds the life of the underprivileged, the straggled illiterates, the confounded pilgrim. In a 1986 article, Barolini recalls she was affected by the notion that a

> [w]riting that touched on what I felt deeply — my estrangement from models of Anglo-American life, my discovery of being outside it — was considered marginal, ethnic, exotic. A ludicrous example of how that kind of down-grading is mindlessly ex-

---

[28] See for instance the discussion by Pivato and the critique by Carrera in *DIFFERENTIA* 6/7.
[29] The issue has been interpreted differently but ever cogently by just about every expert in Italian American studies, from Basile Green to Gambino, from Viscusi to Vecoli,
[30] See for instance Marco Micone's play, *Voiceless People* (2001), where the character Nancy at one point explains: "I teach teenagers who all have Italian names and who have one culture, that of silence. Silence about the manipulations they're victims of. Silence about the country they live in. Silence about the reason of their silence."

tended is the reference to Luigi Pirandello, Nobel Prize winner from Italy and one of the leading world dramatists of our century, as an "ethnic" writer. It was as though to write from the consciousness of an Italian American was not to be "universal" — as though that consciousness were somehow less human than that of the Jew-outsider, the Black-outsider, or the Wasp-insider.[31]

What has been said of the plight of the Italian American woman can be extended to cover the entire subfield of Italian American poetry: Marginalized by the host culture, and silenced by their own, or originating, culture.[32]

11. ETHNIC GHOSTS RETURN

Let us now suppose once again that resistance to Italian American literature from both the "real" American writers and the "real" Italian literati is motivated by an ambivalent understanding of the notion of *ethnic*? Well, fear no longer, help is on the way, for that, too, has been challenged. If we read Werner Sollors in conjunction with Stephen Steinberg, we can actually elide that association, and reveal new colors and hues. For if we view — as we must — Italian/American poetry as a peripheral indeed back entrance kiosk in the great mall of competing legitimized American poetics, then we have no choice but to use this perspective to gauge what is going on in the bustling sunlight of the main hall, where the most important transactions are taking place and where a greater number of people, of histories, of experiences are given. It is true that this also is necessarily a partial view, but counter-discourse jettisoned the all-encompassing *theoros*, for Theory presupposes a supra-temporal almost Platonic viewpoint, whereas

---

[31] Carol B. Ahearn, "The New Pluralism and Its Implications for Italian-American Literary Studies," in Scelsa, La Gumina and Tomasi, 204-05.
[32] See on this an early paper by Mary Jo Bona, "Voices of the Silent Ones," 1991: 97.

theories are effective critical discourse and are by definition articulated *as* a specific utterance in time, space, and situation.[33]

The ethnic parameter can be perceived as an organizing force, as a tense symbolism, for instance, not just in the fiction, but in several active poets such as Jay Parini, Sandra Gilbert, Felix Stefanile and Maria Mazziotti Gillan. However, ethnicity is constantly on the verge of falling into a Social Darwinism that can be manipulated by the media and by politicians at will.[34] Even if we adjust to its "imagined" reality, to its self-legitimizing rhetoric, ethnicity is still perceived and "commonly qualifies as an ascribed, not an achieved identity,"[35] as an ideological fix that served non-literary purposes especially in the last thirty years, but that has now become a smokescreen to divert our attention from more pressing social and political problems.

Ethnicity must be correlated to its anthropological fold first, to its emergence in post-Renaissance descriptions and accounts of the New World. Not that the Greeks did not know of *ethnos* as a differentiating value, but it became a fierce ideology only in recent times. Books are being written on the counter-memory of the Modern, on the fact that it was during and through the post-great discoveries decades of the sixteenth century that certain instrumental discursive formations emerged: colonization, class struggle, capitalism, the scientific ordering of reality and social action, the rationalization of ideologies, the hospital, the penitentiary, the mercenary armies.[36] If in ancient Greek *ethnos* means "race," in

---

33 See the cited articles by Radhakrishnan, Rabasa, and Bhabha. [For an in-depth analysis of the relationship between Theory and theories, see now my *The Elusive Hermes* (2013)].
34 Stephen Steinberg in particular warns of the danger of transporting this complex approach into cultural studies. See also Josef Barton's "The Edge of Modernity" in Tomasi et al, *The Columbus People*, 1994), 323-41.
35 Barton, "The Edge of Modernity," 324.
36 The Bibliography on these aspects of the rise of Modernity has been substantial in recent years. For my line of argument, I have drawn on the works of Michel Foucault, Walter Mignolo, Tzvetan Todorov, Paolo Rossi, and historians of science and politics.

Latin, according to one etymological reconstruction;[37] race, *razza*, is connected to and in fact is derived from *ratio*, that is, from the same word-concept that was to become the hallmark of the Scientific Revolution and of the Enlightenment. To reason means to distinguish, to discriminate, at least in the sense in which philosophically, critically, that is what we want to do. Discrimination, from Latin *discrimen*, means that which serves to separate, in order to tell the difference between two things. But transposed to the social and political arena, it has borne its own embedded violence and apparent contradiction.[38] We might as well be dealing with a mathematical opposition, but social life and aesthetics are not equations, and we can no longer afford the luxury of wandering aimlessly in the *abyme*.[39] The poets are talking *about something*, and as key *topoi*, ethnicity and racism both concern an *excluded third* of sorts. That is what we are after. It is epistemology itself which must bow down to the demands of an effective social, concrete history, and account for the claims it makes on the basis of an ideal of knowledge or coherence. Race and ethnicity are expressions of the manifold in history, the plurality of identities, logical contradictions withstanding. And it is time we stop attaching aesthetic or moral value to an epistemological claim simply on the basis of a self-evident convenient symmetry. As John Hodge has brilliantly written in *The Anatomy of Racism*:

> The many forms of oppression, including racism and sexism, are sustained by an ancient moral concept — the dualism of good

---

[37] See Leo Spitzer, *Critica stilistica e semantica storica*, 230-42 (but with reservations from Gianfranco Contini).

[38] A fate similar to the hermeneutic notion of prejudice, as pre-judgment, which is an ontological primum and actually a positive starting point for interpretation, but which when employed in political and ethical terms bears the signature of condemnation, exclusion, and dogmatism. On this, see Gadamer (241-45).

[39] One is reminded of how most of Jacques Derrida's work consists in exposing how some critical words in our Western culture contain in their very essence the trace of an opposite or contrary meaning and therefore, according to deconstructors, the self-erasing force of what they putatively state.

and evil. Using this pervasive and generally accepted notion, oppressors are able to justify their behavior as joining the struggle between the forces of good against evil. (Goldberg 1990, 89)

For us, legitimation resides elsewhere, not exclusively in the State, not specifically in any single authority, but in the System, *in the network of relations, in performance, in local determinism, in power-at-the-site of utterance*, where we must be alert to and conscious of interlocking communities and the multiverse of struggles.

Thus, if ethnicity can be dismissed, ignored, erased as a recently volatile ideological construct, let us not think for a moment that the idea of nation, and of a national language, are exempt from the same critical rethinking.[40] In fact, one can make the opposite claim: an *ethnos* is more deeply rooted, more primordial, more endogenetic than a nationness, let alone a nationality. If to identify a literature by its nation, by the language it employs with full legitimation by a national literary history collective residing in the universities, is to succumb to the guiles and manipulations of a middle- or upper-class, ultimately trans-national power structure, then why not rediscover the full value of ethnicity as something which one takes with him or her no matter what nation or national language is traveled? But this aspect can only be properly treated if we bring into the discussion the question of immigration, culture contact, and incorporation in the host country.

---

40 Benedict Anderson makes a compelling case for a rethinking of the idea of nation and, with it, the ideology of nationalism, as it is tied through and through to the seventeenth century expansion of early capitalism and the rise of the bourgeoisie. Nationalism creates nations, and not the other way around. Above and beyond the noble if utopistically premature intentions of the *carbonari* and the *Giovine Italia*, Italy, for instance, was constructed from the top down, *a tavolino*, one might say, foreshadowing a trickle down ideology of power which resulted in labor drain in the South and capital gains in the North.

12. Critique 3: Dilemmas

Here is a text by an American of Italian descent, Diane Raptosch:

> Emanuela in the New World Garden
> finds Arizona, Vegas, Idaho pretty
> much one place, one promise: One palm tree
> in every other pot stands an off-chance
> of bearing flesh
> only ripest
> pineapples can boast.
> If she's not
> found bowing among flora, try the wilder-
> ness of green on green, where flocks
> play 21, placing low bets —
> a couple of bucks or so
>
> Watch her
> watch the dealer shuffling the deck so
> fast the cards are blurred
> waves not even the Mediterranean
> she's memorized
> could match.[41]

This intricate palimpsest would benefit from a textual and hermeneutic analysis of the sort John Paul Russo performed on the literary corpus of Gilbert Sorrentino.[42] Clearly, one may extract the "Italian" out of these poems, consistent with a critical orientation that seeks the cultural other in an English text. Yet I feel this and similar poems speak primarily to that complex fate called being an American. Russo's analysis of Sorrentino's "choice" of severing himself from his background, his early rejection of his ethnic "non-history," his efforts at creating himself out of the dialectic

---

41 As cited in Tamburri, Giordano, and Gardaphé, *From the Margin*, 214.
42 *From the Margin*, 338-56.

between a disappearing oral heritage he dismissed as being out of tune and out of place, and the yet unwritten voice of a peculiarly Italian/American literary history, all this speaks simultaneously to the exclusionary and exclusivist aesthetic of American Modernism. Is it merely coincidence that within that camp Sorrentino immediately joined ranks with the radicals, the rebels, the "militant protestors,"[43] in short, the then latest and now last wave of serious avant-gardism, in the fifties? A similar analysis would have to be done on the writings of Diane De Prima, Lawrence Ferlinghetti, and Gregory Corso.

At this juncture we can fold back and tie in with Sollors' notion of what constitutes the fundamental American drama: when you have no past, no empowered ancestry, no relations of substance (by blood or nature) — and we might even add, as a former generation would have done, no fathers to kill — which would define identity by *descent*, then you plunge into the poetics of *consent*, attainable through "law" or "marriage":

> Descent language emphasizes our positions as heirs, our hereditary qualities, liabilities, and entitlements; consent language stresses our abilities as mature free agents and "architects of our fates," to choose our spouses, our destinies, and our political systems. (Sollors 1986, 6)

This is a neat and to some degree fruitful critical grid with which one *begins* to survey the field and determines what goes on this side, and what goes on the other. We cannot avoid, as we saw above, to discriminate in the sense of effecting a judgment! Yet it is also too easy a model, as pointed out at various junctures throughout this and other chapters. Poets of Italian extraction or descent who write in some variation of the English tongue ought to be read for what they have to contribute to the understanding of the American tradition, how they mesh in, and at what cost.

---

43 As Daniel Aaron calls them, cited in *From the Margin*, 8.

"Dabblers, Small Fry, Canon Fodder"

Despite the theoretical limitations of the Sollors model, it is certainly true that if we identify poets by their personal backgrounds and ethnic descendancy we stand to lose sight of what it is that they actually contributed to aesthetic sensitivity, history, and poetics.[44] Moreover:

> If anything, ethnic literary history ought to *increase* our understanding of the cultural interplays and contacts among writers of different backgrounds, the cultural mergers and secessions that took place in America, all of which can be accomplished only if the categorization of writers as members of ethnic groups is understood to be a very *partial, temporal, insufficient characterization at best*. (ibid., 14-15; emphasis added)

This is a workable path, but not the richest among the few we have sketched. If Italian/American poetry is read as being exclusively a semantically marked expression in which something "ethnic" is either presupposed or developed, then certainly we can "increase our understanding of the cultural interplays and contacts." At the same time, however, Sollors warns of falling prey to an "organicist imagery of roots" and never attain what he calls "the pervasiveness and inventiveness of syncretism."[45] Nevertheless, we can still read these poetries as "part of the rites and rituals of this land, as an expression of a persistent conflict between consent and descent in America."

Why would anyone want to erase this locus, this process of social and historical conflict and difference, ignore its presence, undermine its value, cancel its inscription? Let us develop this criti-

---

[44] Sollors here gives a compelling example: if I want to study specific poetries, and each and every time I am cross-referenced to ethnic, national or racial origins, it helps little to see Allen Ginsberg listed as Jewish-American, Jack Kerouac as Franco-American, Frank O'Hara as Irish-American, LeRoi Jones as Afro-American and Diane de Prima as Italian-American, emphasizing, in short, the writer's *descent* (14).

[45] Sollors, *Beyond Ethnicity*, 15. It is unfortunate the author does not develop the critical notion of syncretism.

cal topos. In fact, descent is not simply Italian-sounding last names, birth certificates, genetics and the dubious semiotics of grafted local traditions. Descent is also memory, refashioned old traditions, genealogy, the dynamics of cross-pollination, the development of a tortuous, often hidden, written record, and the slow emergence of an historical cultural unconscious. And in view of that, the dynamics of these attempts, their tentative vocabulary, tugs and pushes from mainstream to multiple marginalities, all would mark consent as eminent sites to witness the struggles of the Italian discourse in America. An Italian American literary history would be obliged to investigate, record, account for what is, in broad strokes, the polylogic of dissent and rejection, of misrepresentation and facile stereotyping, the fear of leveling out by absorption, and even, most recently, the reverse desire of shedding the association with the moniker Italian American.

Without having to resort to Gramsci, one can argue that Sollors' critical model is suddenly too simple when not altogether naive. It is very easy with this approach to demonstrate that Italian American poetics, or a supposed Italian American novel, is theoretically meaningful only if we see it as a "passing" literary category, one whose subject and/or object of inquiry can no longer find a real social substrate, having become a closed historical chapter. If we downplay or refuse the dialectics of consensus, having a name to be identified with, we basically vanish from the radar, we risk not existing. We ought to have learned from the predicament of other sub-cultures and marginalized groups throughout history: if you do not write your history, if you do not bear witness, you risk being pushed into a contrived silence, removed from the scene of history. And Italian Americans are hardly a people without a history.

13. Provisional Conclusions

My contribution at this juncture consists in this critical programme: let Italian American literature stay at the margin, however defined, let us not attempt to mainstream it, let it remain in the shadows and the penumbras of the borders, let it inhabit and haunt the periphery. We cannot believe, not now that we are ankle-deep into the 21st century, in the hallucination of a stable, homogeneous, empowering center or mean or mainstream *of anything*. Such a philosophical fiction reeks with ideology, power mongering, the status quo. It would require selling your services, prostituting your craft, living in the hyperreality of deferred failure or the surreal dimension of wanting to be with their dominant group at all costs.[46] In the fifties, it was sociology's new great methodology, akin to the push-and-pull theory of migration.[47] Those analytic tools have shown their limitation, or better yet, social and historical reality proved to be more complex.[48]

Perhaps we ought to confront the possibility of not only being written off the history books of both modern Italy and America, but of being persistently labeled as "minor," as barely important. One might say of Italian/American literature what James Marcus wrote in a *New York Times* book review about the work and worth of Iginio Tarchetti, as he reviewed a translation of *Fantastic Tales*:

> Call an author "minor" and you tar him or her with a saturated brush. According to conventional wisdom, minor authors are too gifted to dismiss, and too trivial to bother reading. They're dab-

---

[46] The bibliography on the postmodern is too vast and diversified to even consider taking sample positions. For a general historical and critical view, see Lyotard (1983), Rosenau (1992), and Carravetta (1991, 2009).
[47] See for example Stephen Castles and Mark J. Miller, eds. *The Age of Migration*, 19 sgg.
[48] For the conceptual and hermeneutic leaps in sociological theory, compare Edward Shils to Anthony Giddens. Similarly, great methodological issues have been raised in anthropology and ethnography, with the result that the question of the possibility of interpretation of group behavior, values and dynamics without involving the observer/writer has taken front stage. The informant is inevitably caught in a social practice, a praxiological hermeneutic. For studies on this aspect, see the Clifford and Marcus anthology.

blers, small fry, canon fodder. The application of the dread epithet often has much more to do with literary fashion than talent. Authors who set up shop outside the mainstream, who work in some oddball or imported genre, usually find themselves condemned to almost automatic minority.[49]

Yet, however "minor," the writers mentioned along the way seem to be profoundly aware that the age of revolutions, honest presidents, ideology, and moralistic posturing is gone: that change can be effected almost solely through an interactive exchange of ideas and positions in view of specific consequences along the various networks. It requires constant negotiation, symbolic — and often concrete — contractual tugs of war, serious cultural exchanges and initiatives. We must acknowledge that each critical position and every school or movement in the arts and the poetries produced sustain themselves through a multitude of communicative venues and are *ab initio* destined to constant instability.[50]

---

49 Marcus, "Beware the Haunted Raspberry," *New York Times*, Aug. 27, 1992:7.
50 I am implicitly referring to cultural conundrums and paradoxes explored by authors such as Lyotard, Deleuze, Foucault, Baudrillard, and Prigogine.

CHAPTER THREE

THE SILENCE OF THE SUBALTERNS: CONTACT, CONFLICT, CONSOLIDATION DURING THE FIRST WAVE (1880s-1913)

> *Ma noi siam peregrin, come voi siete*
>
> Purg. II, 63

1. FROM EMIGRANT TO IMMIGRANT: THE SENSE OF THE PASSAGE

The number of difficulties and real chances for disasters large and small being endless, one wonders how the Italian immigrants to the Americas withstood whatever life threw at them during their journey and resettlement, and moved on to forge themselves a new life. Perhaps, as befits the etymon of *migrare*, which from the Latin means simply "to move (on)," to go off somewhere or on to something else, their condition as migrants suggests two possible approaches, one literal: moving to another country; and the other metaphorical: engaging in activities such that the immigrant becomes somehow and perhaps inevitably someone else. We know so many never completely severed the overstretched umbilical cord with their provenance, preferring to return, whether periodically owing to the seasonal ebb and flow of particular sectors, such as farming or construction, or maybe permanently for more complex reasons, or even simply because they just "couldn't take it."

But looking back at what will emerge as the silent chaos of origins, we should ask: What was it that pulled them through the trans-formation into functioning members of a different nationality, cobbling a different public self not at all in harmony with the basic cultural brick and mortar of the first self, the one rooted in and shaped by a "fatherland," or the "mother tongue," or the very *idea* of Italy? And to what level or degree did they achieve the transformation required eventually to become American? Or did they ever? I am provisionally using "American" as an uncontested umbrella word, which it is not, since the Italians experienced a variety of often contradictory if not paradoxical aspects of the new country, as we will see below. For we must ask: Which Americans spoke for which Italians? With what purpose?

Now that present-day Italian Americans are four or five generations removed from these humble trailblazers, do they configure a distant model, an *arché*, and inscribe a "founding" rhetoric for what has emerged over the same period of time as a constantly challenged sense of social identity? Furthermore, can the experience of the first generation of the great exodus teach us anything about broader sociohistorical shifts that impact on the very essence of what a national identity is, what modern Western history itself is supposed to consist in?

The physical journey over the Atlantic has already disrupted many "natural" attachments to the earth, their roots. No doubt this affects how the immigrants will see, relate to, and live in the "world" — quite appropriately *here*, the "*New* World". To grasp the symbolic and existential ramifications of what the journey meant, recall the scene in Ermanno Crialese's film *The Golden Door* (2006/2007), when the ship loaded with emigrants edges out from the dock (probably Palermo) to the tune of a gloomy, bone-rattling fog horn. What at first sight appears to be a normal teeming period crowd literally filling the screen, seen from a strategic overhead shot, is slowly but inexorably separated into two: those who stay behind, on land, in Sicily, and those who, with Salvatore and his family, depart toward the United States. Those on the ship experience the growing spatial void being filled by an indifferent dark-brown sea, with the actual tearing away foregrounded in a swirl of kerchiefs. The scene makes the viewer think of what the individual self must have felt at the moment: that this was going to be an epochal, life-altering, uni-directional event, like a death in the family, or going to war, or dissolving a marriage: the separation will scar the self forever.

Immediately afterward: the real drama of the journey. Making it through between ten and twenty days at sea, depending on the number of ports...to pick up more emigrants. This was no tourist cruise. The same Crialese film shows what a nightmare it was, especially for people who had never even seen the sea, as the great majority came from hinterland mountainous regions. That *terra firma* has symbolic affirming power did not need to be explained to them. The majority of emigrants, even those who made their living at sea, like tuna fishers and maritime workers, had a bone-sure sense of what land was like: governments come and go, harsh winters and dry seasons occur periodically, and, yes, the sea is dangerous, but one knows where one plants one's feet. These people, this avalanche of humanity, setting out to sea, consisted, as is well known, mostly of under- or un-employed laborers, *contadini*. They were exploited, undereducated and largely unskilled country folk who knew only their immediate region, only their fields and rivers and woods, and were imbued with various fatalistic beliefs.

Still, among them, something snapped and they decided to leave. And to understand that we would have to undertake a separate and different inquiry into post-Risorgimento Italy.

Upon uprooting they were identified by society as "labor migrants," though the claim being made here is to recall that they need to be considered "dispersed" souls wandering in search of security, freedom, meaning, and *a* home (since they no longer had *the* home). In the old country this class of people, the largest numerically, coming mostly from the South did not enjoy the advantages of the urbanized middle class, which had greater auton-

"The Silence of the Subalterns"

omy and could rely in various degrees on existing government agencies and private institutions. Immigrants from this latter sector should properly be called "expatriates" or "exiles."[1] They were typically more "worldly" in their outlook on life and society, were well-educated and, significantly, most did not travel in steerage.[2] Interpreting the role of those who were employed in still other sectors, from business to government, from transportation to specialized labor, requires a more nuanced approach toward the migration progress, based on the different socio-ideological spaces they navigated.[3] Here we would see a heterogeneous group, which, in general, was less fatalistic or apocalyptic about leaving the land, and was better equipped to enter and explore the "New World." And finally there were also, albeit in a restricted number, some professionals, intellectuals and artists in their midst. Accounting for these groupings one can begin to study the variety of Italian *diasporas* that participated in the historic demographic flow.[4] But it becomes all the more important and more difficult to imagine the experience of the veritable "silent majority" among those who did not go back to Italy, about three million people.

---

[1] See Chapter 1, above, pp. 11-21.

[2] This group includes those who arrived with strong intellectual and political motivations and joined the ongoing struggle for labor reform, immigrants, children and women's rights, becoming activists and ideologues. See Philip Cannistraro and Gerald Meyer, eds. *The Lost World of Italian American Radicalism*; and Rudolph J. Vecoli, "The Italian Immigrants in the United States' Labor Movement from 1880 to 1920" in Bruno Bezza, ed. *Gli italiani fuori d'Italia,* 258-306.

[3] We would have to include in this group professionals associated with the Italian diplomatic corps or consular offices, shipping and navigation personnel, medics and religious representatives, and highly specialized artisans who arrived with a labor contract already.

[4] See Donna Gabaccia, *Italy's Many Diasporas*. (Abingdon: Routledge, 2003). The concept of diaspora introduces a dynamic element in the otherwise static notions of identity, ethnicity, and migrant. For a fuller theory, see Robin Cohen, *Global Diasporas*. Though economic need is traditionally considered the prime mover for the great exodus, diasporas are much more complex and witness a variety of forces intersecting and creating a web of motives, creating "endogenous patterns" owed to peculiar historical conjuncture and remote chance events; see on this Enrico Moretti, "Social Networks and Migrations: Italy 1876-1913."

"The Silence of the Subalterns"

A paradox emerges in the historical reconstruction of this "silent majority." These emigrants did not speak about themselves, left few traces and, over a thirty-year period they were *not* truly represented in American society, though they had become very visible to the host.[5] This was not because they chose not to speak out in exchange for some minimal guarantees, protection and civil status. Instead, to repurpose an expression from the 1980s-90s, this underclass, these "subalterns,"[6] did not speak out *because they could not*: I am arguing for those two-plus million people (out of the 3 million who remained in North America) with no language skills, education, no access to effective social discourse, no access not only to the means of production (obviously, though of course some managed to start their own in-house businesses[7]), but to *the very possibility of communication*. In this perspective, what we have to work with is how they were perceived by denizens of the host country, how they were described and labeled, how *their social and cultural identities were being constructed from the outside*, as it were, once in America. And yet we can only infer or guess what, at the same time, they must have been experiencing on the inside, in

---

5 Of course this changes over time. By the early 1900s there were over 250 Mutual Aid Societies and other local organizations. See Antonio Mangano, "The Associated Life of the Italians in New York City," 1904, now in Lydio F. Tomasi, ed., *The Italian in America*, 153-161. Some were religious and marked by their parishes; see "The American Mission of Frances Xavier Cabrini," *The Catholic World*, April, 1918, reprinted in Moquin and Van Doren, eds., *A Documentary History of Italian American*, 338-42. Two monographs give an idea of the cruciality of religion among the newly arrived: Robert Anthony Orsi, *The Madonna of 115h Street,* and Marco Callaro and Mario Francesconi, *John Baptist Scalabrini*. In a sense, this also contributed to the immigrant beginning to feel "Italian" (as opposed to solely Neapolitan or from a small Sicilian or Calabrian town) whether in Harlem or the North End, creating a social identification bond that did not exist among them prior to embarking for America.

6 I am referring to the much discussed article by Gayatri Spivak, "Can the Subaltern Speak." It gave rise to a field of Cultural Studies called "Subaltern Studies."

7 Much of the early historical research on Italian Americans, beginning in the 1950s, focused on rediscovering the exemplary lives of the entrepreneurs, small-business owners, and artisans who had left a positive mark on American society. See, for example, various early volumes of the proceedings of the American Italian Historical Association.

their minds, their gut, their hearts. For this aspect we usually turn to literature, theater and the other arts, as our last limited yet ever revealing passageway into the psyche of the immigrant.[8]

In some way the sea crossing washed the soil from under their feet. It made for an awareness that reality is an unstable dimension. From the time they landed, they were ever conscious of where they walked. There is a tradition of scholarship that interpreted the role of the individual migrants as passive: fearful and ignorant, they were unequipped to realize what forces and dynamics were at work in their lives.[9] Many did not know they were even "Italians" until they got to Ellis Island.[10] Many found that their most basic sense of identity, their own names, were changed almost arbitrarily before being approved and released to land.

---

8 On the literature of the pre-World War I period written by and large in Italian, again, by that small percentage that could, see Martino Marazzi, *Voices of Italian America*; and Francesco Durante, *Italoamericana: The Literature of the Great Migration, 1880-1943*. For the theater, see Emelise Aleandri, *The Italian-American Immigrant Theatre of New York City*, a multivolume work. For a shorter article on the subject of theater for high versus low culture, see Esther Romeyn, "Performing High, Performing Low."

9 This reminds us of the then ongoing struggle, on both sides of the Atlantic, that functioned as background to Antonio Gramsci's work and ideas. A burgeoning underclass of farmers and a growing cadre of industrial laborers needed to be educated and made aware (so as to "acquire class self-consciousness") of their status as an exploited group or class that had or ought to have "rights" as a first step toward an emancipation and change that might end what was a millennial subjugation. Italian *émigré* intellectuals at the beginning of the twentieth century did much to carry on this work among the Little Italies, vying for better representation and working conditions. See note 4 above and 21 below for bibliography.

10 Donna Gabaccia, "Is Everywhere Nowhere?" This pioneering article alerts us that hitherto historians have operated under "the tyranny of the national" (1116), thus working within a model that imposes homogeneities and sets up an in/out paradigm, while being blind to specific inter- and trans-national flows and relations that reveal migration to be more complex, stratified, and heterogeneous, with unsuspected networks or kinships. Drawing on this and related studies, there is need now for Italian American social and cultural history to situate itself within the broader and more flexible paradigm of an "Atlantic, capitalist, and world economy" (1118).

2. A PATCHWORK OF ITALIANNESS

The Italians by and large spoke provincial or regional dialects, and upon aggregating into communities even their dialects changed, especially during the first decades, as they borrowed words from *compaesani*, pulling in whatever Italian they knew, coining new words, and inventing a new morphology, as the presence of English encroached and became steadily dominant.[11] Though highly uneven, this can still serve as *koine*, or common language, for inter-personal, inter-regional exchanges and affiliations. Looking in closer, we find other aspects which demand *realignments* of practices and strategies to connect and exchange with specific groupings. In finding themselves members of small dedicated groups — such as when hired for work gangs, joining neighborhood political activists, partaking in parochial organizations, or becoming educators[12] — these immigrants, strangers and babbling aliens, were nevertheless forced to interact *across* national language barriers and religious and ritualistic differences. A few scholars have recently conjectured that, unbeknownst to themselves, the first-generation emigrants/immigrants were participating in the larger political economy of the North Atlantic Trade triangle, and as such their interpretation requires a transnational perspective. Moreover, whenever and wherever they found work, except in the cases of older family members working in the back of a small store-front business, these Italian immigrants had to deal with people from all sorts of backgrounds, some also immigrants, but most others already established on the

---

11 Hermann Haller, *Una lingua perduta e ritrovata*.
12 To get a sense of the variety of occupations of this first major wave of Italian immigrants, still useful is the monumental (and thorough for the period) work of Robert F. Foerster, *The Italian Emigration of Our Times*, in particular Book II, "Causes," 47-126, and chapters from Book III, 320-411. Though terminology and social concerns are peculiar to the decades in question, 1880-1915, the book is illuminating in placing emigration within a broader Euro-American dynamic, and compares the immigration to the Unites States to that going on at the same time in Argentina, Brazil, France, Switzerland, Austria-Hungary, and even North Africa.

territory: Blacks and Jews, Europeans and Asians, Latinos and WASPS, the wealthy and the paupers, urbanites and local boors.

This fluid and shifting social reality would have made unexpected demands on the immigrant, as it required engaging this panoply of humanity at work or in the street in order to figure out, or "decode," how best to co-exist with the (very different!) locals. The juxtaposition forced them to constantly self-check, and constantly look for ways to rearrange their own home, work, and living habits. If the koine was the main vehicle for regrouping locally while re-elaborating a now swelling imaginary past, the anxiety-filled and ever uncertain relations of the present, whether recurring or isolated, had to be experienced and experimented with anew, on the spot, on their skin. The immigrant, in negotiating his "belonging" to the broader "American" paradigm, had to become malleable, inventive, with sharper reflexes, essentially a "survivalist." Connecting civilly at any specific point proved a day-to-day campaign: too many the opportunities for swindlers and profiteers to set them back in multiple ways. When local opportunities for growth diminished, or authorities failed them, they retrenched in their neighborhoods. A redoubling or splitting of the self-informed his psychosocial world-view. Immigrants developed a stereoscopic vision of things: everything could be looked at in two ways, the Italian way (or their understanding of what was thought to be Italian) and the American way (or their understanding of what this America was turning out to be).

That migrants in general must be adaptive is a safe generalization, but many of them, not only Italians but also Hungarians, Czech, Germans, and Jews, displayed a clearly pragmatic approach to dealing with the new environment. This became a positive predisposition when beginning the process of incorporation and assimilation in the United States, where a Protestant ethic in principle favored individualism, self-reliance, and initiative. If not before the journey, then decisively after relocating, one became pragmatic.[13] The immigrant quickly realized, moreover, that s/he did not have to be "100% American" all the time in order to live and work in America. The immigrants could adapt to and interact with the *necessary interfaces* (landlords, schools, the police, employers) and still have psychological space sufficient for re-creating an interior world that was familiar, local and full of symbols of belonging. The great number of local clubs and religious feasts attest to this. Yet this personal-familiar world had the peculiarity of constituting a de-territorialized minor culture, one that alternatively loved and resented the grander paradigm called "Italy" that to them was inexorably turning into a fuzzy past, maybe a myth, as old as Jesus or Rome.

Furthermore, what is often not included or thematized sufficiently, in the discussion about migration, is the role of class, both with respect to the immigrant him/herself, and with respect to the existing social class or group in America that were empowered to assess and pass judgment on the newcomer. This is an unfortunate result of the demise of the bipolar world in the 1990s, and with that the waning of an entire critical vocabulary variously associated with Marxism. But, as Marx himself is quoted as saying, echoing a Galileo forced to recant: *eppur si muove*! Who, and from what stump or editorial office or government agency, could contribute to creating an identity for the newcomer? Who would allow them to become active participants in shaping their new environments? To return to the most physical of levels, social psychologists tell us that a standard reaction upon being thrown into a different environment is that the subject sharpens her focus and searches spontaneously for what, in the new habitat, is recognizable, constituting a safe reference point or locus of primary orientation with respect to the basics of life: streets, houses, clothing, iconic images, time schedules, sounds. But did the immigrants all negotiate the transition, which effectively meant going through

---

13 John Bodnar, *The Transplanted*, 46, 52.

the complex stages of culture shock, in the same way [see Chart 2, page 36]? And how did it come about that the immigrants were assigned by the American public a repertoire of semantic/symbolic markers that made rabble-rousing discriminatory statements not only acceptable but quick and effective? What agencies or communities contributed to creating public resentment toward the Italians, a resentment that was bolstered by scientific and juridical authorities, as we will see, and then edged into and complicated the bond between first and second generation Italians?

In order to find further links among these larger concerns, we need to turn to some more circumscribed issues. I would like to begin with a "culture-scape":[14] a sketch of what America was like at the end of the nineteenth century that illustrates the complex dynamics into which the immigrant walked unawares. Then I shall treat the changing *perception* of Italian immigrants between 1880 and 1913: a treatment that requires identifying further discursive subsets that impacted the lives of this first generation. Finally, and in conclusion, I shall examine the broadly philosophical implications of this sketch and of the role of migrations in history.

3. THE CHANGING CULTURE-SCAPE OF AMERICA FROM 1880 TO WORLD WAR I

One must consider some general aspects of the host society into which the immigrants arrived. The Gay Nineties have also been called the Grey Nineties.[15] Jim Crow policies[16] had sealed the fate

---

14 I am loosely adapting the notion, first developed by Arjun Appadurai, in his article "Disjuncture and Difference in the Global Cultural Economy," now in his book *Modernity at Large. Cultural Dimensions of Globalization*, 1996.

15 An alternate well-known moniker for that decade is the "Progressive Era," on account of reactions to financial liberalization, and explosion of social activism and calls for social reform. But historians recently have seen how it could also be called the 'Regressive Era." For period documents and commentary, see Richard M. Abrams, ed., *The Issues of the Populist and Progressive Eras 1892-1912*, Jackson Lears, *Rebirth of a Nation*.

of African American social integration and advancement for another seven decades.[17] In the same decades the Amerindian genocide ended with the total submission of the Native Americans.[18] During these years the Frontier Hypothesis anchored to the Grand Scheme of an American "Manifest Destiny" — which originates in the early 1840s — came to fruition: the country was ripe now for the unprecedented exploitation, coast to coast, of its vast land. These are the post-Civil War decades of the rapid growth and expansion of major industries, such as coal and steel, of the manufacturing and shipping tycoons, and the decades of struggle of the farmers, the "agrarian revolt," against the North-East moguls, the railroad barons.[19] Significantly, America began to take a peek at the rest of the world.[20]

---

16 The second Morrill Act of 1890 continued this "Separate but Equal" policy by permitting states to divide federal funds, nominally in support of agricultural and mechanical arts colleges, between separate institutions for white and black students. In another important landmark case, *Plessy v. Ferguson* (1896), the Supreme Court voted 8-1 that "governments could enforce segregation by statute." See Williamjames Hull Hoffer, *Plessy v. Ferguson*.

17 In fact, matters had gotten so bad with the treatment of African Americans that between 1910 and 1960 some 6 million African Americans left the rural South for the urban Northeast and Midwest, representing one of the greatest domestic or *intra*-national demographic shifts of modern times. Steven Reich, ed., *The Great Black Migration*; Roger Daniels, *Not Like Us*, 35-37.

18 After the massacre at Wounded Knee, in the Dakota territories, in 1880, Black Elk pronounced it "The Death of o People's Dream." See Williamjames Hull Hoffer, *Plessy v. Ferguson: Race and Inequality in Jim Crow America* (Lawrence: University Press of Kansas, 2012)
  The Dawes Act of 1887 — https://www.ourdocuments.gov/doc.php?flash=true&doc=50 — was meant to apportion 160 acres to individual Native Americans, but it turned out to be an administrative and political disaster with unscrupulous whites buying off the land. The Curtis Act of 1898 mandated the dissolution of the right to incorporation by tribal governments by 1906. There is an uncanny parallel here with what happened in Italy after Unification with lands expropriated from the Church and the Bourbon dynasty and ending up in possession of the old estate owners and latifondisti.

19 See Lawrence Goodwyn, *The Populist Moment*.

20 In the periodicals of the era — *Atlantic Monthly, North American Review, Harper's Weekly, Charities of the Commons* — there are many articles that comment critically upon what is going on in Europe in political, economic, military and other affairs. It is easy to perceive a growing interest in "internationalism" as a relevant and timely component of American social and political discourse. It will come to a head in 1898, date scholars consider the birth of American imperialism.

"The Silence of the Subalterns"

One major concern that loomed large in public discourse concerned the millions of foreigners "flooding our shores" who were becoming front-page news, starting by the early 1880s. An occasional optimistic entreaty by the likes of William Lloyd Garrison — the son of the famous abolitionist — to the effect that "Uncle Sam is Rich Enough to Give Them All a Farm,"[21] would be countered soon by an avalanche of discriminatory, racist articles by resurgent nativists representing allegedly "threatened" communities in a number of States. As late as 1896, Garrison could still write "Let them come..." with ecumenical fervor,[22] but the times they had a-changed, for, unfortunately, there were no welcoming committees to greet them — notwithstanding the good intentions of Emma Lazarus![23] Indeed, early on some Italians were treated worse than slaves and denied their very humanity by being assigned numbers:

> ONE ITALIAN PROBLEM SOLVED
> *From the American Railroad Journal*
>
> A fundamental improvement is reported from the works of the West Shore Railroad... We refer to the ingenious way by means of which the contractors on the lines named identify the Italians in their employment. The "linked sweetness long drawn out" of Italian patronymics, so suggestive of Southern indolence and leisure, possesses no such charms in the ears of said contractors as leads them to master the difficulties presented in their memorizing and pronunciation.

---

21 *Boston Daily Globe* (22 October 1881), 5. The headline reworked a folksong about the Homestead Act that went: "Uncle Sam is rich enough to give *us* all a farm."
22 *Boston Daily Globe* (11 April, 1896), p. 6
23 Emma Lazarus's poem, "The New Colossus," with its famous lines, "Give me your tired, your poor, your huddled masses yearning to breathe free...," was originally published in 1883 to raise funds for the Statue of Liberty's pedestal. It was rediscovered after her death and in 1903 it was inscribed on the plaque inside the statue's base. Because Liberty is said to challenge the Old World to "Keep, ancient lands, your storied pomp," with *"silent* lips," and because the immigrants are called "wretched refuse," commentators and cultural critics have remarked upon the poem's ambiguity and the potential for a deconstructive reading.

"The Silence of the Subalterns"

> They therefore substitute numbers for names in their identification of the Italians in their employment, these numbers being conspicuously painted on the most spacious portion of the trousers worn by the men . . . [24]

But these were the years of Wild-West capitalism, which demanded government policies that were supposed to protect American manufacturers and contractors, not the workers.[25] Although the Sherman Act, effectively the first anti-trust law, was passed in 1890, there were Supreme Court decisions that, while curbing monopolies to some degree, explicitly supported industry

---

24 *The New York Times,* August 26, 1883. The article goes on to say that this "ignominy" should and will end "at such a time as the said Italian has developed a proper appreciation of his dignity as one of the sovereigns of the United States."

25 In February, 1886, Congress passed the "Assisted Immigration Act," which regulated the degree to which corporations could contract labor abroad, and protected against undesirables, as laws in 1875 and 1882 had done. The law was challenged in *United States vs Craig,* Oct. 11, 1886, on the grounds that it interfered with the free operation of Commerce, and as free trade was sustained by Congress, the restriction was deemed unconstitutional. No challenge was made to the immigration of persons, meaning labor, in itself. See *The New York Times,* Oct. 12, 1886, p. 1. Interestingly, in arguing for the constitutionality of the Act, Judge Brown spells out the motives for challenge: "It had become the practice for large capitalists in this country to contract with their agents abroad for the shipment of great numbers of an ignorant and servile class of foreign laborers, under contracts, by which the employed agreed, upon the one hand, to prepay their passage, while, upon the other hand, the laborers agreed to work after their arrival for a certain time at a low rate of wage. *The effect of this was to break down the labor market, and to reduce other laborers engaged in like occupations to the level of the assisted immigrant."* [emphasis added] *The Federal Reporter,* Vol. 28 [Cases Argued and Determined in the Circuit and District Courts of the United States, August-December, 1896], p 798. In the opinion, however, the legal reasoning gets murky: "…a careful perusal of the section will demonstrate that the penalty is attached, not to the making of the illegal contract, but to assisting, encouraging, or soliciting the migration of the alien to perform labor or services here, knowing that such illegal contract or agreement had been made." In the end the issue is raised that there are local statutes that interpret parts of the law, especially concerning what "assisting," or "soliciting" mean. One consequence was that, as foreign labor was lured to the US with (basically false) contracts, upon arriving at Castle Garden Immigration Depot in lower Manhattan (after 1892, arrivals disembarked on Ellis Island), a condition for the immigrant laborer to remain on US soil was that he, on the one hand, be not "feeble minded," ill in any way, a pauper or anarchist, and become a charge to the public, a vagrant, and on the other that he did not violate the law by declaring that some firm had actually solicited his arrival with a contract. But the premises for "selective" or "preferential" immigration were already laid out.

in the face of growing claims against workforce abuses and the labor disputes that were connected with immigration.[26] This would have important ramifications when the intellectual component of the Italian migration took a leading role in early struggles to build unions, improve labor conditions, raise wages and advance other social issues.[27]

A tacit, selective anti-immigration sentiment in American social history goes back to the founding of the Republic,[28] becomes more vocal during the Jacksonian era, and reached an early peak with the anti-Catholic Know Nothings of the 1840s and 1850s. Until the Civil War, the greatest numbers of immigrants came from Sweden, Germany, England, Ireland. After the conflicted results of the Reconstruction Era, more attention was focused on the foreigners, and the passing of the Chinese Exclusion Act in 1882 signaled a paradigm change in American immigration history. The American government could legitimately now decide who would be barred from its sovereign territory.[29] During the 1880s the American Protection Association became influential in public debate, and it reached a membership of over 2 million by the mid-1890s. In 1894 the Immigration Restriction League (IRL) championed an "Ideal American" who was juxtaposed against the

---

26 Abrams, ed., *The Issues*, 125 et infra. See also Paul H. Boase, ed. *The Rhetoric of Protest and Reform*. For some period texts, see John A. Garraty, ed., *Labor and Capital in the Gilded Age*. For the broader context, Susan H. Smith and Melanie Dawson, eds., *The American 1890s: A Cultural Reader*.

27 On this major chapter in Italian American social history, see especially Philip V. Cannistraro and Gerald Meyer, eds., *The Lost World of Italian American Radicalism, cit.*; Donna A. Gabaccia and Fraser M. Ottanelli, eds., *Italian Workers of the World*; and Marcella Bencivenna, *Italian Immigrant Radical Culture*.

28 This is the thesis, to some degree controversial, of Aristide R. Zolberg, *A Nation by Design. Immigration Policy in the Fashioning of America*.

29 For the text of the series of statutes and progressively more restrictive immigration laws, between 1875 and 1907, see *Immigration Laws and Regulations of July 1, 1907* (Washington: Department of Commerce and Labor, Bureau of Immigration and naturalization, *Fourth Ed.*, February 15, 1908). The list contains 17 acts. As we will see below, with the publication of the Dillingham Commission report in 1911, there will be a qualitative change in sections regarding who might be excluded from admission to the US.

"hordes" that were arriving. One of the co-founders of the IRL, Prescott Farnsworth Paul, argued that Americans would soon have to decide whether they wanted

> [a nation] peopled by British, German, and Scandinavian stock, historically free, energetic, and progressive, or by Slav, Latin, and Asiatic races, historically downtrodden, atavistic, and stagnant.[30]

An "Anglo-Saxon complex" was slowly being forged in the American collective unconscious. The conviction that the unchecked daily disembarkation of thousands upon thousands of foreigners could not continue, harbinger of a cultural identity crisis, soon demanded that certain distinctions be made:

> Upon the whole, however, the contributions to our population from the Teutonic and Scandinavian countries have been assimilable, useful, and even needful…objectionable immigration is immigration of a people so alien to us that they cannot become Americanized, either in the first or in the second generation, and that threaten to remain here, so long as they remain at all, as foreign colonists. Such is the emigration from Italy, from Russia, from Poland, from Bohemia, and from Hungary. Immigrants from some of these nationalities are found convenient and available, on account of their cheapness, due to a low standard of living, by capitalists in Pennsylvania and elsewhere who are actively engaged in the good work of protecting American labor against the pauper labor of Europe.[31]

---

30 As quoted in Daniels, *Not Like Us*, 43.
31 *The New York Times*, July 26, 1888, p. 4. The complexity of the forces interacting in determining whether immigrants were good or bad for the country is borne out by the history of labor, where even the well-meaning patriotic capitalists could not ignore the advantage of unprotected cheap labor, and obstruct the path of the fledging labor organizations. Immigrants typically got caught in the cross-fire. See Bodnar, *The transplanted*, cit., Ch. 3, 85-116.

"The Silence of the Subalterns"

One strategy that attempted to stem the tide involved legislation to impose a literacy test on immigrants: such legislation was passed five times in the House of Representatives, although it was vetoed by a succession of Presidents.[32] Another strategy involved reporting constantly on the repulsive, unhealthy, and uncouth ways of living of the immigrants: the tenements and slums of New York, Boston, Philadelphia and other urban enclaves. Well-meaning, upstanding middle-class white (North-European) Americans were "shocked" at the way the majority of first-generation immigrants, and Italians first among them, were living in "their" America. And justifiably so![33]

---

32 Sample articles: the *Boston Daily Globe*, Jan. 3, 1896, p. 9: Representatives of the [immigration restriction] league...last month spent three days at Ellis Island...for the purpose of investigating the class of immigrants that arrive in this country under the present immigration laws. The main point that they sought light upon was the illiteracy [in English or some other language] of arriving immigrants...A great proportion of the illiterate immigrants are Hungarians, Galicians, Austrians, Italians, Poles, Syrians, Arabians and Asiatic Turks." Later the same year, the *Boston Daily Globe*, Apr. 25, 1896, p. 9, reports: "Half are Illiterate. Influx of Immigration from Southern Italy Claimed to be Seriously Bad...Prescott F. Hall, secretary of the Immigration Restriction League" went to Ellis Island to see for himself and finding that 7000 out of 11,000 that landed in a three-month period could neither read nor write, added ammunition to his claim that "the great efficiency of the reading and writing tests [are] a means of further restricting immigration." The House of Representatives passed versions of an Immigration Literary Test law — which basically meant to test whether the immigrants had any basic reading skills even in their native tongue — in 1895, 1897, 1913, and 1915, and 1917. Each time it was vetoed by a different president, some say for the sake of political opportunism. It finally was passed by Congress even after President Woodrow Wilson had vetoed it twice, and became law in May, 1917, during the years of the First World War, when anti-immigrant feeling peaked.

33 See various articles in *The New York Times*, "Improved Tenements," June 2, 1887, p. 2; "Inspection of Tenements," Nov. 25, 1888, p. 9; "An Unhealthy District," June 18, 1890, p 8; and so on through the 1890s, with articles bearing titles such as "Tenement House Evils," "Slavery in Tenements," "Unsafe Tenements." New York City was the epicenter of this urban blight. The Tenement House Act, enacted in Albany in 1867, expanded the authority of New York City's Board of Health to oversee construction of tenement housing in 1878. Architect James E. Ware won the competition for a standard model, measuring 100 feet by 25, called the "dumbbell: "Five to seven stories high, the tenement will have 14 rooms per floor, with two four-room apartments in front, two three-room apartments in back, and two toilets near the center of each floor to be shared by the tenants. The bedrooms all have windows, but 10 of the 14 rooms open onto air shafts only three to five feet wide, created by indenting the hallway sections of abutting tenements; little light or air reaches the

But there is a difference between a generic, moralizing indignation, and concrete, effective intervention to improve matters. Improvement, ultimately, came about thanks largely to the initiative of the immigrants themselves, through a growing number of neighborhood and fraternal associations, parochial councils, and social clubs.[34] And the publication of periodicals and local newspapers.[35] Fundamental in this context remains the famous book by Jacob Riis, *How the Other Half Lives*, which was published in 1890. Summing up by then current opinion, but with the verve of the committed reporter, here we read that these Italians in lower Manhattan are undesirables, riff-raffs ("Lazzaroni"), unassimilable paupers, thieves; they were deemed collectively uncouth, unclean, archaic and backward:[36]

---

apartments, the air shafts often become filled with refuse, and they become fire hazards." From James Trager, ed., *The New York Chronology*, 190. For living conditions in nearby Philadelphia, see Emily Wayland Dinwiddie, "Some Aspects of Italian Housing and Social Conditions in Philadelphia," in *Charities*, Vol. 12, 1904, pp 490-93, reprinted in Lydio Tomasi, ed., *The Italian in America*, cit., p 175-79. For conditions in a smaller city, see for example *The Hartford Courant*, "Expert Speaks of Tenement Houses," Nov. 16, 1905, p. 12. The topic was on "sanitary inspection." Same newspaper two years later reports "Calls Tenement Loathsome Dirty," Jan. 14, 1907, p 6. In 1912 we read that "Poor people who live underground…[in] some vile basement tenements on Pleasant St. Park Street Family Has No Sunlight All Day Long. Children Living Like Moles, Must Wear Glasses," Feb. 23, 1912, p 5. But see in particular the Introduction and various places, in particular chapter 4, in Jacob A. Riis' 1890 classic *How the Other Half Lives. Studies Among the Tenements of New York.*
34 See Silvano Tomasi, "Militantism and Italian-American Unity".
35 See Peter Vellon, *A Great Conspiracy Against Our Race*; Joseph Velikonja, "Family and Community: The Periodical Press and Italian Communities," 47-60; and the beautifully edited and commented collection by James Periconi, *Strangers in a Strange Land.*
36 Jacob A. Riis (1849-1914) was an immigrant from Ribe, Denmark, who arrived in New York in 1870. He became a journalist, photographer and reformer. In his book, he traces the origin of the tenements as the result of the population explosion of New York City first in the 1820-40s, then again after the Civil War, where the "new" popular housing model debuted. More than half the population of the city lived in what became veritable slums, and the majority was foreign-born: "The one thing you shall vainly ask for in the chief city of America is a distinctively American community. There is none; certainly not among the tenements." "A map of the city, colored to designate nationalities, would show more stripes than on the skin of a zebra, and more colors than any rainbow." See James P. Cosco *Imagining Italians*, especially chapter one; and Ilaria Serra, *The Imagined Immigrant*. The latter uses, besides the *NYTimes*, the *San Francisco Chronicle*. While these two studies devote

> In the slums he [the Italian] is welcomed as a tenant who "makes less trouble" than the contentious Irishman or the order-loving German, that is to say: is content to live in a pig-sty and submits to robbery at the hands of the rent-collector without murmur.... Like the Chinese, the Italian is a born gambler. His soul is in the game from the moment the cards are on the table, and very frequently his knife is in it too before the game is ended. No Sunday has passed in New York since "the Bend" became a suburb of Naples without one or more of these murderous affrays coming to the notice of the police.

However, Riis also points out that these new unkempt and slick tenants have some positive qualities:

> With all his conspicuous faults, the swarthy Italian immigrant has his redeeming traits. He is as honest as he is hot-headed. There are no Italian burglars in the Rogues' Gallery; the ex-brigand toils peacefully with pickaxe and shovel on American ground... The women are faithful wives and devoted mothers. Their vivid and picturesque costumes lend a tinge of color to the otherwise dull monotony of the slums they inhabit. The Italian is gay, lighthearted and, if his fur is not stroked the wrong way, inoffensive as a child.

And finally he zooms in on the real culprit behind this deplorable state of affairs:

> An inspector of the Health Department found an Italian family paying a man with a Celtic name twenty-five dollars a month for

---

space to how the Italians were perceived, a comparison with how other groups were described by Riis, in particular the Chinese, the Jews, and the Czech (and as non- immigrants, the African Americans and the pestiferous hordes of homeless children and teen-age gangs, called "Arabs"), shows that some of the adjectives used for these latter were even more stirring, and by today's standards, almost insulting. To Riis' credit, however, it must be said that his object was to show the average Americans, and denounce to policy makers in particular, that it was the tenements that bred such unfathomable conditions, and he was merely using the accepted public language of his day.

three small rooms in a ramshackle rear tenement — more than twice what they were worth — and expressed his astonishment to the tenant, an ignorant Sicilian laborer. He replied that he had once asked the landlord to reduce the rent, but he would not do it. "Well! What did he say?" asked the inspector. "'Damma, man!' he said; 'if you speaka thata way to me, I fira you and your things in the streeta.'" And the frightened Italian paid the rent.

It is the greed of the landlords that is the problem, and before we point the finger across the ethnic-national divide, it isn't just the Irish, who are now up on the pecking order having arrived *en masse* half a century earlier, who exploit the ignorant immigrant: what's often overlooked is that it is also the Italian "padrone" who enslaves his helpless charge:

> The padrone — the "banker," is nothing else — …. receives him at the landing and turns him to double account as a wage-earner and a rent-payer. In each of these roles he is made to yield a profit to his unscrupulous countryman, whom he trusts implicitly with the instinct of utter helplessness. The man is so ignorant that, as one of the sharpers who prey upon him put it once, it "would be downright sinful not to take him in."[37]

Reading the entire tract, and coming to terms with the fact that more than half of the population of New York City lived in slums,

---

[37] Elsewhere Riis write about "the dreadful padrone system, a real slave system in Italian children, who were bought of poor parents across the sea and made to beg their way through France to the port whence they were shipped to this city, to be beaten and starved by their cruel masters and sent out to beg…" For sample reporting on the issue, see "Padrone Slavery. An Evil Which, to a certain Extent, Exists in Boston. Methods Adopted to Keep Many ignorant Italians Under Subjection. How Immigrants are Bound Out to Unscrupolous Taskmasters,' in *Boston daily Globe*, Jul. 4, 1884, p. 5. See also, "Deluded Immigrants. An Italian and Family of 13 at the Mercy of a Usurer ["one Ciroceni"] — Stonecutter Here Under Contract," in *Boston Daily Globe*, Jul. 1, 1888. For another example, "Padrones and Laborers. Why Italian Immigrants Come to America. Testimony Heard by the Congressional Investigating Committee. Leaving Ten Cents a Day for a Mythical Dollar and a Half," in *Boston Daily Globe*, Jul. 28, 1888.

it is too easy to say that Riis used what today appear to be some politically incorrect qualifiers when describing the Chinese, the Jews, the Czech, the Hungarians and so on. At bottom he was trying, perhaps in the spirit of the many other social crusaders at the time, to offer a spectrum of an urban underclass that hardly reflected the lofty ideals of a country where the streets were paved with gold: *that* myth, it might now be argued, proved to be a farce! Exploitation reigned, demoralization and abuse were the norm, and being blamed for this condition was thrust back upon the hapless immigrant:

> Pauperdom is to blame for the unjust yoking of poverty with punishment, "charities" with "correction," in our municipal ministering to the needs of the Nether Half.

The major press in English from various cities furnishes a great observatory to gauge dominant public opinion and corroborate this assessment. Although patterns emerge, they are not necessarily trans-historical or atemporal, and are perhaps better understood as inter-class and trans-ethnic. However, in tracking an increasingly negative view of the Italian arrivals it is possible in the press to mark out a period that began with the widely discussed 1891 lynching of eleven Sicilians in New Orleans,[38] and continued over the years with reportage that concerned the insidious Italian "Black Hand," or that emphasized Italians who got into violent scuffles.[39] Such articles appeared about as frequently as others that

---

38 The entire story is told by Richard Gambino, *Vendetta* [1977]. An HBO teleplay version with the same title, starring Christopher Walken, was directed by Nicholas Meyer and released in 1999, with a DVD issued in 2004.

39 For a representative selection of articles see the collection in Salvatore J. LaGumina, *WOP! A Documentary History of Anti-Italian Discrimination*; Wayne Moquin and Charles Van Doren, eds., *A Documentary History of the Italian Americans*, cit.; and commentary throughout Richard Gambino, *Blood of My Blood* [1974]; Lydio Tomasi, ed., *The Italian in America: The Progressive View 1891-1914*, cit.; and various pages throughout Jerre Mangione and Ben Morreale, *La Storia*; and Francesco Cardasco and Eugene Bucchioni, eds. *The Italians. Social Backgrounds Of An American Group*. Considering that Italian American studies have grown

concerned the hunting down of a stray Sioux or Comanche in the Far West, or about the lynching of a Negro in the South. Matters get more complicated when we add reports of the growing presence of Italian immigrants among the anarchists, socialists, union organizers, labor disputes, strikes, demonstrations, and riots that were the source of so much middle-class and government anxiety in the first fifteen years of the twentieth century.[40] The tenor and ideological depth of popular prejudice against Italians would continue to grow in this manner until it culminated, in the post-World War I decade, in the case against Sacco and Vanzetti.[41]

4. MAKING ITALIAN-AMERICANS

It is difficult today to comprehend how a national government and, by reflection, the people it presumably represented as "Americans," could come up with and endorse blatantly racist and exclusivist policies against Italians (but other groups as well, as we saw) to the point of making them a widely accepted background scape-goat and despicable social value or frame of reference. But if we recall briefly the role played by the Dillingham Commission (1907-1911) in the fate of all immigrants, not just Italians, things become clearer. The Commission's work was a crucial socio-historical event where identities were shaped from the outside, and measured and pinned on the body of the immigrant, both metaphorically and literally.

According to Desmond King, in 1882, out of 650,000 European immigrants who arrived in the US, 13.1% came from southern and eastern European countries comprising Austria-Hungary, Greece, Italy, Montenegro, Poland, Portugal, Romania, Russia, Serbia,

---

considerably in the past thirty years, it is remarkable that there have not been further collections of materials of this kind. The dearth of original documentation is what prompted the D'Amato Chair at Stony Brook to launch the Italian American Archive Project.
40 See the above cited works by Cannistraro and Meyer, and by Bencivenna, and sources therein.
41 Herbert Ehrmann, *The Case That Will Not Die: Commonwealth vs Sacco and Vanzetti*.

Spain, and Turkey. Twenty-five years later, in 1907, which was an all-time peak year for immigration, we notice an epochal change: of 1,207,000 immigrants who arrived in the US, 81% came from these same southern and eastern European countries. It was cause for alarm.[42]

The growing public chorus[43] that something be done about this "invasion" eventually forced government officials to take action. It's not that there weren't Italian immigrants who had already incorporated and assimilated by the beginning of the century, and distinguished themselves in various sectors of society. There were successful bankers, politicians, wine growers, artists, political activists on the scene.[44] It was that great mass at the bottom of the socioeconomic hierarchy which, together with their *confreres* from other countries, represented a veritable human tsunami arriving at the various ports, from Boston to New Orleans, from San Francisco to Los Angeles, with New York being the major hub. In 1907 the numbers peaked at nearly 300,000 thousand! As a result, President Roosevelt was lobbied heavily to take action, and in 1907 the Congress approved the creation of a US Immigration Commission, known by the name of the Vermont Senator who chaired it, William P. Dillingham. What was perhaps most remarkable about this gargantuan undertaking was the coordination and collaboration of hundreds of scientists, demographers, anthropologists, sociologists, medical researchers, and criminologists who went on to conduct interviews, recordings and photographs, summarizing, and eventually testifying before other

---

42 Desmond King, *Making Americans*, cit.
43 I my research, I have plied the pages of major dailies, such as *The New York Times, The Los Angeles Times, Boston Daily Globe, The Hartford Courant, The Chicago Tribune*, and others for the years 1880-1914.
44 See for instance, "Lots of Italian Banks. North End of Boston Full of Them. How They Do Business Without Any Legal Restraint. American Banks Patronized Only by the Educated Minority," in *Boston Daily Globe*, Jan. 28, 1894, p. 11.

experts and officials about the most diverse aspects of the nature of the European mass exodus to the United States.

Lasting nearly three years, the results were delivered in 1911, in 42 volumes. It is by far the most exhaustive, thorough, and we might even say scientifically "accurate" investigation of such a huge topic to date.[45] Paradoxically, the Italian intelligentsia contributed to strengthen the Commission's conclusions that Southern European and East Europeans were "inferior," relying among scientific authorities on the work of the Italian criminologist Cesare Lombroso, and of his younger peer, Alfredo Niceforo. The latter made a case for "two Italies standing in stark contrast," and whereas

> The Aryans, northern Italians, have a more developed sense of social organization rare among Mediterraneans, southern Italians [...] have by contrast a more developed individualistic sentiment.[46]

---

[45] This remains a problematic issue because the Commission allegedly employed the top scientists of the day, though in retrospect scholars have identified two kinds of problems. One is intrinsic to the nature of scientific discourse, especially concerning the typologies of race and intelligence, which existed at the time and dovetail into the question whether these have (or according to some, have not) been superseded by later and contemporary research (just think of recent publications in sociobiology and the genome project). The second problem is extrinsic to science, in the sense that the results were appropriated by ideologues and politicians to make the case that certain people are naturally inferior, unteachable, unadaptable, and so on, and who could therefore be justifiably excluded from entering the country. See on this Oscar Handlin, *Race and Nationality in American Life* (Garden City: Doubleday, 1957); King, *Making Americans*, cit.; Jon Gjerde, ed., *Major Problems in American Immigration and Ethnic History. Documents and Essays*; and the monograph by Robert Zeidel, *Immigrants, Progressives, and Exclusion Politics: The Dillingham Commission, 1900-1927*.

[46] See the detailed analysis in Peter D'Agostino, "Craniums, Criminals, and the 'Cursed Race': Italian Anthropology in American Racial Thought 1861-1924". On Lombroso and his theory, see the thorough study by Mary Gibson, *Born to Crime: Cesare Lombroso and the Origins of Biological Criminology*.

"The Silence of the Subalterns"

By the time they got through the hearings and testimony, this assessment was adopted by the Commission as scientific, a factual truth.

We recall how, in official immigration statistics, "Italians" were listed next to other nationalities and "races" in the late XIX Century as "undesirables" and "unamericanizable," but by the early 1900s a further distinction was introduced between "Northern" and "Southern" Italians. The Commission thus legitimated as unvarnished truth a distinction between more bourgeois northern Italians and more rustic, Arab-looking southerners. In other words, the Commission confirmed and reified a descriptive characterization that had already become popular belief and would remain the basis of stereotyping until only a few decades ago.[47] The impact was felt by the immigrants not only on arrival, but also in the course of these early decades of constant negotiation with the social reality with which they and their children interacted and competed with other groups for a seat at the table.

One area of investigation and reflection that is often overlooked is the complex relationship between newly arrived Italians and the African Americans who were already here. Though both groups were seen with suspicion in the early 1900s, Italian immigrants were grouped with an increasing frequency with the "whites": disgusting as they might be, the opinion went,[48] they

---

47 See for instance the contested thesis of Edward Banfield, *The Moral Basis of a Backward Society*, which argued that the Southerner's allegiance primarily if not solely to the family, at the expense of social investment in a broader "civil" society, was "amoral." The problem with this book is that it is ahistorical, and the fact that the sample population had been oppressed for centuries was immaterial to his point, which was to prove that the poor are morally inferior and don't behave like middle class suburbanites. Less prejudicial in its premises was Eric Hobsbawn, *Primitive Rebels*, which shifted the emphasis from the moralistic to the anthropological, with reference to the same areas studied by Banfield. For an Italian history of how the "inferior" Southerner was "constructed" over time, see Vito Teti, *La razza maledetta*.

48 Implied in the exhortations to be "good Americans" by the likes of Gino Speranza of the *Progresso italo-americano*, and the Italian consular personnel.

were at least *"not* black."⁴⁹ Things such as feeling or "being Italian," and feeling and "being American," though still pressing concerns at this stage, made room for a new overarching concern, passing for or "being White."

And in terms of society at large, moreover, what took place was the emergence of a conceptual distinction, adopted even by the highbrow intellectuals and labor reformers, between those in the "New Immigration" whom they thought acceptable or at least "Americanizable," and those whose basic set of qualities were "unwanted," "dangerous," and "unassimilable."⁵⁰ The nation's founders and their descendents up to about the period of the Civil War were clearly constitutive of what then was referred to as the Old Immigration, so there was no stigma attached to the fact that, if we pursued it far enough, they also could trace their origins back to Europe, specifically to Holland, England, Scotland, Germany, the Scandinavian countries. The issue became who, among the New Immigrants, was acceptable.

I have argued elsewhere that after four or five generations, it seems that wherever they re-planted roots or re-settled, people feel they *own* the land and, with it, its history, and are therefore entitled to calling themselves natives.⁵¹ As the great majority of the New Immigrants - Italians, Croats, Slovaks, Greeks, Bohemians (Czechs), Turks, Romanians, Poles, Russians, and Polish and Russian Jews — came from southern and eastern Europe, the Commission concluded that we were taking in the "refuse" of

---

49 Revealing work has been done in this topic, often seen as problematic in Italian America, by Thomas Guglielmo, "'No Color Barrier': Italians, Race, and Power in the United States," in Jennifer Guglielmo and Salvatore Salerno, eds., *Are Italians White*? 29-43. On the role the Italian language press played in this scenario, see the important book by Peter G. Vellon, *A Great Crime Against Our Race*.
50 Cf. Handlin, *Race and Nationality*; King, *Making Americans*.
51 See the Introuduction, "Migration, History, Existence,"above, 11-22. See also the beautiful essay by Hans Magnus Enzensberger, "The Great Migration". His analogy with the attitudes of passengers in a train compartment, who treat each new passenger as an "intruder" but who in turn, after establishing community with those already there, will perceive a new later passenger entering the compartment as an intrusion, is very instructive.

other nations, worshipped in Orthodox churches and synagogues, that they were heavily illiterate and impoverished, that they now lived together in "Little Italies" and "Little Polands" and "Jewtowns" and "Chinatowns" in the jam-packed and unhealthy and dangerous inner cities, and implicitly had no desire to "Americanize."[52] Moreover, whereas the Old Immigration movement was conceived as being essentially one of permanence, as entire families settled the land, the New Immigration, the report continued, was made up largely of individuals, a considerable proportion of whom apparently had no intention of establishing a permanent domicile, their only purpose in coming to America being to temporarily take advantage of the greater wages paid for industrial labor in this country. This claim has been contested, since as we gleam from other sources (including worsening conditions in the sending country), by early 1900 the majority came to stay, no matter what the odds.

The Dillingham Commission was important for another more theoretical reason. Two of the most important and powerful discursive formations of the country, science and jurisprudence, had joined their authority and created a *de facto* legitimate stereotype. In principle, science seeks to find what is called knowledge, whereas the law seeks what is the truth of a particular state of affairs in social interactions in view of what is legitimate. Thus we witness, on a grand scale, how institutions of higher learning and the professions (the scientific community comprising some ten different specific disciplines) present their findings, and another fundamental body (rooted in ethics, the law, and setting standards for moral compass), meaning the Congress of the United States, have now proved and approved beyond the shadow of a doubt that some groups or races or nationalities were inferior to others: stereotyping is legitimated! Historians of the period corroborated

---

52 This can be followed as ongoing topic for years in *Harper's Magazine*, setting the prejudgment that Italians were to be distrusted and in general not good people.

"The Silence of the Subalterns"

the conviction.[53] And the then dominant field of geography also supplied further ammunition.[54] One need only consider the representation of Italians in the early silent era movies to get a glimpse.[55] Thus by the time World War I broke out intellectual and political élites could state that what had made America great were the values of the legitimate heirs of the immigrants hailing from northwestern Europe, an idealized White Anglo-Saxon Protestant, and that it was scientifically accurate, politically advantageous, and socially acceptable to discriminate against people coming from Mediterranean and eastern European countries.[56] As historian Oscar Handlin concluded in his path-breaking work, the

---

[53] While he was President of Princeton University, Woodrow Wilson, later to become the 28th President of the United States (1913-1921), wrote a five-volume *History of the American People* published in 1903), where we can read the following assessment: "The census of 1890 showed the population of the country increased to 62,622,250, an addition of 12,466,467 within the decade. Immigrants poured steadily in as before, but with an alteration of stock which students of affairs marked with uneasiness. Throughout the century men of sturdy stocks of the north of Europe had made up the main strain of foreign blood which was every year added to the vital working force of the country, or else men of the Latin-Gallic stocks of France and northern Italy; but now there came multitudes of men of the lowest class from the south of Italy and men of the meaner sort out of Hungary and Poland, men out of the ranks where there was neither skill nor energy nor any initiative of quick intelligence; and they came in numbers which increased from year to year, as if the countries of the south of Europe were disburdening themselves of the more sordid and hapless elements of their population, the men whose standards of life and of work were such as American workmen had never dreamed of hitherto." Vol. V, pp 212-13.

[54] See E.G. Ravenstein, "The Laws of Migration," cited by Zolberg, *A Nation by Design*, cit., p. 202. In the age of positivism, there was a broad application of theories and methods derived from geography, biology, and the recent science of evolution. Leading anthropologist Franz Boas, who edited Vol. 38 of the Final Report, wrote on "Changes in bodily form of descendants of immigrants," deploying the tools of the new science of anthropometry. Other volumes contain research on somatic and other physical characteristics and their at the time presumed direct correlation with the potential for learning, criminality and other proclivities, including moral aspects.

[55] I am thinking of films like *The Black Hand* (1906), *The Organ Grinder* (1912), *The Italian* (1915). *Tony America* (1918). See Carlos E. Cortes, "The Hollywood Curriculum on Italian Americans: Evolution of an Icon of Ethnicity," in Lydio F. Tomasi *et al*, eds., *The Columbus People* (New York: Center for Migration Studies, 1994), pp 90-92; and Giorgio Bertellini, *Italy in Early American Cinema* (Bloomington: Indiana University Press, 2009).

[56] The actual documents can easily be retrieved online by going to the Open Collection Program, Immigration to the United States, 1789-1930, at Harvard University.

Commission only proved what everyone believed even before it started its lengthy, laborious, "scientific" research, and its equally lengthy committee work.[57]

A number of people and associations protested the misuse of the results of the Dillingham Commission.[58] But once the Commission's report was circulated, overt xenophobia became standard fare in the press. Patriotic groups and associations began to craft rules and procedures for Americanizing the immigrants. As had been done with the Amerindians, the pressure was on to forget the ways of the old world, of the immigrant parents, and learn "the proper way we do things in America." Patterns also began to emerge in the ways in which Americans undertook to think about assimilating the immigrants. Historian Desmond King has drawn attention to three competing models of assimilation: (1) An *Anglo Conformity Model* under which assimilation means instilling all members of the polity with Anglo-Saxon values and interests. (2) A *Melting Pot Model* in which the group that is longest present or most dominant does not determine an overall national identity, which instead remains open to negotiation. And (3) a *Salad Bowl Model* that views assimilation as a form of cultural pluralism in which a multiplicity of ethnic groups and identities coexist.[59]

---

57 See Oscar Handlin, *Race and Nationality in American Life*, cit. The theses of Handlin's most famous book, *The Uprooted*, 1951, were critiqued by later scholars and, concerning Italian Americans, by Rudolph Vecoli, for generalizing about, and minimizing the relevance of the places of origin of the immigrants. But in this sense he was already pointing to the necessity, recently underscored by Gabaccia, of breaking beyond the restrictive "national" paradigm for interpreting migrations.

58 For one thing, people started differentiating between culture and race. The Immigrants Protective League made it known to congressmen that they meant to "aid in the Americanization of immigrants." Its director, Grace Abbott, "threw cold water on the non-historical notion that the older immigrants had been perceived at their time of their arrival as any less assimilable than the new immigrants were now judged in 1912." Abbott reported that "when you come in close daily contact with the newer arrivals, you find that they are men and women just like the rest of us, some good and some bad, and it is impossible to discriminate against them as a whole." (King, *Making Americans*, 63)

59 Ibid. 85.

Interesting point here is the growing popularity of the Melting Pot ideology, as per the title of the influential play by Israel Zangwill, which premiered in 1908. This was to create a narrative for large sectors of popular opinion, as some lines seemed to be perfectly etched:

> America is God's Crucible, the great melting-Pot where all races of Europe are melting and reforming...Germans and Frenchmen, Irishmen and Englishmen, Jews and Russians, — into the crucible with you all! God is making the American.[60]

This ideology was viewed quite positively by the assimilationists and the pro-immigration leagues, notwithstanding that it was an immigrant Jew who advocated it: he all but wanted to cast off his origin and literally start anew, construct the new citizen of this exceptional country. And it would be another immigrant, this time an Italian, Frank Capra, who a generation later would shape for common consumption the American Dream.

The paradox for historians, social and literary alike, is that, broadly speaking, *at the same time* that Americans were vouching for *both* the conformity model *and* the melting pot assimilation schemes, they were also "deliberately controlling who was to be eligible to assimilate."[61] The fact that some of these groups found solace or validation or security within their own enclaves only heightened the discrimination and racism against them. The process of a coercive, warped, or incoherent assimilation into America had also political and economic aspects to it, because lots of funds were made available from private foundations as well as government agencies and school districts, to educate the immi-

---

60 See Israel Zangwill, *The Melting-Pot*, 35.
61 This recalls the thesis, already mentioned above, advanced by Aristide R. Zolberg, *A Nation by Design. Immigration Policy in the Fashioning of America*, cit., according to whom there has never been a moment in our national history when our leaders and representatives did not explicitly, or tacitly, promote a selection process that favored certain incoming groups over others.

grants themselves and/or their children into the American way of life, often in traumatic ways.[62] Schools were set up even in factories and offices, so that everyone spoke English, learned white Protestant mores, and by and large tried to live up to the values of the dominant Anglo Conformity Model. Multiculturalism was far in the future. Second generations Italian Americans learned to love white bread and peanut butter and jelly. Some, following the entreat of people like Gino Speranza and the *Progresso italo-americano*, thought it best to cut off their cultural and linguistic roots and become champions of the American way of life.

5. CONCLUSIONS

In closing one might reasonably ask: Why did they stay? Of those three million who did not go back, given the culture-scape we just sketched, what motivated the immigrant to remain? Perhaps the experience of migrating brings one closer not only to what is essential to human survival, but also to the instincts necessary for co-existence, instincts that may actually pre-date the construction of our social identities that now seem so important to us. Identification with a country of provenance — with its many language-and-history marked social worlds — dies when the migrant dies. Contrary to some accounts, I do not think of the Great Migration of the Italians who came to America in the years from 1880 to 1920 as a wave of people who arrived bearing a sword or a torch like Aeneas, who arrived foreordained on the shores of Latium. This was instead a transitional historical generation that was disseminated almost at random in the most varied environments — farming, railroads, construction, fisheries, mills, and so on. They planted the seeds of a generation that, in growing up American, would carry a complex symbolic load, or "charge," or field of expression. But their parents were *no longer* "Italian" and *not yet* "American." They might be called "Atlantians."

---

62 See Gary Gerstle, "Liberty, Coercion, and the Making of Americans".

"The Silence of the Subalterns"

Many the writers who have tried so valiantly to "re-construct" or "re-imagine" or "reclaim" what the lives of these people, the first generation of immigrants, were like.[63] But in these texts one often hears an echo chamber, a hollow space that is approached, tasted, teased, and yes, given a voice, but one which somehow sounds distant and, as it were, from the "outside." In an effort to regain some authenticity, some contemporary researchers have turned to the eloquent few of the period, to persons who claimed to represent "their own people" and who furnished partial mirrors, "in their own language," of their living conditions and of the profound social problems they faced. I am thinking of the radical organizer and writer Arturo Giovannitti, and popular writers such as Bernardino Ciampelli, Riccardo Cordiferro and others,[64] and the plethora of activists and well-meaning "patriots" who peopled the pages of the very active Italian language press.[65] Still, like veteran actors on the stage of Italian American history, these persons end up as "figures" or "characters," not as real people.[66] Their story is destined to be recounted a generation later — maybe two or three generations later—when the net results risk romanticizing and idealizing our stoic, self-less, impenetrable grandmothers and grandfathers.

The experience of the first generation of immigrants has been by and large safely labeled either as an epiphenomenon in the lives of nations or as a preliminary, indeed transitory, step *toward*

---

[63] I am thinking of fictional or family-autobiographical works produced by writers who were the children of the immigrants, and who by expressing themselves in English, make up what is really the "first" generation of Italian Americans literature. See, for instance, the writings of Garibaldi La Polla, John Fante, John Ciardi, Jerre Mangione, Pietro Di Donato and Helen Barolini. In scholarship, see also by Barolini, *The Dream Book.*; Mary Jo Bona, *Claiming a Tradition*; Fred Gardaphé, *Italian Signs, American Streets*. Of special importance is the Ellis Island Oral Histories project (1892-1976), which recorded, to the degree that it was still possible with an aging and disappearing generation, the accounts, and songs, of the first Italian immigrants.

[64] See Francesco Durante, *Italoamericana*, cit.

[65] See Peter Vellon, *A Great Conspiracy*, cit.

[66] See Ilaria Serra, *The Value of Worthless Lives*, cit.

becoming Italian American. It is quickly subsumed as a "natural" thing, complicated and dramatic of course, but subject to laws of economics and ultimately not the stuff that makes history and civilizations. Yet the magnitude of the tidal wave of Europeans to the Americas, and of Italians in particular, touched on a greater set of social institutions and cultural mores than could ever be contained within any one national discourse. It involved the entire world of the Euroamerican *oecumene*, the North-Atlantic trade and development, ultimately the troubled when not diabolic relationship between capitalism and democracy. Survival, labor, dignity, and the desires for a functional justice system and the improvement of one's family, were predominant among the culture-shocked immigrant arrivals, and these were matters that cut right through the epistemological grids of race, gender, language, and identity affiliation that modern scholars have created for them.

Considered historically, the silent majority to which I have been referring seems to puncture rather than reinforce the cultural structures we normally work with, such as pride of flag, or descent, or place, or religion, or language. Here the crucial components of what makes a culture were experienced at their base value, at their lowest possible denominator, so to speak, at the locus where a belief system — the value of certain rituals, the reassurance of origin, the identity of names, a memory which was *not* that of the grand paradigm called Italy, that of the *alta cultura* — was anchored to a material, life-sustaining process, implying above all concerns for a real job, a safe family or loved one, a peculiar often illegible system of beliefs and social dynamics. These people knew, in their inability to get a hearing in the host society, that nevertheless there was no going back, for migration is truly a one-way trip, and all the romanticizing about their "having made it" in the host country will never cauterize the wound of being forever in-between. The new credo that now, in this country, if wrong was done there would be an authority to which one could turn —

a democratic government (!), bad apples notwithstanding, — was just that, a credo, a hope, a force pulling them onward into the unknown, chart it, dig the ditches, lay the rails, erect the buildings, sell the newspapers, hawk their meager products somehow.

It is only with the American-born that the question, "What is an Italian American?" truly arises. But the Atlantians, those who "came before," were locked in the silent and inner-life roiling effort of making do, of living, and of paving new pathways (both metaphorically and literally), opening up concrete venues for themselves and their families and communities, true explorers without maps and compass, inglorious and unsung builders of the new empire. Still, they managed to draft their own blueprints for survival, they found self-determination in the face of a stripped self, they offered models of adaptability to new mores and devised ingenious ways of resolving problems, and undoubtedly contributed to the process of planting new seeds and grafting where possible different shoots, premises for seeding ever new gardens.

But this silent crowd of misunderstood and maligned individuals on both opposing shores of the Ocean sea called the Atlantic existed in a twilight world. They never fully entered and partook in the much touted and dreamed New World. When the next generation finally came of age, and aspired to validate its own past, it could obviously see the remains of what had taken place, but their interlocutors, if they spoke at all, spoke a different idiom, and I don't mean just English. These ocean-crossers, these lower-case explorers and pioneers, this transient generation presents formidable problems of interpretation, being more a *trans-latio* — literally "a carrying across" — between and among contrasting and conflictual world-views. Today's Italian Americans are in this sense the heirs to an origin that is fundamentally a translation from a non-language to a non-place, from a powerful silence to a babel of possibilities. Theirs is the task to give voice and relevance to the silence.

PART TWO

Geographies of Identity through Literature

CHAPTER FOUR

PLACES, PROCESSES, PERSPECTIVES IN
ITALIAN AMERICAN POETRY AND POETICS

> *the war of the worlds hang here,*
> *right now, in the balance*
> *it is a war for this world,*
> *to keep it*
> *a vale of soul-*
> *making*

Diana Di Prima, "Rant"

1. CRITICAL FIELDS

Taking a cue from a recent and most fruitful spate of papers fired in response to Gay Talese's provocative "Where Are the Italian-American Novelists,"[1] I have been asking myself "Where are the Italian American Poets?" For an adequate response, I began a three-fold process of inquiry. The first concerns the necessary qualifying epithet attached to any cultural or more specifically poetic group or gathering or network. It cannot be denied that some of the most piercing and revealing literary and cultural criticism during the past quarter of a century came by way of anthologies, scholarly articles, and monographs dedicated to, for example, Black Writers, Black Women's Writings, Asian-American literature, Caribbean writers, Chicano Writers, Chicana poetry, Literature by Latinas of the United States. It would come nearly spontaneous to then ask oneself: why isn't there a more diffuse discus-

---

[1] See Talese (1993) for the original article, and *italian americana* XX, 1, (1993), for responses, as well as Viscusi (1994).

sion, publication, critique of Italian American writers, and specifically poets? Unlike novelists, poets are proverbially blind to their audiences, which are small and idiosyncratic for the most part. On top of that, the identity, role and recognition of poets and poetry has been undergoing noteworthy — often confusing, contradictory, ever culturally meaningful — shifts in this country since the end of World War II.

This is especially detectable if we focus on the necessity, on the part of poets, to play up to the paradigms imposed by newly fangled institutional agendas and missions (creative writing majors, composition courses, news media, public founded organizations, etc., needed for "survival") while protecting their kin in whichever way — preferring certain tropes to others, pursuing newly configured ideologies, or inventing a particular style.[2] This sets the premises for the creation of an archipelago of localized, often barely visible subcultures,[3] but which permitted poetry as a threatened species to survive.

I. We are interested in understanding how poetry — among the general public elbowed out by new contending arts, some extremely powerful, such as cinema and videos — reaches its audience, and the broader though often subliminal effects it has and might have. From another related angle, I am wondering how a less constrictive or elitist notion of public might respond to contemporary poetry. It is not technically a demographic of readers we are seeking, but the description and possibly the charting of a taste and a politics, a recognizable influential discourse. The study of a poet's reception and transmission is, after all, one of the main-

---

2 This applies to the various poetries or "schools" as well which allow us to recognize (or organize) poets according to whether they are Bay Area poets, New York poets, Angelino poets, etc.

3 Dana Gioia's *Can Poetry Matter* is a most recent recapitulation of these complex changes in our society, an analysis of competing poetics especially since World War II, and a considered invitation toward a different kind of aesthetic-critical commitment, one attuned to and participatory in the postmodern culture grids and which alone may restore poetry as a meaningful art form, giving it a more pervasive presence.

stays of literary hermeneutics, a critical hypothesis seeking and tracing a sense which in part transcends my own subjectivity and speaks to a broader community or constituency.

II. The second set of critical references will concern a topology or topography of what these Italian Americans poets actually do write about. It is time we begin to (re)read and critique literature *as if* the words still (or: yet again?) referred to something/someone outside the text, as if the text were nonetheless referential in some guise, allusive to an outside or other place of sorts, allegorical enough to warrant the effort to circumscribe engaging clusters of meaning, a sense, some icons and figuras of contemporary poetics. This will see us through a spate of sample readings below.

III. The third background concern in this paper is of a strictly historiographical, academic nature, and aims to explore and reflect upon the relationship between thinking, language, and reality, within the context of European and North American cultures in the second half of the twentieth century.

IV. Among the most essential tasks of a poet is that of polishing and fine-tuning the language of a society, ensuring that its words, and their capacity to interest and innovate, do not degenerate into automatic ready-made phrases, endlessly repeatable until they lose their range, richness, their predisposition to be more than univocal messages or, worse, signals. In this view, the poets who attack long-encrusted locutions or splinter everyday words or word-clusters would be automatically avant-gardists, convinced as they are that the province of poetry is the Word, actually the Noun, the *lexis*, Greek *onoma*, essaying to shock it out of its torpor, and recharging it with political, symbolic, visual, enigmatic allusions. No doubt, however characterized, Italian American poetics can count among its practitioners eminent representatives of the canon of Modern American Poetry tout court. In some cases, this has meant that their poetry acquired a currency and an aesthetic collocation within the parameters of what is now long associated with the Beat Generation label and a score of thematics that our cultural memory associates with that designation. Among these authors: Ferlinghetti, Sorrentino and Di Prima. Deploying an *ad hoc* categorization, we may call this an *ontico-political poetics*.

Though this line of inquiry can yield revealing results, there is another approach to Poetry as the realm of the Word, and this consists in reworking the part of speech in terms of another of its fundamental functions, namely, that of Naming reality (or, better, the Being of the Real). From the Bible and Homer and down through Aristotle, Vico, Nietzsche, and Heidegger, the poetic word has been conceived and experimented with in terms of its founding capacity, foregrounding its somehow "magical" power to in-vent or devise a "world" of sorts. This poetry by and large focuses on the possibility/eventuality *that* it can and does create with words a "world" no matter how feeble and fleeting. We can call this *ontological poetry*.

At other times, the poetic word has been looked at in terms of *what* it brought out, what it highlights amidst the noise and the silence of language, of the world borne out of language. This type of poetic has a political soul markedly different from that of the avant-gardists. A poetry in which isolating, touching, lighting up the naming function of the word is a poetry intrinsically concerned with naming the concrete world, pointing toward reality, and a social historical symbolic life-world at that. We can call this a *gnostic* or *cognitive* poetry. To name something actually existing corresponds not to merely mentioning a word-that-refers-to-something the first time, in a casual sequence of "new" words or things we discover. *To name something is to bring it into existence from the void or nullity of non-Being,* it is very much like creating or inventing an idea or feeling or psychohistorical knot. This is intrinsically a question of identity because if I mention the proper noun Italy or name a cluster of critical problems as somehow related to Italy, I have already excluded all other possible nations or ethnic or cultural backgrounds. And that affects and pre- or co-determines the sense of the ensuing reading. But beyond that, we would have to ask *why* a writer needs to express this identity, and how it is wrung out of the chaos, how it is fashioned, what pathways or better said labyrinths of the soul must be traversed before the poet can frame or chisel or utter this memory, this image, this claim.

2. Preliminary Overview

There are, upon first considering the field, a great variety of poetics, an intriguing variation in styles, vocabulary, and reappropriations. We will discover that often some of these poets write about things that have nothing to do with their "Being Italian American" — or being American! or being Italian! — and speak rather to broader and less ethnically marked or "nationally" positioned concerns.

We may include in this grouping some poets who belonged in some way to the Beat Generation and/or other more circumscribed avant-garde movements in its wake, such as Lawrence Ferlinghetti, Gilbert Sorrentino, Leslie Scalapino, Diane Di Prima and Paul Vangelisti.

Some poets prefer to focus on the everyday, on life-situations, spontaneous juxtapositions, miracles and mirages of otherwise gratuitous or ignored encounters, hauntingly sentimental and subtly philosophical. Think of the poetry of Richard Milazzo.

Others choose to belabor their family history as the master trope, the generator metaphor for the life both personal and social of the poet. We can think here of some aspects of the writings of Maria Mazziotti Gillan, Felix Stefanile, Anna Bart, Janine Veto, Sandra Gilbert, Carmela Delia Lanza, Rita Ferrarelli, and Daniela Gioseffi. In these poets personal memories, family history, the attempts at understanding and resolving conflicts and defeats are poetized — "texted" we might say — against the often subliminal reminder of two tensions and torsions produced in the subject by unevenly distributed (or understood, or desired) yet co-enabling cultural codes, rich in linguistic substrates but also wrought with endless situations of miscommunication, violence, resentment, a tormented stoicism of sorts.

Gender is certainly emerging as a key *topos* in Italian American poetry. Poets who come to mind whose work is in need of critical evaluation and support are Phyllis Capello, Rose Romano, and Vittoria Repetto. These poets explore the language and the events of an "Italianness" no one cares to hear about, as it cracks the more amenable stereotypes of the Italian American woman.

In other instances, the poet turns to history, generating a layered quilt of voices and versions. There is of course always the nostalgic, preachy and moralistically outdated "national epic" poetic. The poetry of Rose Basile Green is an eminent example of this ever-popular genre of well-intentioned and melodramatic, acceptable lyrical narrations, typical of the earlier generations bent on a poetics of historical transference, of political deference, and of assimilation by denial.

Fortunately, there has appeared in more recent times on the scene a radically different configuration, a post-colonial rewriting of an Italian experience that comprises Europe and indeed the entire West. I am thinking of the brilliant sequence by Robert Viscusi, *An Oration...*, a short long-poem that situates and relates the Italian American experience beyond the chronologically defined migration trope of earlier generations, while metamorphosing various avant-gardist agendas, suggesting a radical revision of both modern Italian history (the selective memory) and American ideology (and its mythographies).

There is also present on the critical horizon the unexpurgated excavation of misery and political outrage, of unflinching social critique and the haunting self-realization of the nihilism that pervades everything, and with that the need for yet deeper energies and creative powers. Here we may think of the writings of Gregory Corso, Diane Di Prima, and Justin Vitiello. At a certain point, in the poetry of Pasquale Verdicchio, one senses how the question of history, one's auto-biography, and the philosophical quest for an ontological ground coincide:

> Something moves within the failed
> field of vision   disallowed fragile rose
>
> The intolerable absence of innocence
> an alternative proposal of
> questionable practices
> a sterile avant-garde poses
> in the lap of the executioner
>
> Beyond any approved limit
> to the undoing of the old world:
>
>> a group strategy
>> the fall of all alibis
>> all components undermined
>
> Monologues of desperate analysis
> diverse rebellion
> in itself the place   nothingness
> no longer an illusion
> but an unconfessed word
>
> Marked condition   immutable faith
> muted   something foreign
> become history
> in a posthumous hell   (*The Posthumous Poet*, 21)

Of course, there are also lyrical poets, who by definition are writing about the fleeting moment, the sweet and sour and unrepeatable sensations of a deeper or higher truth about being in the world and being with others, the snapshot that nails the image and is ever ready to stir us outside of space and time. Yet that is a classic, indeed romantic, and even worse a belated modernist conceit. Though lyric is shot through with metaphysical doubt and dilemmas (cf. Carravetta 1995b), it is not to be excluded that, with keener instruments, we might be able to read *in filigrana* different sorts of stories, trace invisible networks of signification. Much depends on the critical model adopted, even more on the categories devised to reframe the poem and have it emerge anew to the reader's consciousness. The poetry of Pier Giorgio di Cicco and of Joseph Maviglia lends itself to this type of inquiry. Let us, for example, take a look at this poem by Felix Stefanile:

"The Wedding Photograph"

They are stunned into poise. Their fixed eyes stare
at something strange...
They are used to waiting.
In her wedding gown my mother's face shows pale
beneath her blazing veil, the flying fillets.
My father glares. Confined in a gaudy peace,
he seems to be thinking this is serious business.
......

.......I remember them now,
heads nodding, pondering, or with gesturing hands
one or the other exclaiming, "Life is work."
They never saw that picture but they laughed out loud.[4]

Then there are the poets who describe their places of origins or non-origin, actually — in lyrical form, as in the case of Sandra Gilbert, in

---

[4] From *From the Margin*, 158-59. Hereinafter cited as FM followed by page number.

"In the Golden Sala"

> Sun of Sicilian hillsides
> heat of poppies opening like fierce
> boutonnieres of Apollo
> light of Agrigento, fretting the sea and the
>   seaside cliffs
> light of the golden *sala*.
> the great *sala* of the ruined *palazzo*
> where my Sicilian grandmother and her nine children
> camped outside Palermo   (FM, 169)

From a seemingly different context, we read, in Jay Parini's "Grandmother in Heaven":

> It's always almost time for Sunday dinner,
> with the boys all home: dark Nello,
> who became his cancer and refused to breathe;
> her little Gino, who went down the mines
> and whom they had to dig all week to find;
> that willow, Tony, who became so thin
> he blew away; then Julius and Leo,
> who survived by their wits alone
> but found no reason, after all was said,
> for hanging on...   (FM, 173)

In this sense, one can develop the notion of *italianità* and discern how it emerges, struggles, changes, what kinds of metaphors it calls for, what kind of map it inscribes, and then whether it is disseminating, or vanishing. And finally, what is it telling us about...America? about Italy? Nowhere is this more dramatized than in Maria Mazziotti Gillan's poems "Arturo" — which ends with the well known: "Listen, America,/this is my father, Arturo,/and I am his daughter, Maria./Do not call me Marie."[5]

---

[5] See Maria Mazziotti Gillan, *Where I come from*, pg. 51. See a fuller analysis below, ch. 6.

Once beyond this preliminary, hardly exhaustive reconnaissance segment, the best approach is to delve into the texts themselves, or should I say, the poetic experience itself, registering what strikes the critical mind, evoking the semantics of images, the costumes that dress up meanings, the filters that encumber experience. I begin my study discussing selected poems by contemporary, living poets I have encountered recently.

3. INTERTEXTUALITIES

In a poem titled "A Man Talks to Me on the Bus" Claudia Menza writes:[6]

> If you intend the path to my house,
> > best you take another road.
> > The only prints upon this doorstep
> > belong to me or the overruling rain.
> > I have but one chair — a passerby
> > would find not even a cup
> > to spare — now go!
>
> Love has been put out of this house like a cat
> > you don't mean to let back in.
> > Touch is merely memory across the skin.
> > Footsteps cause my hair to rise,
> > my claws extended — see:
> > I am also that cat put out.
> > ....
> > Don't, don't, don't
> > come closer. This conversation is ended.
> > There are other hearths
> > at which to ring.
> > No voice but mine breaks the silence of stone.
> > At last the pleasure of my own thin song.
> > Should anyone intrude upon this house,

---

6 Text given by poet to author during a reading, not included in *The Lunatics Ball*.

"Italian American Poetry and Poetics"

> I close the door,
> and the door shuts out.

Powerful stuff. It speaks to coincidence much more than to accident, it relates to perception as interpretation, to the rhythm, the *rhusmos* of assertiveness of the self in the strands of causality, it bespeaks a moment of attention, reception, response, decision, choice. It is an allegory of finitude.

Let us problematize this characterization even further. First of all, if it "works" it is owed to a critical presupposition, namely, that we believe we can describe the poet's poetics and, slowly and by degrees, figure out the poet's intentions, what she or he thinks, what the underlying metaphysics is. Flying into the bifurcate wrath of the critics of "the fallacy of paraphrase," this is also a valid critical path, indeed a necessary *risk* the moment the critic assumes the responsibility of reading-for, referring-about, explain or teach such-and-such subject or method. It is, in short, an enabling hermeneutic precondition. The receiver should train the critical sights of what it is — or seems to be — being talked about in these allegories: you too, dear reader, have a world view, or, with a few lines from Diane Di Prima:

> You cannot write a single line w/out a cosmology
> a cosmogony
> laid out, before your eyes
> ("Rant" in FM, 154)

Here we should focus *not* on the fact that these writers are writing from within the domains of a pre-established category, and have such and such names,[7] and therefore probable descent,[8]

---

[7] I agree with Gioia (1993, 64) that "Life experiences not a surname is what determines ethnicity in literature."
[8] This is one of two major critical concepts developed by Sollors, the other being consent. For a critique of this model, see the previous chapter.

ghosts of yesteryear's identity,[9] *but*, rather, being we in the postmodern epoch of fallen gods and splintered centers, we ought to ask: what do they see from there, from that nook, from that raft, that switchboard, that splinter they cannot help being on? from what ultimately is a privileged position? what can we sense and understand and what are they saying about us all?[10] Thus, we move from the poetic to the philosophical and then finally converge on the social, the political, the concrete. So to return to "the thing itself," that is, the text, let's read the poets *at the same time* for their ideological and political value at a time of untenable ideologies and utterly unbelievable politics and policies. In the same poem, Di Prima writes these lines:

> the war that matters is the war against the imagination
> all other wars are subsumed in it
> the ultimate famine is the starvation
> of the imagination
> ....
> the ultimate claustrophobia is the syllogism
> the ultimate claustrophobia is "it all adds up"
> nothing adds up & nothing stands in for
> anything else
> ......
> the taste in all our mouths is the taste of our power
> and it is bitter as death
> bring yr self home to yrself, enter the garden
> the guy at the gate w/the flaming sword is yrself   (FM, 155)

---

9 As is the case with many of the Chicano writers in the Sánchez study and the Fernández anthology.

10 I am not forgetting the cruciality of the in-between-ness of the relation, and in fact tension in Allen Tate's sense will be found to be a key element in all the poems analyzed. Equally important is an awareness of the diaphoric nature of poetizing, as sketched in Carravetta (1991). It is just that, "for argument's sake," I choose here to focus on what the possible *references* of the poems might be, in light of the three tasks sketched at the beginning of this paper.

The reader will contextualize, will expand, will relate and recreate and hypothesize, it is a hermeneutic principle to be responsible for the dialogue, as the reader/critic acknowledges at every tract of the pen: I am the other half responding, I scan it once and say: yes, it is talking about the imagination, the image-making faculty, the capacity to dream and invent and see. Leaving aside for a moment the question of how this text fits in with the pre- or non-ethnic characterization of avant-gardism in America,[11] what's being said is that there is a war against the imagination that influences all other wars.

Let's see: are we being told that the imagination is threatened, that someone is warring against our capacity to imagine, our freedom to dream? is real-war less important than that? Well, no, it is just that if you work on the imagination, then even the *other* war, the one with guns and F-16s, can be controlled, can be carried out in a particular, in an alternative, way (perhaps consider not having war at all...)! This is plausible insofar as the text supports a canvassing of the semantics of the word imagination, its potential and borderline dimension, its threatening force, unleasher of secrets. Moreover, there's the phrase signaling the fact that *that* is the primary concern, what truly matters. In a second movement, we then proceed to connect with the fact that ours is a society of images, of advertising billboards and video and cinema and glossy pictures. At this juncture what's being addressed is our very capacity to imagine things, taking stock that imagining (creativity, dreaming, phantasy itself) is under siege, that the problem is a major issue. After all, how many articles and TV programs have been dedicated to the issue of how much coverage the Gulf War really got, and which images we were made to see, and

---

11 Di Prima's presence among the Beats is well known, though too many times scholars who deal with one or more of these writers seem to forget to mention her name, or exclude her from anthologies. In A. Charters, ed., *The Beat Reader*, she gets 8 pages out of a 620 page volume.

which images of our leaders and political representatives were studiously chosen for general circulation over many networks?

4. URBAN METAPHYSICS OF CLAUDIA MENZA

Menza dedicates her book "To New York and Her People" adding right below "brave city." Deconstructive undecidability notwithstanding, the dedication *can* be read also as saying these linguistic experiences, these terse constructs that we ordinarily call poetry, are situated, are comprehended within, an urban/social/historical environment called New York, and that within this horizon of comprehension, this necessary and as yet unspecified *contextual background* there will be talk of people, references to something pertaining to their lives, interpersonal exchanges whether told in the first person (as if the poet were talking autobiographically) or the third (as when reporting a seen thing or phenomenon, canceling the speaking subject while allowing the things-in-themselves-as-language to in-form our reading).

Otherwise said, this poetry is often lyrical, at other times photographic, at other times yet meditative on the facts, the myriad experiences of a profoundly urbane spirit wandering listlessly, recounting, seeking to chisel another trace-of-presence into the elusive, manifold temporality and geography of an ever-mysterious cityscape. Let's read from *Apples*, p. 31:

> We step off the subway/caved in from work/the promise of dinner/hanging in the air/at day's end to raise the spirit/this evening in early summer/filing toward the light/no more the long coat of winter...

A stanza which sets a balance and seamless continuity among a typical downtown day, when heading home with an inner sense of relief and pleasure, which can be typical of many possibly all human beings, a "natural" dimension we might say. At this point, a sort of semantic metonymy links the actual time of the year, early summer, with a sense of moving toward *or* being illumined by the light (passage from sunlight to light as a metaphor for "seeing" or more prosaically understanding), plunging suddenly into a comparison-rejection of the season just past, one which required a coat, which spelt winter, and the rich allusiveness of this word (cold, dormant, frozen, inactive, being covered, as imposing a limit on the body's expression, and so on).

To close the circle, the book of poems dedicated to New York and its "brave" breeds of individuals and groups and subcultures and communities is written also to stir up mind and sense, to communicate a certain understanding, to make us aware and share something. But in order to more fully recompose or refigure this critico-creative reading of the poem, we should reread the next stanza:

> no love
> no vote
> get battered
> get shammed
> got drugs
> got armed
> so what
> not ours
>
> children shoot us from the IRT
>
> this time it's apples. (32)

A cruelly concise description of urban life for a certain group of people, scripted through the disquieting negation: no love, no vote. The so-called jungle requires immediate adaptation, immersion, awareness of facing the constant risk of extinction, capacity to become a barely human form of social interaction. *There are no leaves of grass in this world*, there are cracked menacing sidewalks, unsafe streets, trick conversations, the constant possibility for one's imagination and thought to fly off and reconsider the whole, the totality, the meaning of it all, the just as inevitable realization that it's all a mystery, a tragicomic game. The logic of the children's mutiny on the IRT, the political theorizing that justifies leaving the lepers, society's rejects, to their own predictably (self)destructive destiny, the piercing "rational" sequencing of the explanation for coming to terms with certain behaviors, with certain social forces, leaves no room for ambivalence: if one gets battered, gets slammed hither and thither in hopelessness, gets into drugs, one must do so to survive, and once there one must arm oneself, and acting before the real threat to life and limb. This may mean a preparedness to violence, to having to use weapons at any point during the day: these become real, tragically real concerns to these inner city dwellers.

There is no single statement, poetic or otherwise, which does not bear in its semantic womb a motivated, interested political end, an effort to establish some sort of upper hand, or advantage (however "rhetorical" this may turn out to be). Once armed, if the Great Voice of Society, the ever present Grand Ideal were to force a justification for this particular state of things, the response is no less politically aggressive: "so what[?]/[what's around, life, possibility] not ours." *Not specifically marked for gender, race, ethnicity, or party affiliation, the text revolves around a broader frame of mind and experience.* From this vantage point, *poetry turns philosophical*: you cannot get more categorical, more devastatingly effective, than this: that sorry shameful social sub-condition present in the city is somehow also our own responsibility, our own doing. The stark irony of the final two lines makes this truth compelling: "children shoot us from the IRT//this time it's apples" (32).

Another truly enticing, subtly comic and yet darkly serious poem is "Helicopters" (38-40). It starts again with a "typical" lower Manhattan apartment setting, with "normal" early morning flights of the fancy.[12] Then suddenly, the narrating voice says, something strange happens: "This morning, for instance,/a man strung between two helicopters,/a crucifix,/a prayer across the sky." Notice how though using everyday language the poet is capable of fixing a set of referents, and images, to create an enveloping sense for the whole, a layered photograph. The poet then proceeds with a list of questions one might ask in trying to figure out this unusual event, followed by another stanza in which she leaves her subjective pondering in order to reposition herself within his mind, and what this human being suspended over the city streets might be thinking. This includes phantasies about being an eagle, and the panic assessment of being in real danger of dying.

In the next movement, the poet zooms in on how one might actually be convinced (in a flash encompassing the pre-conscious, the physiological and certainly the mythical) of still possessing the gift of flight of our biological ancestors, the birds! The depressing irony of having to come to terms with this impossibility, neither physically nor (and more problematic) spiritually or intellectually attainable, leads the poet to explore the metaphysics of life through the recalling of emblematic, allegorical figuras, such as Daedalus and his son Icarus. The mythemes here disclose intellective, cognitive fields, those implied under the metaphoric use of the images of Daedalus and Icarus. The poem about a man hanging by a wire in the thicket of Manhattan's architecture can make one think of the relationship between flying (as liberty, as untrammeled wandering) and being predetermined and bound to the earth, "grounded," between the reasoned schizophrenia of the practical social dweller, and the unreasonable alienation of un-

---

12 This poem brings to mind another one by Joy Harjo titled "The Woman Hanging From The Thirteenth Floor Window" in which the poet recounts, while witnessing the rescue, many possible lives for the person "hanging by her own fingers, her/own skin, her own thread of indecision."

bound desire, the tragic flaw that surfaces with unremitting types, absurd visionaries, and infantile dreamer poets:

> Daedalus was thinking
> the illusion of flying,
> to be buoyed suddenly upward,
> poised on beaten air.
> And Icarus was thinking: I am a bird. (40)

The engaging, often unsettling suggestion the poems make throughout the collection is that our contemporary reality hosts many like Icarus, paradoxical prophets, as they can take the form of cult leaders, great though little known authors, or simply an everyday expression of deeply psychotic delusions. The "brave" know it. Their resilience is embodied in the invisible glue that attracts and binds the magic of these events, which allows Claudia Menza to halt time and natural cycles in order to dwell and roam in one of the many feasts, reunions, happenings that make the city what it is. But notice the ending that brings us back to a concrete self-conscious need to speak out in the second person, positioning the ego on the ground, telling its counterpart to probe deeper into one's self:

> In love we are all beggars.
> And if you don't believe that,
> watch yourself next time
> hope beckons. (18)

To venture an overall impression would inevitably do injustice to the variety and richness of sketches in verse. Yet whatever these few words about *The Lunatics Ball* may contribute to a deeper appreciation of this remarkable poetic voice, I stand fast to the belief that as critics we must *risk* an evaluation of sorts, with a clear intention of not wanting to misrepresent the sense of the text.[13] A critical discussion and evaluation partakes of the socially acknowledged and empowered discourse of literary criticism. As such, it searches for and creates meaning for a broader constituency, and it reflects on the meaning of things. As throughout *The Lunatics Ball*.

5. CITY (E)SCAPES IN KATHRYN NOCERINO

Another original poet of the New York area who has read often at the monthly literary *appuntamenti* of IAWA (Italian American Writers Association) is Kathryn Nocerino. Working within a personal adaptation of the gnawing, often glacial, at times biting irony of high Modernism, and not unreceptive to the most interesting verse experiments of the Fifties and the Sixties, Nocerino's text is yet another voice arising out of/responding to the inner city, a riveting of images beyond grammar and logic, a journal of phenomenological snapshots:

> half a block away, the sidewalk
> rumbled. the thing turned right at Broome
> and shifted north: a diesel truck two
>   buildings long, a double-axled
> juggernaut, its platform open to the sun; for
>   once, the contents visible. at the far
>   end of the truck, in the
>   seat of honor, there was a great
> big, feisty machine: meters, knobs, and
>   dials all over it. sleek
>   ("Triumphal Barge; West Broadway," *Wax Lips*, 13)

Nearly all of *Wax Lips* and *Death of the Plankton Bar & Grill* are made up of poems about New York, its myriad faces, its endless surprises, its peculiar dis/ordering of the universe. Identities here

---

13 I analyzed this problem in some detail in Carravetta (1991).

are ever captured *between* two points, meanings ripped from some mysterious origin, headed toward some unclear locus. It seems that movement itself is featured. Appropriately, the opening text in *Wax Lips* is titled "Hermes: West 14th Street," which we should read in its entirety:

> when the Gods begin to go to
>   seed, they should move on
>   discreetly. truth
> is, they never do. the way we
>   live, we're a kind of homeopathic
>   medicine for them, so that I'm
> almost at the point where I no longer
>   disapprove of rhinestone
> Hermes; his paunch; his motorcycle
>   helmet from which the fiery
>   wings protrude. sunlight brings him
> out in a Hawaiian shirt covered with
>   tikis and erupting volcanoes, wings of
>   silver kid tied, above running shoes, to
> ankles which have managed to retain some
>   delicacy. he hangs
>   around, he has nothing to
> do. this is understandable, since he
>   spent himself on the sport, spent
>   everything on it. the
>   body can't be blamed for not knowing how to
> read. it is we who are
>   faithless and essentially superficial, we who
>   tolerated you only so
>   long as you continued to be a
> slow drink for the eyes;
>   revivifier of limp awarenesses
>   old before their time. (*Wax Lips*, 11)

Our modern day messenger of the gods, patron of commerce, of "a good deal," jester and chameleon, child and sage at once, forever in transit between sender and receiver of messages, Hermes is now, in this poet's realm, nearly jobless: he has nothing to do because he has already *been*, having lived uncompromisingly he is now spent, burned-out, the mask of a bygone moment of glory, perhaps an invisible monument to what is no more, a floating ghost of the passing, the tormenting reminder of the decline of metaphysical Being, of any Grand Truth.

In the same vein, we read a brutally realistic and ethically discomforting assessment of inner city life, of urban politics, laced with a recurring sense of alienation: "our situation, in which ... land,/currency, and capital are unobtainable: the/entrepreneur resolves to use the/human being as final source of wealth; people/are not scarce," after which the narrating voice alights on the currency of salesmen, pseudogentlemen or pimps, political canvassers, gypsies, dreamy "normal" citizens "prospecting/love or its facsimile," in the end "thinking hard about/valuation, mediums of exchange, and desperate/bargains made among strangers." Life is no longer protected by or entrusted to omnipotent deities, and so in the concourse of human exchanges the telling signs of incertitude, of hopelessness, of absurdity, of the unexpected and incredible encounters emerge and constellate these texts. This displays further evidence of their own resistance to silence, resilient being-in-the-world that seeks to circumvent — when not actually going through — the distance, the strangeness, the untouchable ordainment of the cosmos, the constant declining of social life forms. A poet who sings to the sporadic traces of bygone gods but refuses to escape to, or find solace in, sentimental lullabies or pat retroprojections. This poet has re-embodied Hermes – perhaps as Iris – for the current age, a world in which where one comes from or where one might want to go, are less important, certainly no longer compelling, than where she is, than the locus of the unveiling of being, which finds its motive force in the ecstasies of quotidian revelations ("Transfiguration of a clothing store dummy." "The magic greaser,") the stupor before the endless surprises of the living ("I walked with a zombie," "Cowboy in the city,"), or — especially in *Death of the Plankton Bar & Grill* — the amazement at how the urban sieve has modified the parameters and the very sense of coexistence.

If Hermes/Iris no longer warrants narrating the irretrievable origins or the future utopia, then in the now-time of being what better classical figura to...reflect upon...than Narcissus? The nihilism that gnawed within the restless folds of modernity reemerges with the compelling conclusion that the essences are gone, that the indifference of entities, of virtual images have become concrete impenetrable realities, in fact they dominate and impose recognizable paradigms. Survival is possible, yes, but life must wring out its vacuous exultant promises, humble itself before the gaping abyss. In a poem appropriately titled "The Mirror," we read:

> gaze into it, but not too deeply.
> this is the lake of Narcissus,
>   always full.
> some fall in, never to emerge:
> you see them on the other side,
> to the right of your reflection,
> preening endlessly:
> windless lake, as smooth as...glass,
> featureless vessel,
> it lies dreamlessly,
> waiting for the imprint which will give it life.
> look, now, here's your doppelganger -
> twin who threatens usurpation.
> you are substance and merely exist;
> it is form,
> which dances without cease, before your vision.
>   (*Death of...*, 61)

And then, midway through the poem, the tone shifts. We hear the urging yet plaintive call out to a "you" which can be the narrator's interlocutor, the face of Destiny, an alter ego propped up and spurred not to give up, the poet's self perceivable as a returning but blurred, unreadable vision, a stirring yet muffled voice from the uncharted penumbras of reflection itself:

> take heed:
> many have sailed on this whirlpool,
> to starvation -
> solipsistic death.
> once engaged, you drift like a somnambulist
> ...
> inside, there is no room with silver candelabrum,
> no log-fired hearth;
> instead, a pool of stars in which you float forever.
> your eyes are now wide open,
> dull coins held in the traveler's palm -
> coins from the bottom of the ocean - green
> the symbols ancient and unreadable.

There is no doubt that in many ways Nocerino's poetry pays homage to the great lyricists of the tradition, from the Metaphysicals to the Transcendentalists, from the High Romantics to the mercurial Symbolists, finally closer to us to the existential politics of disillusionment and the vanishing cause. That "you" which transforms Being-I into a Being-with-others, which places the (first-person) subject into the care of the object (the mirror-image) or the other (the necessary second person), that life now pictured is disclosing its wide open eyes, a metaphor for someone seeking, or reckoning with something strange. That "you" is found to cling to "dull coins" (an exchange contract), validating icons (money, the ability "to buy" and therefore "to possess") which are useless, no longer *current*, first because they are in the hands of the traveler, the roving unmoored subject who cannot pretend to have its coin, its capital power-token, accepted everywhere, and second because this currency is dredged up from the "bottom of the ocean," the depths of the past, forever tarnished — "green" — therefore no longer legal tender, worse than that, "unreadable."

To provisionally conclude this installment, let's return to Dana Gioia's question: can poetry matter? We must respond in the affirmative. Nocerino's poetry certainly reasserts the cruciality of the poet's role in today's society, as "purifier of the language" who may speak freely across sectors, professions, classes and hierarchies. And as representative of a small clan of poets destined to read and print one another as if belonging to a semiprivate club of aficionados. My point here is also to short circuit the enclave and bring poetry to matter most (yet again) among a broader intellectual horizon which would legitimate it beyond the confines of academic criticism, and be circulated and performed in tandem with other art forms, from music to theatre, from academic meetings to radio shows.[14] In the end, however, as a critic I hope I have stimulated further interest in these intriguing contemporary poets, and to have realized for them what Robert Frost called "the utmost ambition [of a poet, which is] to lodge a few poems where they will be hard to get rid of" (Gioia 1992, 22).

---

14 This is nearly what is suggested in Gioia's *Can Poetry Matter?* (19-24), especially in order to give vitality and renewed appreciation to poetry beyond the confines of the university or the club of aficionados, mostly the poets themselves. Gioia (1994) makes some of these recommendations also in the specific context of Italian American literature, listing several "steps" (all of them having to do with constructing a readership, a variegated but persistent intra-cultural conversation) that Italian Americans ought to undertake. This is a marked transition if not altogether a poetological swerve from the *VIA* article a year earlier in which he identified the major trait of an Italian American literature to be the migration saga of the first two generations, making it therefore (at least at the theoretical level) a "transitional category" (1993, 61).

CHAPTER FIVE

ANTHONY VALERIO AND THE REAPPROPRIATION OF AN "AMERICAN" IDOL

A first observation concerning Anthony Valerio's *Valentino and the Great Italians* is whether to call it fiction in the high modernist sense of the term, a story or stories narrated on the basis of certain widely accepted formal rules and rhetorical devices, and not rather something else, a literary construct, a writing that makes you think of an autobiography, creative journalism, or semiserious *scherzi* worthy of the highest journal tradition, pictures drawn through words, frames of life. The title of the book, at the typographical level even, creates a perplexity. I cannot decide where the title actually ends, so I must posit interpretations almost like scientific hyotheses. I have at least two possible meaningful evaluations: Hypothesis (A) *Valentino and the Great Italians*, by Anthony Valerio, where the "by" is the convention for something like "Anthony Valerio is the *author*," a social entity or category detached from its construct, from its product." Hypothesis (B) would instead read like this: *Valentino and the Great Italians According to Anthony Valerio*, where I introduce two things: "according" as an intended alternative to "by" in that it signals a more pointed direct rapport between the writer (the person) of the text (of the book) and the subject (theme, topic) of the text (the actual writing as activity, as being in the world with others). And I introduce a no-longer-author "real" person named Anthony Valerio, someone I have actually met, who does exist and is in fact a legal resident of New York City. If this reading is accepted, then this new full title which incorporates its maker is making a statement about a specific cultural referent, namely concrete, "real" persons and events in the common American heritage, such as Valentino, Cuomo, and Sinatra. The reader is both informed and warned that whatever will be said about Valentino and the Great Italians is so *only* according to someone named Anthony Valerio. In this key, one is tempted to call this book non-fiction, creative journalism. Or a book about the social imaginary of a binational, bicultural group, melding History with Fantasy. The actual history of the famous Italians referred to in the book is well known, as historians and critics of every stripe have time and again sculpted all sorts of memorable and not always disinterested images of them. Here, though, they are four-dimensional. As happens almost predictably with great works of art, of the art of writing, Valerio's prose sustains different levels of perception in the world-within-the-text, and suggests several possible critical viewpoints as text-within-the-world. The following are some of the possible preliminary hermeneutic gestures toward a fuller appreciation of Valerio's *opera*.

In a sheaf of short stories the author gave me to read, part of a planned volume *Conversations with the Godfather*, Valerio re-reads through the stereotype called Italian American. Yet in working with the common place, *locus communis*, Valerio makes us realize and accept that we do indeed dwell and dream in a common, known, habitual space. Only, it is uncannily so, reverberating with something else, not just a musical note — there's a lot of music in these tales — but an echo, a stir, a smothered clanking, a persistent hum. The living space we inhabit daily is full of cultural icons, of tangible meanings. Working with the stereotype and making it come back to life, evincing its recognizability, stretching the logic of its typicality, rupturing in selected places its surface, its style. That appears to be one of the tasks this writer has taken upon himself. He ponders the genesis of recognition, of what lies behind a belief, a type. Mention something, an idea you have, 100 times and it'll slip from out of the shadows onto your feet, ready at your service; share a rumor as many times and you've created a conviction, a "truth" about a person, or event, or nationality. In casual conversations we may hear something like: men are animals. For a particular character in the story, deep down, men are vicious, or untrustworthy, you can only trust them so far. Thus the character: "Especially non-Italian women are drawn to the animal in us." But what does a great writer do with stereotypes? He transfigures them. In the short story *Animal Magnetism*, a man's pseudo-identification with the animal is turned into a phenomenology of male types, or if you wish a metamorphosis of male metaphors. "There's Jake the Bull. Sly the Stallion. Each and everyone of us is a fox. But the winds may be changing. Stallone has a script on his desk about the life of Giacomo Puccini." "Me? I'm an animal, too. I'm several animals in one. First and foremost, I am a chimp. No, not a chump, chimp." Further on, the character speaks as if he were a horse, then an elephant, a steer. All pretexts to set the narrative machine going, loci communes to retell the story of glorious sexual encounters, springboards to recover some moral or affective association with your loved ones.

Stereotypes and common places have been explored in hermeneutic philosophy by Greeks and Romans within the context of a civil rhetoric, but after the Renaissance our culture decreed them utterly unreliable, insidious, *doxa* in perilous contiguity with paradoxes, fodder for old maids and drunken salesmen. The value attributed to characterization slowly moved onto aesthetic terrain, creative pursuits, and in recent times modern middle-class moralists have been so arrogant as to think themselves above them, as that which denotes the uneducated, the faceless crowd, boors and bums and backyard social critics. None is too eager to begin a conversation by admitting candidly that he or she has a preformed opinion about another person, or artwork, or national origin. Stereotypes are rule of thumb notions that we acquire to pave the floor of our subliminal social and cultural maps, so that we can waddle and totter through the everyday with the aid of an automatic pilot, talking ourselves to exhaustion about how our four or five itineraries through existence are really what counts whereas everyone else's, especially the stranger you meet on the subway platform or the goofy looking bystander at the corner, really ain't worth their salt. If you can fence out your course, then so much the better, as everyone beyond is just a marass of inferiors, history *docet*: those natives, you know, they all look the same (you can find similar demeaning assertions in the Almirante's logbook, as in Captain Cook's, or in *Heart of Darkness*, or recall General Westmoreland's view of the Vietnamese). Yet stereotypes have been unwittingly bestowed a founding and enabling force, connecting a cluster of traits which one may cast in the metalingo of the semioticians, or the sociologist, or worse yet the sophomore who took Psych 101 and armed with his "Freudian Primer" walks around the campus judging and labeling friends and taxonomizing the strangers from strange lands (often the neighborhood down the avenue). The common place is also at the base of prejudice, that preconscious response to an other person's way of being which is, alternatively, imprinted, impressed, imposed on us as we grow up and which it would be foolish — scientists have made it their credo for centuries — to pretend one can ignore or, devise strategies to neutralize them. This state of affairs can be observed at various levels, from the most physiological to the most psychoanalytical, that is, from mere neural response to sophisticated phenomenological reduction.

The interest and novelty of these tales by Anthony Valerio consists in part in the way he spins out prejudices on common places and with a light hand unknot them in a variety of settings and situations, leaving us to savor the disturbing possibility that these stereotypes may indeed be, if not pre-determining the fate of certain encounters, probably co-determining the unfolding of the semantics, disclosing newer understanding.

"The Reappropriation of an 'American' Idol"

The stereotypes of course concern the Italian Americans. What the Italian American characters say, and what is said about them, are part and parcel of the same cultural experience. Stereotypes and national or ethnic mythographies go hand in hand. You need plenty of the first to stitch a consistent net for the second. Italians are colorful, interesting, ambiguous, but not all alike. For the mythography to turn into a sensible network of recognizable icons, the images must be worked and reworked, they must be visited relocated reupholstered to suit the times, to speak to a different generation, to respond in tune with, or as an antistrophe to, a waning or tarnished or demeaning picture.

Right from the first page of the first chapter (essay? article?) titled "The Sicilians," Valerio seductively engages: "According to Dante, Frederick was a wise and noble gentleman, and he chose as the seat of his throne not Swabia but Palermo. He preferred the southern clime, hot and dry, the cooling shade of the ombu tree, and he was enthralled by the beach at Mondello, which still stands and has sand the texture and glitter of star dust." It is hard to put down. His writing takes Italian American literature onto a new terrain, one which has not been explored so directly, so explicitly, so evenhandedly. Whatever can and has been said about certain highly visible figures of the Italian and Italian American cultural panorama is fair game for a different kind of telling. And with a low key and haunting humour.

Valerio is a city writer, gracefully urban and ironically urbane, though the irony never takes the upper hand while the grace is polished and spontaneous. In his text you are at home, you recognize your stock of typologies, but somehow you are not angered oppressed or vilified by them: you are in the company of a seasoned storyteller whose short takes on village life, historical memory, and popularized anecdote sketch a realistic setting where his characters can inter/play with their attributed identities, their socially created myth, with a light hearted and often matter of fact attitude. But beyond the formal, stylistic — to which we will return — the exploration of the stereotype is also, in Valerio's hands, its explosion, its coming apart and reconstituting in a different key, wearing a different hat, sketching a picture that can be at once a corrective and a stimulus to further adventures. One of the ways in which this is achieved is through a narrative which intersects the lives of several of these mythical Italians.

Let's take just one example. The story titled "Frank Sinatra" begins this way: "I come to Frank Sinatra midway through my life when I'm happy with my woman, when I've learned to dance the tango and when I discover that Frank Sinatra lost his mother in a plane crash, depriving him of the opportunity to kiss her forehead one last time, run his fingers through her hair. Italian boys are not accustomed to their mothers flying" (15). The narration moves on to talk about Sinatra's Hoboken childhood, then the personality of Natalie Sinatra and a microhistory of organized crime, then the narrator tells a story to a priest about his troubled relationship with an Argentinian woman, then shifts without warning to a visualization of Sinatra's youth and the importance of words, how they must be felt and understood. We read that the attention Sinatra pays to lyrics is in harmony with Enrico Caruso's attitude toward them (17). Then the narration shifts to a global view of Sinatra's career, in a way praising him for having survived a "million leeches," and for not having followed in his father's footsteps. It was his mother, the narrator informs us, who bought blue eyes the first p.a. system, mike and loudspeaker. The fact that she died on her way to seeing him sing suggests that the mythical singer carried emotional scars like any other of our fellow humans. The narrator sympathizes with the subject. Then there's a digression on names, on naming sons like fathers and children like the saint on the calendar that day they are born. "A name day is a day of truth. Just as on their daughter's wedding days all Dons grant any wish whatsoever, on their name day they are obliged to tell the truth"

(19). But the next sentence leaps onto a different plane. "The truth is that St. Anthony was not born in Padua, he performed his miracles there. He was born in Portugal"! And then, seemingly out of the blue: "The truth: is it possible for one man, even an Italian one, to romance the likes of the following women...?" and then a list of fifteen famous women Sinatra loved, from Lana Turner to Mia Farrow. And then the narrator returns suddenly to his own life: "A name day is also a festive one, but the truth is I've been alone all day with northerly gales blowing pollen in through my window. Dark clouds are rolling over." The next two paragraphs contain a tight dialogue, then we're back to names and naming, the rarified social and personal life of Sinatra, anecdotes retold through the narrator's father, who in turn brings him to speak again of Caruso and of how once he got arrested, something having to do with professionally unacceptable situations concerning his not showing up at concerts (perhaps to launch a singer to a captive audience), then the possible origins of the singer's association with the underworld, memories of special encounters with in/famous types, all this narrated with a flair for spontaneity, quick strokes that allow the characters to flesh out on the page quickly, in their humanity, pride fear twitches and taboos included:

> "Tell me, how's your uncle, Joey Gaff," Lucky Luciano asked me in the car.
> "He passed on."
> "What a guy, Joey Gaff: flashy dresser, great driver. He was the best driver I ever had. In the old days we were tough, it's true, but, you know, we loved to dance. Joey, me, George Raft, we'd dress to the teeth and go uptown and dance. George, he was the best of us."
> "Where did he learn the tango, do you know?"
> "The tango was the rage. It was a new import from France. Valentino had danced it in *The Four Horsemen*." (32)

"The Reappropriation of an 'American' Idol"

Thus *Valentino* is part story, part history, part anecdote, part personal musing, part cultural geography. The naturalness with which Valerio shifts point of view, blends the sacred and the profane, the official and the officious, hard facts with volatile beliefs is remarkable and highly distinctive. His is not a narration of the unconscious, a stream of consciousness magma, but rather a conscious if bemused juxtaposition of mythography and desire, set in a continuity whose logic of framing is more attuned to casual, every-day, incidental exchanges between people. The syntax and the images are drawn from what we recognize as "normal" situations, or likely "conversations," such as two friends meeting at a bar who while away an hour by comparing Cuomo to Iacocca, Mario Lanza to Caruso, or how the Mona Lisa one night visited them in their beds. Fantasies of history, the imaginary of a cultural identity, the musical chords of our background. As suggested by the list of sources on the last page, one might be inclined to calling these stories free hand sketches of Italian Americana, an as yet unseen or unheard mosaic which is freed from plot and morality, and which adds a seductive voice to the complex Italian American human comedy. There is a need to re-trace back, or be aware of carrying on a heritage, and the spiritual life of those who passed away. The creation of tradition, Gadamer would say, requires a common-place valued for its capacity to link us across the brief bodily lifespan. Our sense of continuity with the great deeds and values of our past are represented, for example, by the statues and annual celebrations we devote to particular individuals, such as da Vinci, Columbus, Garibaldi, and so on.

But the allegories here are also to be constructed by the reader, by the interlocutor, by the included third of any worthwhile human exchange. The reader follows the path of this persistent exploration, exemplification, and symbolization of the limits of language and the existential angst at not being able to do anything about it.

We cannot do anything about changing the irreversibility of time precisely because we have not yet invented the language to express the reality of this paradox. What we can do is figure out ways to retrieve the traces and the symptoms of meanings that constitute our collective memory and which are not always reassuring. How can a narrative escape the probing eyes of the historian: they are, after all, both telling a story.

The issue of the relationship between reality/fiction reemerges, but it is no longer useful. History of the main character cannot but land, at some point, on the reasons for their being there, in America. The group is not homogeneous, the travellers have travelled different routes, the destinies were not necessarily meant to be common.

Chapter Six

Naming Identity in the Poetry of Maria Mazziotti Gillan

> *Listen, America,*
> *this is my father, Arturo,*
> *and I am his daughter, Maria.*
> *Do not call me Marie.*

During the past two decades American poetry by Italian American women has experienced a remarkable growth and established itself as a major complex field of inquiry for literary analysis. The keystone book that brought the field of Italian women writing into the limelight and practically set the agenda for years to come is, of course, Helen Barolini's *The Dream Book*.[1] In her Introduction, Barolini identifies and situates the main forces, and as a result the topics, which inform this literature: the question of silence, the ambivalent patriarchal order, the obsession with lost origins, surviving stereotyping while reconstituting a new cultural identity, and basically the issue of (re)discovering the woman author. The anthology was usefully subdivided into the following sections: memoirs, nonfiction, fiction, drama, and poetry.[2] Among the poetesses that were active in the eighties and who have since continued with even more engaging works, we can list Phyllis Capello, Diane Di Prima, Maria Mazziotti Gillan, Daniela Gioseffi, Kathryn

---
[1] See Helen Barolini, *The Dream Book*, whose "Introduction" (pp. 3-56) is a truly brilliant social, historical, and methodological essay.
[2] This model was followed by the two other milestone anthologies that have come out since then: *From the Margins*; and *The Voices We Carry*.

"Naming Identity in the Poetry of Maria Mazziotti Gillan"

Nocerino, Claudia Menza, Rachel Guido de Vries. Women poets[3] who have emerged in the nineties include: Gianna Patriarca, Rose Romano, Donna Masini, Adele La Barre, Vittoria Repetto, Maria Fama and Giovanna Del Negro.[4] To be sure, if one merely peeks at their production, the diversity and range of their diction and the topics explored makes it difficult to place them under the same aegies. One can easily argue that the poets just mentioned can also be anthologized under such established or improvised critical categories as, respectively, avant-gardist or of linguistic dissolution (Diane Di Prima), social protest (Daniela Gioseffi), ethnic lesbianism (Rose Romano and Vittoria Repetto), lyrical identity search (Gianna Patriarca), urban parodic metaphysics (Kathryn Nocerino), imagistic contemplation (Claudia Menza), or psycho-sexual loss/ search of self (Donna Masini). And, of course, if one were to develop a multiperspectival hermeneutic, many stylistic aspects of these poets criss-cross not only among themselves but, and perhaps more importantly, with the poetry of women poets that one would find grouped under other, broader sets of critical/archival paradigms, such as ethnic literature, post-avantgardism, psychological fragmentation of the Modernist ethos, and finally the demise and recomposition of subjectivity.[5] *Dulcis in fundo*, the perennial issue of identity. Of all shapes, forms and stripes.

---

3 The reader is reminded that I am concerned solely with poetesses, and that many other Italian American women writers, most of whom have chosen as their main artistic venue different genres, such as fiction or non-fiction, cannot because of space limitations be referred to here. This field would include writers like Diane Cavallo, Tina De Rosa, Mari Tomasi, Rita Ciresi, Dorothy Bryant, Ann Paolucci and Helen Barolini herself, among many others. See for instance the many younger women writers introduced by the journals *VIA Voices in Italian Americana* and *Italian Americana* since the late eighties.

4 Once again I must caution the reader that these "lists" are merely indicative of a burgeoning field of women writers of Italian American descent, and it does not absolutely intend to be exhaustive. A complete annotated bibliography of Italian women poets is still lacking. For fiction writers, including men and women, the situation is not so bleak; see Serafino Porcari, "Italian American Fiction: A Selected Bibliography, 1950-1993," in *Italian Americana*, 1995, and Fred Gardaphé, *The Italian-American Writer*.

5 The observations that follow have been inspired in part by similar inquiries in contiguous social and ideological spaces. See for instance Henry Louis Gates, Jr., *Loose Canons*; Gugel-

"Naming Identity in the Poetry of Maria Mazziotti Gillan"

A poet whose work seems to span several territories and not always in predictable ways is Maria Mazziotti Gillan.[6] Leaving aside the knotty and often ambiguous pursuit of how to locate and characterize identity politics in a general way, I would like to focus on this poet's specific poetic experience, isolating the themes and the stratagems deployed in the text, and attempt to sketch what appears to be a paradoxical poetic, one which takes off from the same terrain all of the women poets mentioned above cohabit, but which takes chances in constructing or at least subscribing to a vision that succeeds in wedding the old and the new, the traditional and the radical, the simple and the complex, a poetic which refuses to take sides because it seems to perceive the possibility of making contraries co-exist. And defiantly so.

In the poetry of Maria Mazziotti Gillan, the naming[7] is carried on not simply or exclusively as a defiant screaming for long overdue public, social, communal acceptance, tolerance of one's difference, or specific cultural subtexts. The naming is just as crucially dependant upon a phrastic construct, a verbal texture that makes it possible to refashion a sequence, (re)construct the possible meaning of an experience, give it a memory because a story, however short and brilliant, is always already a history of consciousness, an indelible account, a complex of thoughts and situations. In the poems the loci of memory make up a sort of series or suites on specific interlocutors, such as the daughter, the mother, the husband, interspersed more or less chronologically in the recent collection *Where I Come From*. These sequences therefore establish a cluster of

---

berger, Georg M., "Decolonizing the Canon;" Ahearn, Carol B., "The New Pluralism and Its Implications for Italian-American Literary Studies"; and Richard Rodriguez, "Mixed Blood. Columbus' Legacy: A World Made Mestizo."

6 The main text of Maria Mazziotti Gillan's I will be referring to from hereon is *Where I come from* (Toronto: Guernica, 1995), abbreviated 1995. Other texts referred to or implied are: *The Weather of Old Seasons* (Merrick (NY): Cross-Cultural Communications, 1993); and the anthology she co-edited with her daughter, Jennifer, *Unsettling America: An Anthology of Contemporary Multicultural Poetry*.

[7] See above Chapter 4, pp 146ff.

themes, and circumscribe a poetic journal, a phenomenology of feelings, of the feelings of a woman who ushers a new typology, a more complex picture of the Italian American woman, and the Italian American woman poet at that. We can take the cue from a line of "The Crow" (67-9), "We are driven women,/ and we'll never escape/ the voices we carry within us."[8]

The voices borne in the bosom of these women speak a different language from that of earlier generations. In Mazziotti Gillan's case, the voices that speak inside her cultural (un)conscious(ness) register a set of polarities in fluid dialectical relation as they attest to an emotional and existential development (the poems that deal with "accepting" reality, the "passing" of time, the "foreknowledge" of emotional storms to come). They also evidence a conflict to be resolved: the evolution of her feelings toward her mother, oscillating from resentment and distance to the recapture of her deeper self later on in life, as she becomes a (the) mother herself. Yet another poetic journey could be attempted by re-tracing the painful emergence of the author's social and cultural identity, and the corresponding sense of entitlement and respect. Let us briefly explore this last topic.

In the poem "Public School No. 18, Paterson, New Jersey," (12-14), the poet or narrator recalls in quickly sketched images what must have been a painful experience as a child:

> Miss Wilson's eyes, opaque
> as blue glass, fix on me:
> "We must speak English.
> We're in America now."
> I want to say, "I am American,"
> but the evidence is stacked against me.

---

[8] It is this last line, incidentally, that returns in the title of the next best collection of Italian women writers, Mary Jo Bona's *The Voices We Carry*, cit.

The following stanza relates how her mother "scrubbed" her scalp, how she was made to feel "dirty" and "ashamed." The third stanza returns upon the struggle with language, with being forced by external pressures to forget Italian and focus on "proper" English. Nevertheless, the sense of shame is carried on beyond language: "Without words, they tell me/to be ashamed./I am." The condition of the self is imposed upon by the gaze, the forbidding authoritarian Master panopticon. Being poems of reminiscence and confrontation/acceptance, the next stanza leaps ahead, only to recall another ready-made external label: "Years later, in a white/ Kansas City house,/the Psychology professor tells me/I remind him of the Mafia leader/on the cover of *Time* magazine." Clearly this person has had to struggle against all sorts of diminishing stereotyping, and for a long time. The next stanza is in fact constituted solely by two verses but delivering an eruption of the growing gnarled emotion: "My anger spits/venomous from my mouth" followed in the next two stanzas by a defiant declaration of one's ownness, no matter what, deploying a bullying, indeed threatening counterattack:

> I am proud of my mother,
> dressed all in black,
> proud of my father
> with his broken tongue,
> proud of the laughter
> and noise of our house.
>
>
> Remember me, Ladies,
> the silent one?
> I have found my voice
> and my rage will blow
> your house down.

"Naming Identity in the Poetry of Maria Mazziotti Gillan"

We have here a great many topics that will return in Mazziotti Gillan's later poems, and are present also in a number of other Italian American poets. The complexity of the necessity to show pride in one's family and customs (no matter how 'imperfect' or 'different') is of course a topos that extends to other ethnic and cultural groups as well. It is a first stand, a fundamental positioning. The family is what Mazziotti Gillan's poetry is mostly about, and the complex emotional dynamics among its members. From the standpoint of a core identity, the poetic I finds security, trust, and a sense of purpose in the parents, in the house, and in their irreplaceable specificity.[9]

But time doth pass and changes do occur, as the formerly cowered and shamed bright little girl is now a grown person. And this adult poet has earned her right to speak, demand respect, show her wounds and laurels: "Here I am/and I'm strong/and my skin is warm in the sun/and my dark hair shines" (56-57). Pressed so hard to become some vague emulation of a WASP, or the generic American, some culturally, very deeply ingrained "American" traits surface through the text: defiance, readiness to fight, capacity for fairness. At the same time, however, one gets the sense, in re-reading the poems in *Where I Come From*, that the discovery, acquisition or reclaiming of a cultural identity requires (or at least highlights) an analogous if not parallel search for and conquest of one's own I, the person's (or the speaking persona in the poem) sense of self, her subjectivity.

We can see both developments, that of the search for the poetic center, or ego, and that of the social-cultural identity associated with being somehow "Italian," if we were to regroup the collection. Poems like "Arturo" (50-51), "Growing up Italian" (54-57), "In Memory we are Walking" (58-59), "Columbus and the Road to

---

[9] Yet the "myth" of the "security" of the Italian American family has slowly been eroded, especially through the increased critical attention paid to the social history of actual case studies. See Barolini *The Dream Book*, 6-7 et infra. See also her recent collection, *Chiaroscuro: Essays of Identity*, especially 37-50.

Glory" (80-84) revolve around experiences or type of emotions we would call of ethnic identity and validation. A growing and ever more complex topos of recent intellectual and political discourse, an author's ethnicity sooner or later must be dealt with, exposed, talked about. Whatever this turns out to be, it should be defended, publicly circulated. It is a sacrosanct right of every citizen. Against this recognition, a certain degree of *ressentement* is perceivable, of course, and at times even a note of bitterness, yet there is also in the background an emotional predisposition to healing, to silent participation. Being made to feel a stranger, a foreigner, in one's own country is of course a deeply alienating experience: "I woke up cursing/all those who taught me/to hate my dark, foreign self" (56). It polarizes an inside (the home) / outside (school, work) dialectic, and evidences that the continuity is unsteady, fractured somewhere, or that someone thinks it is so. In any case the very acquisition of a consciousness requires also an inner split or capacity to distinguish between the concept of one's I and *how* that individual I defines itself against the members of one's family, parents foremost. Here the freshly regained sense of a positive social, cultural identity crosses over into psychological space. The life-world of subjectivity is inhabited by several nodal forces. In Mazziotti Gillan's poems the speaking persona develops her female subjectivity against a problematic relationship to the mother, who appears distant, introverted, predictable, and soon outgrown. We can clearly perceive how it is the daughter, one autonomous and rational woman never caught in the more traditional claustrophobic bond with her mother, who chooses in full awareness of the chasm to reconcile herself with her mother. And without any guilt, the speaking persona forges her own self, a different self, an independent ego. There is an Electra resolution of sorts going on. Indeed it is thematically pertinent and, more broadly, culturally significant, that in Mazziotti Gillan's poetry the Italian American woman deals explicitly, tenderly yet resolutely, with those proverbially unspeakable situations or feelings within the Italian American *domus*, as when a daughter has her first heartbreak — "The Shadow Rushing to Meet Us" (16-17) — or has to accept that her son will be moving out of the house — "Poem to John: Freshman Year; Drew University, 1983" (28-29) — and even a tender love note to her husband (37-38).

Another salient characteristic of this poetic voice is that this female speaking persona has a deep love for her father, which discloses an emotional aspect of Italian American poetics and writing that emerged only recently, as Mary Jo Bona's anthology clearly attests, and represents I think an interesting field of artistic expression. Not all Sicilian Americans, for instance, have been monsters to their wives and daughters.[10] In reviewing *The Voices We Carry*, Signorelli-Pappas wrote:

> I am struck by the pattern of strong, nurturing father-daughter relationship that emerges. This pattern seems to reverse the more usual tradition of Italian American daughters who have close, even claustrophobic, bonds with their mothers but reject the authoritarianism of their sterner, more domineering fathers.

In Maria Mazziotti Gillan's poetry, the father is a strong moral model and a loving person. The lines are simple as they recount with a few efficaciously cadenced everyday phrases:

> My father was grateful
> to get a job as a dyer's helper in a silk mill.
> And when he hurt his back lifting
> the heavy rolls of silk,
> he became a night watchman in a school
> and when he could no longer
> walk the rounds ten times a night,
> he got a job in a rubber factory,

---

[10] See the interesting journey *à rebours* through her mother's peers by Giovanna Del Negro, *Looking Through My Mother's Eyes*.

> gauging the pressure on steam boilers
> to make sure they didn't explode.
>
> He worked the night shift for nineteen years,
> the boilers so loud he lost 90%
> of the hearing in both ears.

After such an intensive, knuckle-breaking blue-collar curriculum, the account frames the social, political, and ethical dimension of the person:

> My father, who at eighty-six still balances
> my checkbook, worked for a man
> who screamed at him
> as though he were a fool,
> but by teaching himself the basic laws of the USA,
> he learned to negotiate the system
> in his broken English,
> spoke up for immigrants
> when they were afraid to speak,
> helped them sell property in Italy
> or send for their wives and children. (81)

The father appears to embody character traits which are positive and morally inspiring, whether they be Italian or American. Indeed it appears that, of the two parents, the father represents America and the mother Italy.

As we saw above, the relationship with the mother was marked by silence, or non-communication. The one with the father makes several references to speaking, to entering into a dialectic relationship with one's society. We could even say that in a way the American self (half?) gains access to speech (however "broken"), while the Italian self (half?) remains hidden in the silence of the shadows. This quasi-chiastic symbolic arrangement can be imagined or de-monstrated if we follow the two paths separately. To continue with where the speaking persona is now looking at her father, dressed "in his one good suit," we shift from the personal/familiar recalling to the social/cultural inscription of a dream, a faith, "loving America, believing it to be/the best and most beautiful country/in the world,/a place where his children/and the children of the others/could go to school, get good jobs" (81-82).

The poem then follows with the apparently necessary but by now predictable shortlist of contemptuous epithets aimed at Italian Americans for the past two centuries. I don't particularly see the need for, or understand the compulsion of, the writer, at this juncture in history, to have to rehash these misnomers in public again as if to cleanse oneself through some exorcism, or as if to throw them back "in the face" at the society that formerly employed them for vicious stereotyping. This act of linguistic counterpelting hides a vicious irony built into it: the degrading words get mentioned again: the very presence of the word will recall, *also*, those negative connotations the poet is clearly attempting to deconstruct.

To continue with the poem, the next stanza represents yet another shift in this father/social world/America interrelation, heightened by the concrete reference to the cultural icon of Columbus, and the tradition of its now contested or threatened (Quincentenary Celebrations of 1992) celebration:

> For those Italians, living
> in their tenements, surviving ten hours a day
> at menial jobs, Columbus Day was their day
> to shine, like my father's tuba, polished
> for the occasion, my father, grinning
> and marching, practicing his patriotic speech. (82)

A new sequence can be opened here concerning Mazziotti Gillan's position on Christopher Columbus as an Italian American cultural icon of inestimable depth and importance. We can call it middle of the road tolerance, multicultural privilege, historically "corrected." It is not as belabored and tormented as Viscusi's take on the same issue.[11] Nevertheless, in this social space in which the subjects are called to interact, negotiate and celebrate, the speaking persona shifts frame and re-calls her mother, who had entirely different ideas on what a good daughter ought to do: something along the lines of: shut up and don't make a fool out of yourself. Here the female subjectivity of the speaking persona crosses over to her father's territory, a needed leap to break off the unsatisfying relation, end a dependency:

> Let us pick up our flawed hero,
> march him through the streets of the city,
> the way we carried the statue
> of the Blessed Virgin at Festa.
> Let us forget our mother's orders,
> not to make trouble,
> not to call attention to ourselves,
> and in honor of my father and the men of the *Società*
> ....
> I say: No to being silent... (83-84)

The father figure is the sole focus of the poem "Arturo," a poem where the conflating of self/father/social identity (as an Italian American) attains another level of clarity:

> I told everyone
> your name was Arthur,
> tried to turn you
> into the imaginary father
> in the three-piece suit
> that I wanted instead of my own.
> I changed my name to Marie,

---

11 See Robert Viscusi, *An Oration upon the Most Recent Death of Christopher Columbus*. See next chapter for an analysis.

> hoping no one would notice
> my face with its dark Italian eyes. (50)

This particular daughter not only is not berated or abused by her father, but is also actually feeling guilty for having desired at some point he'd be someone else. The poignancy of this sense of self-loathing, created by racism against Italian Americans, needs no elaboration at this juncture, having been explored in other contexts.[12] The poetic persona is ready to re-collect, to disclose herself to, a renewed bond or a newfound bond of affection and inspiration: "Arturo, I send you this message/from my younger self, that fool/who needed to deny/the words" (50). As in the previous poem, here once again we are told of his humble and honest virtues: "At eighty, you still worship/Roosevelt and J.F.K.,/read the newspaper carefully,/know with a quick shrewdness/the details of revolutions and dictators," and his love of family: "For the children, you carry chocolates/wrapped in gold foil." It is high time for final re-cognition, sealing an identity and a relationship, as well as an historical and ideological vindication:

> I smile when I think of you.
> Listen, America,
> this is my father, Arturo,
> and I am his daughter, Maria.
> Do not call me Marie. (51)

If we turn our gaze now to the second hypothetical path sketched above, we notice that not only mother and daughter have little linguistic exchange, but that if we only go back two generations, we meet up with a wall of silence, the unspoken silent awe of troubled origins, the invisible yet deeply felt past. In fact, a key poem to resonate with this primeval silence, "My

---

12 See, for example, the chronological account by Jerre Mangione and Ben Morreale, *La Storia*; and *The Columbus People*, Tomasi, Lydio et al. eds.

Grandmother's Hands" (64-66), begins, emblematically enough, with the line: "I never saw them." As a result, the entire genealogy is marked by rupture and indefiniteness, even though it is entrusted to the filial link, to the traditional weavers of a common tongue, at least a homespeak of sorts. A woman's genealogy is constantly threatened by censure, troubling gaps, indifference and silence. Her grandmother is clearly from another world, a faraway somewhere:

> Once she sent a picture of herself,
> skinny as a hook, her backdrop
> a cobbled street and a house
> of stones.
> In a black dress and black stockings,
> she smiles over toothless gums,
> old years before she should have been,
> buttoned neck to shin in heavy black.
> Her eyes express an emotion
> it is difficult to read. (64)

How could it be read, this emotion, if it has never been spoken: the eyes alone, the idea by itself, do not suffice. The poem in a way reminds us of the limits of visual representation, of the paradoxes of photography. The description is obviously a re-projected construction, an imagined simple but cohesive social view, humble and yet noble. But notice also how the break in the threadbare narrative of history occurs violently, in mid-breath, suggesting a destinal event:

> I think of my mother's mother
> and her mother's mother, traced
> back from us on the thin thread of memory.
> In that little mountain village,
> the beds where the children
> were born and the old ones died

> were passed from one generation
> to the next, but when my mother married,
> she left her family behind. The ribbon
> between herself and the past
> ended with her,
> though she tried to pass it on. (64)

A memory grounded in nothing less than the archetypal bed where generations are conceived, born and die in continuity, irrespective of external configuration or at least unmarked for ethnicity, nationalness, specificity of provenance.[13] History breaks into this simple, silent cycle when the mother marries and migrates. Her leaving signals a dramatic repositioning of the subject, who attempts to keep alive the cyclic continuity through the practical administration of home life, as recounted in other poems of *Where I Come From*. But the ribbon is broken, despite her doomed attempts. Seeing and doing alone perhaps do not suffice: words are needed, a speaker speaking, someone who may listen, perhaps understand. The genealogical experience takes a different route, one fraught with consternation, frustration, the hand of inexorable change:

> And my own children cannot understand
> a word of the old language,
> the past of the village so far
> removed that they cannot find
> the connection between it
> and themselves, will not pass it on. (64-65)

---

13 Compare Barolini, *Chiaroscuro*: "My own conviction is that I am an American writer writing through my material for everyone, not just for Italian Americans ... Italian Americans are not writing only to be read by Italian Americans any more that African Americans write only for African Americans, or the West Indian Novel laureate Derek Walcott is writing only for West Indians Americans! We all write as Americans for everyone who will read us..." (69).

"Naming Identity in the Poetry of Maria Mazziotti Gillan"

The speaking subject takes stock of this situation by placing herself in the space in-between, with a view and a sense of the old silent faraway of her foremothers. At the same time, there is a marching toward a future family space which cannot even begin to understand, listen, absorb, or somehow touch that elusive origin. The tone is absorbing, melancholy, disquieting:

> They cannot possess it,
> not in the way we possessed it
> in the 17th Street kitchen,
> where the Italian stories and the words
> fell over us like confetti.

Consistently with a property of poetry to evoke huge philosophical issues in deceivingly simple phrases, the itinerary can be understood as an attempt at assigning experience a value, or giving one's past a name, a continuity, a symbolic coherence. Yet as rooted as it is in hard reality, the consequences seem inevitable, and the speaking persona squares off with her own role in all this, being as she is in-between two worlds, two incommunicable realities, the silent foreign past and the noisy common future:

> All the years of our growing
> were shaped by my mother,
> the old brown rocker,
> the comfort of her love
> and the arms that held us
> secure in that tenement kitchen,
> the old stories weaving connections
> between ourselves and the past,
> teaching us so much about love
> and the gift of self
> and I wonder: Did I fail
> my own children? Where
> is the past I gave to them
> like a gift? (65)

There is a dead end here, where the background drama of migration is consummated, where the origin, the original, the provenance, the recognizable din of history is ripped off its axle. And there is little else left to forge new recourses.

Now, the journey requires that we deal somehow with this wound, with this fading memory, with that unnarrated because unnarratable chapter of the Italian American poet's social and cultural unconscious. And much like her mother did with her, the most the poet can do is try to give her children something of that continuity, although at this juncture it does not — it cannot! — find expression in anything cultural, ethnic, national, socially or historically marked. The poet turns inward, breaks onto the tenderness and closeness of the familial, mother-to-child universe. Finally, the acceptance that the weaves and patterns of one's history are variously configured, tenuous perhaps, and permeable, but still a home of sorts, a deeper trans-historical, indestructible *domus*:

> The skein of the past
> stretches back from them to me to my mother,
> the old country, the old language lost,
> but in this new world, saved and cherished:
> the tablecloth my grandmother made,
> the dresser scarves she crocheted,
> and the love she taught us to weave,
> a thread of woven silk
> to lead us home. (67)

The identity of the self and the naming of the home coincide. It is a poetic that explores precise dynamics in the social/emotional characteristics of Italian Americans, and women of Italian descent in particular. A poetic that reveals new facets of Italian American writing, hints at possible cultural rhetorics, attempts a manageable, dynamic, affirmative yet compassionate ethos. It also illuminates us on analogous cultural situations among other hyphenated literatures, or "minor" literatures in Deleuze and Guattari's sense of the term.[14] Not to make the poetic we explored universal and applicable to other fields, but to suggest that it is translatable. It can be moved. It moves.

    Names can be translated, but can the essence remain the same?

---

14 See for example Anzaldúa's article in the anthology edited by Fernández, *In Other Words,* listed in the bibliography.

Chapter Seven

The Historical Poetics of Robert Viscusi

1. Poetry

Robert Viscusi's *Oration Upon the Most Recent Death of Christopher Columbus* was written or better crystallized in the heat of the contested 1992 Columbus Quincentenary celebrations. This lyrical-narrative text is a major addition to the growing body of Italian American literary culture. There is no doubt in this reader's mind that Viscusi's *Oration* will stand out as a rich, problematic, indeed troubling and yet unavoidable critical ganglion in the current literary history network. In Fred Gardaphé's estimation: "'An Oration' could be read as an Italian/American 'Howl,' that monumental epic of Allen Ginsberg which spoke for a whole generation." This is a perceptive starting point: Viscusi is speaking for, as well as to, this our generation, his being a poem about America, primarily. Yet America is a complex geohistorical construction, its political and aesthetic discourses evolving at asynchronous rhythms and with unpredictable multidirectional speeds. Ginsberg's re-writing of Whitman aimed at rocking post-WWII, post-Korean War America, which was optimistic and arrogant, totally convinced that the lofty values of its mostly petite bourgeoisie were a divine right. The Beat generation did much to shake the country from its blatant contradictions and narcissistic denial, especially as we edged into the Sixties. "Howl" and "The Fall of America" as well as Ferlinghetti's "A Coney Island of the Mind" are rare examples of combined linguistic experimentation and ideological, political incisiveness only thinly veiled as aesthetic constructs. Their invective sent ripples across a broad cultural range within the alienating geography of McCarthyism and big business driven pseudo-consumeristic endorsements, the *topica major* of poetic exploration focusing on political opportunism and corruption, homosexuality, alienation, rebellion by non-participation, the problematization of imagism and the revaluation of minor and foreign music. Today, with the decline of the greedy-yuppy Reagan cycle, the dissolution of Cold War politics, and an alleged ideological bankruptcy, we have an entirely different vocabulary to contend with. The *Oration* comes at a time when confusion about what multiculturalism means is at an all time high, set against a diffused and uncanny self-awareness of origins and belonging, a broad and world wide explosion of nationalisms, ethnic solidarity and/or cleansing, and a hotly debated reframing of the meaning of colonialism, national mythologies, and social stratification. So it came as no surprise that among the idealized if not idolatered icons of social consciousness to be contested there would be Christopher Columbus: history, it is held, must be rewritten from the point of view of the excluded and the silenced, the uprooted, the "victims" of someone else's past "victories" and glories. The semantics of standard, textbook keywords of Modernity is deconstructed to underscore the negativity of social and historical processes: discovery becomes intrusion, achievements signal the belief of superiority vis-à-vis some other group, commerce means exploitation, spreading a religion is an act of ideological imposition, and progress very often entails subjugating and/or erasing other cultural practices and traditions. In short, civilization itself reeks with violence, prejudice, conformity to an external (and typically Western-European) organization of society and cultural practices. The need and search for difference against the centripetal, alienating pull of transcendental values based on Identity has degenerated into a myriad of cases and positions each voicing its right to be heard and, more than that, the right to accuse someone else of having violated, at some such point in history, their personal rights or cultural heritage. Yet wanting to be different *and* integrated into the mainstream at all costs exacts a toll, as the perversion of political correctness demonstrates. For, in the meantime, the academic orthodoxy, the silent majority, and official government policy, continue to vociferate, legislate, and implement their "ideology" of distracting, disinforming, and *divide et impera*. Up to ten or fifteen years ago, marginalized constituents clamored their right to a stake in Main Street, to be included in the Canon. Today, the question of being marginal is relevant to some groups, at least in terms of social and political empowerment, but critically and philosophically it is fast becoming a jaded issue. For those enmeshed in the self-annulling network of middle America, marginality is now actually something to be yearned for, it becomes an ontological necessity, proof of a visual angle, limited but not abstract topology, there being no credible Center or Grand Value any longer. In fact, when it comes to reinterpreting the value of certain symbols, or emblems, or metaphors, or images, the stakes are high, complex, disorienting, and risky.

Columbus is one such iconic, multilayered figura.

Columbus is central to the very history and myth of America, and he is *giocoforza* a major point of reference in the cultural unconscious of the Italian Americans, even the earlier unassimilated generations. Yet though in the history of America, Italian Americans have played a relevant if minor role, some of their cultural heroes did in fact represent, simultaneously, Italy *and* America, and with that their necessarily multifaceted reciprocal relationship. As these fields or domains resurface in Viscusi's text, the poetic persona recalls them against the fibers of a disturbing historical tapestry, one which is still pointing the finger at the upper classes for their cynicism and greed, and is also downsizing the excesses and the hypocrisy of America the great this and that. A political poem, in short:

> the fact is columbus day will go the way of the dinosaur
> along with everything else
> meanwhile what about garibaldi
> who was fighting for the poor of italy
> but after the revolution
> lived to see the rich steal italy
> and starve the poor
> selling them to labor gangs in suez
> shipping them to new york to dig subways
> in return for cheap american grain
> they brought back in the empty ships
> the italians went to america in steerage (stanza 4)

Here we have a very concise history of Italian Americans origins. And as offended, insulted, resentful as a poet and critic who hails from these beginnings can get. But no less compelling and, above all, true, as a look at a good history book will confirm. Tragic, cynical history. The allegory of the text is not contained in a parade of traditional, folksy, discounted images, but in its prying and then subverting of a host of self-serving and marketable platitudes that our confused modern day American cherishes. For example:

> the americans loved columbus in those days
> he was the *right* kind of italian
> not like those dirty dagoes...

After a rehashing of all known violent and denigrating stereotypes leveled at these people, the poetic persona continues with its social-political reassessment:

> the americans preferred columbus
> our man who wore a telescope in his pants
> who bought america from the indians
> and gave it to the bankers

And for which the official culture could not but reward him with glory everlasting:

> they named sixty or seventy cities and towns columbus
> columbia a university a country
> they called a world's fair
> columbian meaning *forward-looking*
> *inventive daring not afraid of fools and bigots* (stanza 5)

The conundrum disclosed at this juncture is that making the myth so much greater than the man entails creating a symbol-making machinery which cannot always be controlled, as in fact it strives above all to reproduce itself, like a generator, like capital, making a mockery of national ideologies and moralizing aesthetics. In stanza 6, we are reminded of how Columbus found a congenial atmosphere in Puritan households, "passing" in contorted discursive formations from one Mediterranean and Catholic mold into a Northern European and Protestant one. In fact, Columbus turned into a symbol of the progress of science and inquiry, although even before the final desecrating irony, the reader is fast becoming aware of how the Columbus myth contained a darker side:

> in those days they would sic columbus on the priests
> they would have a play in which the inquisition said to columbus
> *the earth is flat, it says so right here in this book of theology*
> and columbus would stand there all smug like galileo
> signifying the progress of science and the freedom of inquiry
> while the priests competed to see
> which of them could say the dumbest thing
> people loved these plays
> in a protestant country
> where they were afraid of priests
> because they hated them
> and found they hated priests
> because they were afraid of them
> this particular logical slave-bracelet
> often called itself the history of science.

"The Historical Poetics of Robert Viscusi"

This is a brutally accurate encapsulation of three centuries of American history, and how it strove to equate scientific progress, imperialism, and self-serving morality.

However, "the times they are a-changin'." The next stanza zooms in on the aftershocks of the crumbling of the American dream:

> nowadays of course this history of science includes
> a lot more chapters than it had a hundred years ago
> in those days they never heard of auschwitz
> they never heard of hiroshima
> they never thought someone could kill lake erie
> ....
> so of course it is no longer so wonderful
> to be the patron saint of science.

As befits the poetic form of old, the oration proceeds by deploying a demonstrative rhetoric, one which conflates several aspects of our social and aesthetic reality. The organization of semantic clusters typically begins by stating an issue, then retraces it in the labyrinths of both world and American history. After that, these semantic clusters deftly illuminate the paradoxes and bitter-sweet aspect of this tentacular, hypothetic nature, and finally return, over and over and with a heart neither deluded nor destroyed, to how in the mind and heart of an Italian American, Columbus will always be "ours." But because Viscusi employs a variety of metrical and stylistic devices from stanza to stanza, each and every time a conclusion is reached, the text avoids turning into a catalogue of complaints or sculpted statements, and manages thus to sustain the dynamism, the serious playfulness and semantic polyvalence that make it so enjoyable and interesting. For example, in stanza 3 the poetic persona responds to the dethroning of Columbus with the resonant participation of children's songs:

> we will learn to get along without columbus
> whom we used to love so well

> there's mcdonald's in columbus
> but colón has gone to hell
>
> there's an awful smell
> where he must dwell
> we will live without columbus
> whom we used to love so well

Yet at a later point in the poem, after having rearranged European and early American fantasies with Columbus, the poet draws for us some of the rituals from more recent memory, from the sixties and seventies:

> at first everyone thought it was the end of civilization
> the day columbus died
> forty thousand italians came to the funeral in black cars
> and afterwards ate heavily
> because it had been a long day
> but the new regime turned out to be good for tourism
> well-heeled germs coming to new york
> to see stockholders who wear beaded moccasins

He then links up with the personal dimension of the myth, and the procession of the national or binational mythical heroes it spawned:

> columbus by my reckoning
> died in seventy-one
> when my grandpa died
> the last i knew
> who believed mussolini
> a god among other gods
> caruso vespucci
> da vinci colombo
> and cut the cord
> that held the continent
> america drifted into the pacific
> where it has rested and stayed

This polarized link between the personal and the national, the private and the public, is picked up a few stanzas later:

> we have been living in a theoretical country
> a mapmaker's metaphor america
> this expression means
> a mere european riding in columbus's afterglow
> america has been a sort of outer space
> where people come from other places
> to try out dangerous ideas
> while working on the railroad
> according to my grandpa (stanza 17)

The *Oration* is singing the disintegration of America with bitter and melancholy tones, and though it does not conflate the myth of Columbus with that of America, it does expound how one has been the *analogon* at times, at others the *allegory*, of the other, how both have been shorn of their former grandeur and recklessness, and how Columbus Day is sinking in the popular estimation. Maybe soon America becomes a ghost of its more demonic self: "america will not die so quickly as Columbus," essentially because "people sort of got used to america"! But these are no longer times for tragic remedies, and no amount of irony will sweep the truth under the rug, as the poet asks, "who will weep for america/when america passes away" if there is no one, no saint or hero or natural wonder creature to do so: "will the duck or the moose or the bison/where the deer and the antelope play," reattach memory to the endless and endlessly challenging vastness of its land, drawing culture into its natural spring folds? At this point, the poet brings his Viconian hermeneutic one step further still, and pictures a futuristic situation where America is only an archeological subject, a topic fit for a new edition of an ancient mythology. In the poetic logic of the *Oration*, this nihilistic though probable slide that our social reality has taken reveals itself as the appropriate, present-day context within which to reconsider who or what the Italian Americans are:

> will the italians go back to italy
> some have left already for other destinies
> eternal nomads who live in the wastes of australia
> or teaching chemistry in china
> many will stay however
> more confortable as indians
> than ever they were as theoretical objects   (stanza 21)

Perhaps, once again, being marginal, as all immigrants have been and as their ethnically marked descendants are, is not so bad when compared to being a fully integrated and functional "theoretical object," an allusion I believe to the Risorgimento dictum of having to forge the Italians once national sovereignty had been attained.

Note also that calling the Italians "eternal nomads" is not inconsistent with the poet saying of them, earlier in stanza 8, "italians are a family people/not as in some political speech/but as in the caves of desolate matese/as on the frosty mountains of gran sasso/family people since the days of visigoths." Because what is highlighted here is the difference between the ethical values and social patterns of a people as it more or less remains put in one geographical site over generations, and the necessarily mercantile, experimental, stoic and frugal dimension of the lives of those who must take the voyage or journey away from one's roots. On the other hand, Italian nomads are not entirely new to what is dangerous, foreign, or strange because their own very history is laced with the language, weapons, and rituals of an endless catalogue of invasions and subjugations:

> family people since the days of visigoths
> and the roman legionaries
> families protecting their own
> from the soldiers and the police

> even their so-called criminals
> even their real criminals
> because who were the soldiers
> they were worse than criminals
> they were <u>foreigners</u>
> they were foreign soldiers
> whom no one was watching
> they came where they came
> and they took what they liked

In other words, there is a way of reading this brilliant mini-epic as a philosophical poem. As their long and complex history tells, Italians seem to have occupied all possible slots on any political or social hierarchy, their cultural unconscious appears to have a sense — or the encrypted memory – of what it means to be on different sides of the fence at different times. This may underlie both the resilient character traits of the Sicilians as well as the tragicomic masks of the Neapolitans, and it may underlie as well the socially constructed demeanors of merchants and farmers, aristocrats and their servants. This may sound Hegelian, but it is not a spiraling progressive dialectic of history I am extracting from the *Oration*. Rather, the capacity, in the face of adverse destiny, to accept and embody a belief in change, take existence as constant becoming, full of risks and fears but also potentially more rewarding, a particular choice of itinerary, a will to dis/cover, to ex/perience, an aesthetic rooted on sensing, on being-there. That sets the stage for a possible ontology, which can be expressed in Heideggerese as "being-in-the-world-*with*-others." This means accepting movement, change, risk, a constantly shifting landscape. Stanza 24 in particular makes epochal predictions on what will happen against some unsettling aspects of this becoming. America is going to wither, decay and vanish, becoming the mythical memory of itself. But here myth and history conflate, as is wont to happen in prophetic or allegorical texts. The *corsi* and *ricorsi* of scripted memory, from Genesis through Babel all the way to technologyas-world view, reiterates emblematically some basic patterns in human social development. They are picked up again in Stanza 28, where with a more traditional and song-like rhythm the *recourse* is made, specifically, to the cultural construct, or the hermeneutic figura, of Columbus, the traveler who knows death is a real possibility, the migrant who wonders and wanders at once, the exile whose words go unheard: "the sails of columbus were straining the mast/till the wind simply tore them away/and the dead disappeared in the wake of the past/as night disappears in the day." This overarching philosophical take is further sounded in stanza 30, where echoes of *Finnegan's Wake* are entwined with Allen Ginsberg, Flann O'Brian and Nietzsche, scansion in classic English tetrameters and pentameters, even reviving an ABAB rhyme scheme. There is no doubt, as I mentioned earlier, that this text will keep us busy for some time to come: "vast anxieties grow in the populace/a movement to revive columbian time" in the main because "it seems he can never stay dead/whenever he thinks he is slipping away/they come and they find him in bed" (stanza 30). Columbus, then, truly suffered another "recent death," but he is far from dead and gone: Columbus is also the museum of iconographic, pictographic, allegorized figures, the philology of its textual representations, over a period of time, through many social groups, and in terms of effective symbolic power. Perhaps as Italian American critics we should explore in greater detail the motivations behind the desire for wanting to kill Columbus yet again, five centuries later, especially in North America.

2. FICTION

Judging by the quantity and quality of reviews it received, a second reprint a year after its publication, and the innumerable readings its author gave over the past three years in New York and elsewhere, Robert Viscusi's *Astoria* has become a text that Italian American literature has to reckon with. Right off, the novel adds formidable ammunition to the battery of responses fired against Gay Talese's provocative yet timely and fruitful article: "Where are the Italian American Novelists?" The mere implication that there might not be any such thing, requires that we consider whether it is indeed true, and if so why. Immediately we go back over critical terrain. We read various hypotheses that may help us approach the text of *Astoria*, "get an idea" or "feel" for the history and context before we try to navigate it.

Scholars have argued that, on the basis of sociological and historical reconstructions of Italian American literature, it typically takes three generations for a writer of immigrant origins to "emerge" and finally initiate the creative/political labor of construing a past, a tradition, a language, and ultimately recognition by the Establishment or the avatars of the National Literature or a Mainstream (whatever these may mean at any point in time). Moreover, Richard Gambino, Gay Talese, and Fred Gardaphé, among others, have given personal accounts of the complex processes of assimilation, self-negation, invisibility, which "ethnic" writers go through before they can gain access to the language of the tribe, or the Canon. Or the Department of English! Of course, a cogent argument can be made that "ethnicity" in literature is not necessarily bad, containing elements that transcend regionalisms and ideological constructions of what is the "right" cultural identity and what is not (D'Alfonso 1996). It will always remain, in the background, precisely because it is literature, a question of language:

> Any new language entails, if I may put it so, its set of burdens on the minority writer. Obviously this weight is rarely felt in a conscious manner; it is present, nonetheless, and no writer can ever exempt of carrying that weight. Every word an ethnic writer positions on a piece of paper is therefore laden with ideology, whether he or she likes it or not. Art for art's sake is as poor an

excuse as is the one which propagates the superiority of one culture over another.[1]

As we shall see, this argument is also central to *Astoria*'s cultural unconscious, its sub-text, or subtle allegorizing.

Moreover, it is now widely accepted that a contemporary critical approach to Italian American texts or "topics" can reveal how these implicitly or explicitly "Italian American Writers" can disclose imaginary *and* critical loci from which to re-view our very traditions, relying on the "positioning" at the margin to exercise a cultural/political critique *through* a novel. Some exemplary readings by Boelhower, Cavaioli, Tamburri, and Gardaphé, among others, attest to the rich critical and semiological terrains that "ethnic" writers can pinpoint and depict. Elsewhere, I have argued that "being at the margin," on a "borderline" situation, may be a fruitful locus from which to scan and analyze our shiftless contemporary society (Carravetta 1991 and 1995). Moreover, in what we might call the "high circles" of critical and philosophical reflection, of a "Continental" flavor, many writings by Jacques Derrida, Gilles Deleuze, Franco Rella, Giorgio Agamben, and Julia Kristeva deal precisely with the ontological status of being/living "in-between," or of "belonging-to-no-one," and with the perplexities ushered by having to construct such belonging *through* literature. And this even before we reach the very issue of what is or might be an ethnically or nationality marked literature.

Nevertheless, a sort of underlying actual social dynamics has been identified. The Italian American writers, in short, could not come out and say they were in any manner or shape "Italian." From a historiographical point of view, this cultural struggle has required peculiar semiotic arrangements. Earlier attempts at identifying, describing, and situating such a literature include important efforts by Flaminio Di Biagi, Ahearn, Tomasi, Viscusi (1981 and

---

[1] Antonio D'Alfonso, *In Italics*, 59.

1994), and the recent D'Alfonso. Theoretically succinct and fruitful approaches sensitive to the very semiotics of writing have been submitted by William Boelhower (1982) and Anthony Tamburri (1991). Fred Gardaphé's recent *Italian Signs, American Streets* explores the circuitous ways in which some specific authors "dealt-with" the issue of becoming, over many decades, socially acceptable literature professionals, no longer ignored owing to their "Italianness," and whose books actually suggest that, above and beyond their highly personal styles, novelists of Italian extraction collectively exhibit a cultural identity in continuous metamorphosis. Framed against the Viconian notion of social history, with the multistage dialectic of *corso* and *ricorso*, the phases which an emergent literature must go through entail an Early Mythic Mode (consisting of autobiographies and autobiographical fictions), a Middle Mythic Mode (represented by the creation of grand identity qualities, Heroes and Godfathers), and a last (and to us the contemporary) stage Gardaphé calls "Later Mythic Mode: Reinventing Ethnicity." As we shall see in the following pages, there are several elements in *Astoria*, which satisfy all three levels, suggesting thus a diachronic, if polycentric, textuality, or narrative line with multiple meanings. In fact, anyone familiar with the theoretical approaches of the abovementioned critics will soon discover, in reading *Astoria*, that the novel fulfills a diversified palette of aesthetic expectations and political and historiographical reinterpretations. In Gardaphé's insightful hermeneutic model, for instance, Viscusi's text activates and plays out themes and styles from all three epochal stages. But to proceed to the actual reading, we can assert that, in general, there exists a significant presence, in our cultural unconscious of the last fifty years, of novelists whom we have no problem calling "Italian American." This writing, this literary presence comes dressed in different costumes. Some Italian American novelists have in fact often chosen denial of their ethnic-cultural roots (Sorrentino, De Lillo), or were forced to become "invisible," "blending into the background," legitimized by the reigning Canon of English Departments (consider the careers of Jerre Mangione, John Ciardi, Mary Caponegro, and Frank Lentricchia). Novelists such as Carol Maso, instead, prefer to (re)construct mythical interactions between past and present, between different tribes, across the years. And there have been those who quasi-cynically exploited certain disturbing commercializable stereotypes (Martin Scorsese, Mario Puzo, and Talese himself), i.e., mafia stories.

Or silence.[2]

Robert Viscusi, on the other hand, dares to "break the silence," to borrow from the title of one of his seminal essays (1990), speaking a different dialect while addressing a radically alternative set of parameters of cultural production and signification, in a way inaugurating an open-ended cycle in the forging of a "minor" or "marginal" culture.

Astoria is a paradoxical and protean text. To call it a novel is just a necessary, albeit ever reductive, editorial convention. It is more than that. The interplay of its palimpsests will exact deployment of several and often conflicting critical grids, as it can be read to accommodate a variety of sound judgments, and reviewers have hailed it as the quintessential Italian American "saga" of the immigration memory, as Eugene Mirabelli once remarked, or the most advanced step in the use of literature to expand and redefine ethnic identity (cf. the American Book Award statement by the Before Columbus Foundation). More technically, and following the syllabus we intend to write, we can classify it as an essay (cf. the beginning and its references to present day critics and issues, such as Gianni Vattimo and articles in the weekly *L'Espresso*), an autobiography (cf. *Astoria* 134), a memoir (cf. Preface), a psy-

---

[2] The "Question of Silence" can easily turn into a major topos in the Italian American literary unconscious and artistic practice. See for example the penetrating analyses by Gambino, Ahearn, Viscusi (1990), D'Alfonso (1996): 77-83, and extending the issue to women studies, cited works by Bona and Barolini.

chohistory (148), a metanovel (133, 161), an epiphany (there are many Joycean moments), a *biographia literaria*, an Italian American *mythologie*, a revisionist historical fiction (akin to some feminist writings), a metafictional post-colonial allegory (in the mode of some Caribbean or Central American authors), a postmodern declination of Being (in that it pushes the envelope of high modernist writing to register yet again the decline of Western logocentric metaphysics, and the European mind set of Modernity). Yet from metaphysics to microhistory, the book is everywhere alighting upon debris, residues, and leftovers.[3]

Astoria is an autobiographical novel insofar as the author clearly identifies the personal impulse behind the narrative itself, which happens to be nothing less than his mother's death, and the strings of painful associations it frees up both forward and backward. In fact we read in minutest details of the organization of reality created by the mother-son relation, and the accompanying expressions of affection, fear, and grief. It is a memoir, a tortured recounting of the irreparable loss, a testament of filial love. The inner drama seeks articulation, hunts for a sense, demands to be told. Once existence, memory, love, and sorrow enter language, they inscribe a story. The author becomes narrator, and as narrating voice can finally let go, uttering the portentous question: Who was my mother? and therefore: Who were my forebears? Who, what, am I as a result of being the descendant of these and only these special people? Can an understanding of their languages, and gestures, and beliefs as embodied in their rituals and idioms and stereotypes, yield a different picture of their origins, a more intricate palimpsest, an appeasing sense of one's belonging? Could it also disclose an alternative History?

---

3 The characterization of the post-modern age as being an age of residues, reduplications, left-overs and finally excretions, has been discussed widely in the literature on what was (or still is) postmodernism, especially in the eighties. See Carravetta 1991 and now 2009.

Astoria is also the account of an intellectual epiphany experienced while sojourning in Paris, visiting the Louvre and Napoleon's tomb. From the beginning, the reader is introduced to a trilateral hermeneutic geography: Astoria/Queens — Paris — Italy. It appears that the main character can rearrange and can sound the connection between his Italian origins and his more immediate life in Queens only when physically away from both, in Paris, in fact, short circuiting the play of mirrors of a bi-lateral identity and escaping dichotomies of all sorts. This discloses newer horizons and prompts hitherto untried conceptual leaps. It allows, for example, for an intriguing gender doubling: mother is like Napoleon, tireless, swift, dedicated, and proud. But she is also an outsider, someone who has had to struggle in silence, buy or conquer everything, someone marked by an accent, constitutive proof of being from somewhere else, easily a parvenue. And the novel recalls that there are several Napoleons available, depending on who is writing the national allegory: *Astoria* mentions four explicitly.[4] It permits a clear contrast and reciprocal annulment of dichotomies such as rich/powerful/male (Napoleon) versus poor/powerless/female (the mother). It also permits the narrator to consider whether, if Renaissance and Enlightenment and finally Romantic absolute values are to be the guiding ethos of both Italians and Americans — as embodied in the French Revolution's *Liberté Fraternité Egalité* and in Napoleon's being its ultimate consummate consequence, then we are not capable of re-viewing this (hi)story profitably, or meaningfully:

> Nature does not reveal nations to themselves. Nations are made through language and through war. One does not touch a nation. One lives in it, as in a language, completely subject to its effects as to the laws and to the value of money." (50)

---

4 Cf. *Astoria*, 114-119. All subsequent citations are from this first Guernica edition and will be incorporated in parenthesis in the body of my text.

Observing with thirsty gaze and fine tuned critical tools, eventually assessing with incredulous gasp the overpowering riches of the Louvre, the narrator writes:

> You are caught here in the circles of l'Astoria, in the sense that it was invented by J.J. Astor: here you are inside the dungeon of reference and the referent built into an ocean of money and will and violence. (51)

Astoria, I might add at this juncture, is also a meta-novel, for the author inevitably turns to its coming into being, its realization as narrative text. In this sense, it can be read as a treatise on the philosophy of language. The question about the reference and the referent in the above quotation is picked up later when the narrator ponders somewhat bewildered what Europe ultimately had achieved through the experience of Napoleon, through the social political phenomenon, or event, called Napoleon. That is, through his having redrawn maps, rewritten legal codes, renamed streets, and rechristianing himself Emperor Holy and Eternal. And through his routing patriotic rhetoric further and further away from the material conditions of the *citoyens*. Something that Saussure would take another hundred years to discover: that, alas, *there is absolutely no necessary connection between words and things*. Acutely aware of this dilemma, Viscusi's narrator deploys many different "I's" depending on who (or what) the third person is, never letting go of a haunting but dynamic intersubjectivity, a multilayered personality acknowledging the necessity of the masks, of the figures of thought we have come to know as memory, history, or justice, but hardly consider the true protagonists of a work of fiction.

Specifically, *Astoria* foregrounds not only the narratological problem of translating or embodying the speaker *in* language, but also *what* language to create and *from* what stoop or pulpit or balcony one can utter anything at all. Ultimately, it is the problem of narrating what has not been told, the story of those who did *not* have a language, but whose lives made up and made possible the reality of the European mindset and battlefield.

As I have argued elsewhere (Carravetta 1995) and above, the emigrants are by definition an individual deprived not only of their land and traditions, but possessing no linguistic/literary memory in common with the nation, no "Alta Cultura," they dispose of no idiom to voice/write anything, beginning with existence itself. The emigrant is to be distinguished from the refugee, the expatriate, the exile, and the nomad, whose just as complex sense of identity and difference does however leverage a sense of history, a political tradition, access to a given society's predominant values (see Introduction). Viscusi's narrator engages and explores directly and indirectly all four levels. But this is no mere modernist dress rehearsal of the eternal or atemporal masks the contemporary subject is condemned to wear. There is a history; it must come to be written. Going against earlier fictional reconstructions of the glorious Italian past, this narrator is not so convinced after all that Italian American roots can claim aristocratic, larger-than-life precursors, such as Aeneas, Dante, Foscolo, Mazzini, or even the ennobled populist hero of national unification Giuseppe Garibaldi. For, as Jerome Krase aptly phrased it, "Paradoxically, for most Italian Americans 'Italian' culture is 'foreign'." Their folk origins are local and regional, not national, and for many the loss of their cultural baggage was a liberation" (Krase 1995). That cultural baggage in short would be the equivalent of what Gramsci called *"cultura negata* (denied culture)," of which there exist scores below the guarded ramparts of *both*, Italian and American (*capital*ized) Culture. But that's too reductive and at any rate an outdated fashion of framing the issue, relying on a romanticized, dichotomized interpretation of Antonio Gramsci.[5] Rather,

---

5 The tendency to construct cultural criticism employing rational methods of inquiry and explanatory procedures from the sciences or logic has been contested widely already from

we have here a more dynamic, contrapuntal, and metaphoric process.[6] The narrator in *Astoria* searches along shifting paths, above all keenly aware of being privileged in some specific way, as he realizes that his success results from several concomitant factors: his unquenchable thirst for knowledge since he was a child, his growing up in an environment that believed in and fostered social advancement, and crucial to all his family's efforts to keep him on that path. And that means the founding stable structure is home, more primeval than the culturally construed archetype or mythological hero. This Italian American is a protean figure, a multifaceted protagonist, degrounding false, though to the masses, reassuring myths of origins, while simultaneously confirming and denouncing the inexorable presence of authority that defines reality, and the "proper" interpretation of reality. For the protagonist's dwellings do exist in concreto, in Astoria and Sunnyside, Queens, and to this *domus* are anchored all other allegiances, appurtenances, transitory fatherlands or *patrie*. As the following quote makes clear, he has lived in many cities, although there's a feeling that he had not adopted and could not adopt any of them as "his":

> I cannot leave Long Island. I was born in a hospital in Brooklyn in the rain ... Once I lived in Ithaca ten months, Bronx a year,

---

the sixties and through the seventies. In this light, even Gramsci's dualistic, dichotomic juxtapositing of "high" versus "low" culture is limiting, as it cannot see an intricate network of cultural representations between the two poles. See for example the cited works by Radhakrishnan, Balibar, Pivato and some of the contributions to Stuart Hirschberg's anthology. Moreover, as John Hodge makes clear in his penetrating essay, "Equality: Beyond Dualism and Oppression," one of the profoundest moral dilemmas in the whole of Western history has been caused precisely by casting the argument on the basis of all-out exclusive pairs: one is either good or bad. The other is necessarily bad. Pre-judice, in short, is ingrained at the very core of intellection, cuts a space, and releases an energy or power, right from origin of Western philosophical discourse.

6 The link between the *due culture* (not to confuse with the "two cultures" paradigm in American intellectual life, which refers to the science versus humanities debacle), and the connexed political and ideological insights it brings to bear in cultural critique, has been explored by Viscusi in several of his critical essays over the years and would require separate treatment.

Manhattan a year and a half, weeks in London, weeks in Rome, weeks in Paris, where I am writing this swiftly because it is a narrative of exile. Sort of.

Though leaving the reader with a perplexing afterthought with that "sort of," what may be sought here is a definable or recognizable cultural identity which, however, is repeatedly found to be appropriated and manipulated by others, by superior, entitled, and authoritative — when not authoritarian — external forces. From this the pages dedicated to the Stendhal Syndrome, that uncanny experience of sublime otherness, terrifying familiarity, distorted *dejà vù*, that inexplicable tearful expression and gaze before a canonical Italian painting, without knowing why such an emotion is even registered. In *Astoria* this fuels the rhythms of some of the most beautiful pages on Paris, "a city of philosophers" with its myriad shapes and arrangements, the austere or proud or stoic yet ever complicitous architecture, its being "the throat of Europe" (75), its being the remorseless de-construction of its own structuring discourse, of its own facades ... Napoleon included.

Alternatively, this traveling through time, geography, and history both personal and national, yields no definable model or rational grammar. Its voices are nowhere to be heard, its narrative a self-defeating enterprise, as there seems to be none to speak it to: "My father's stepfather, whose ear I have been constructing all these years, not to catch it, but to hear it with it." (73) Perhaps it is only by indirection that these voices can be construed. And so we do find, in tightly woven pleated and preened passages, fast-paced descriptions of the "interni" of the narrator's humble immigrant roots. (105) However, unlike the novels of the earlier generations — which have tried the stylistic of brutal disturbing (or "magic" some say) realism, as in Di Donato's earlier work, genteel "aesthetic" representation, with John Fante, for example, and serialized, sociological storytelling (Gambino, Talese) — in *Astoria* there is no longer a pretense of either recapturing or objectively reconstructing this unheard and unsung dimension of social life. What we find is instead the painful awareness that silence is not just an interrupted break in an endlessly possible string of words, but a deeply buried ontological precondition for the very emergence of such a as yet unspoken and/or to date unnarratable work/world. Otherwise put, and consistent with some recent developments in ethnography and hermeneutics, the narrator in *Astoria* never presumes to attain the point of view of a detached positivist observer (of the human heart or the human condition), nor can he be exclusively a participant observer (a writing best suited to autobiographies and epistolaries). Here the narrating subject and the narrated object/event are irrevocably part and parcel of the unfolding of the personal/social/historical moment, forcing the reader to accept an objective line of reference and a subjective constructing and measuring of the same line of reference, at the same time. If *Astoria* can be read as an ethnic novel, and it certainly can, we ought to be careful not to fall into the dualistic epistemology of Werner Sollors, with the descent/consent dichotomy of an all too facile sociology inexorably reductive when applied to literary study. Descent is not merely numbers, genetics, or voting statistics: descent is also and perhaps principally trans-mission, genealogy, a magma rich in untried and unwritten historical epistemes. Descent means having inherited two national languages ever "at war" with each other though, if we should take a Foucauldian view, with striking similar backgrounds in grammar and exclusionary practices. Descent means going down, catabasis, Hades, the Inferno (270) of shades and shudders of who (and what) is no longer living yet is symbolically present, persistent, pervasive, painful. Descent also entails having ancestors, claiming gods or heroes which we saw exist not, but who cares? a local "padrone" or saint, or even a "carabiniere" or a mechanic, would do too, to be sure. Ancestors are a problem, often *the* problem.

Viscusi's novel is not a myth of creation, which would require a re-enactment of the original conditions for a given cultural meaning to ensue. Consistent with what we observed above, he is cavalier about the value or tenability of refurbishing Aeneas as a god-head for Italian American history. I infer that what's pressing at this juncture in time is, besides the necessary recounting of the why, where, and when of the Italian American diaspora, also the rethinking, reviewing, and rewriting of the same whys and how it turned out the way it did, with certain traits and not others. Thus, more modestly, but also more disturbingly, *Astoria* can be read as a sort of post-symbolist allegory of the fall of modern nations, Italy, France, the Americas. Against this background trestle of culturally determined mythemes and autobiography with history, the novel never loses sight of the more philosophical and formal issue of how to identify the languages and practices of an emerging subjectivity, one which we might say is condemned to invent and organize everything, from its lexicon to metaphoric connections to semantic valences without a viable or worthy precursor, or master trope. Thus the unraveling and conflating of diverse strands of meaning, the calling into question the self-assuredness of creations or of foundations of any sort:

> The truth, as it turns out, cannot be said to exist or not to exist, but only, but persistently, to work as a name for the space between two things that need to have a connection if you are not going to disappear into a hole in the air as you walk past the restaurant. (165)

The earliest moment in the phenomenon of human speech, the naming of objects, or subjects for that matter, the enabling practice of discourse as a primal pulse constituting the world in its meaningful immediacy, the inventing of the language, inventing oneself. Which may amount to the same thing. For the novelist, possibilities now abound, especially when rhetorical artifact is, indeed, a factual art, a willed construct, a personal semantics made general theory:

> La storia, their own passion for children; la storia, his own surprise at the saddenness of fame; la storia, his words, his reading of the ribs of the drive wheels in the Victorian machines; la storia, l'Astoria: the passion not only of constructing a memory in the form of a ritual — all of this in my retrospect as rich in gesture and pattern as a portrait of Napoleon by David — not only making this, but made by a prior, chronicle of separations. (60)

As Michael M. J. Fischer observed, "ethnicity is something reinvented and reinterpreted in each generation by each individual ... it is something dynamic, often unsuccessfully repressed or avoided."[7] And Stanley J. Tambiah has enriched the notion by pointing to the "processual" changing nature of ethnicity, as well as its being "porous" and "segmented," highly responsive to specific political-economic situations. On another plane, according to another distinguished ethnographer, James Clifford, it is no longer the case to even consider whether a narrator can be suitably protected against rhetorics: as long as one speaks/writes, the writing will be ethnographically informed, intersubjective, and allegorical at that.

The disquieting news for literary historians here is that having accepted this possibility as a precondition — "ethnographic texts are inescapably allegorical" — we may (re)discover that the same canonical texts yield unforeseen interpretations, in fact we are likely to find that the great majority "enact a redemptive Western allegory" (99).[8] No such analogue can be teased out of *Astoria*, for

---

7 Cited in Clifford and Marcus, 195.
8 If that is true, then there is plenty of revisioning to do. A recent article by Cavaioli on *Leaves of Grass* points out that Whitman's wholesome, free, absolute man, or I, or primal energy – up until recently championed against both the modernist's fragmentation and dissolution of the subject as well as the more recent overdetermined regional or marginal

it is a novel about roots aware before hand that there is no one privileged rootedness, or genealogy, or politically correct history — as for example was attempted by Jerre Mangione and Ben Monreale's *La Storia*. Rather, what the writer (and literary historian) of the postmodern age has to contend with is a shifty and hardly reassuring or redemptive interplay of transfigured facts and faces, ideas and images, powers lost and gained amidst the shadows and specters of national(istic) capitalistic European nations. In this novel's historic sweep, it is not the inexistent ancient mythology of setting sail toward unknown magical lands, nor the more recent amply chronicled humiliating disembarkations that occupy the main character's mind, but a little explored in-between spatiotemporal frame, that is, again by allegorical indirection, Paris, the French Revolution, Napoleon, the Risorgimento (cf. 71 & 240-43). In the novel's unflagging and often cruel self-examination, what is stitched together is "the archeology of removals and rearrangements" (36), a stratification of unreconcilable identities in which language once again takes center stage:

> Thus it is that Italian remains for me the language of the gods, the masters of l'Astoria, which is, as a town, the physical form of la storia, the shape in English recollection of an Italian reality. (46)

La Storia, in other words, needs to be heard by the prefects and judges of la storia's personalized and differentiated events, feelings, and life stories:

> each departure a rupture in the seamless silk of la storia, and each arrival a stitching of l'Astoria, the very condition, in me, or him, of what they ripped and tore in order to make my uninter-

---

narratives – does little to hide a grandly metaphysical unitary I, as Eurologocentric as the myth of progress and of the frontier that politics and capital needed to charge against.

rupted, sedgeless afternoon in the company of Brother Sun and Father Montezuma. (69)

Thus, if on the one hand the novel succeeds in avoiding the "petrifying poverty in the heroic glamor of naked origins," on the other it burns with the revelation, or discovery (often outright belief, evoked through allusion, sarcasm, with blistering invective tones) that the mythical French Revolution – the locus of Modern beginnings – is now a vacuous specter, fake symbol, a failure, a flaunted grand mythologeme:

> The only thing truly clear about it thus far is its success as a consumer of barriers, boundaries of nations, definitions of divine powers, centers and peripheries in schemes of influence and maps of commerce, borders and passes of every kind and, among these for historians of consequence, the supposedly impassable divide between the past and the future. (164-65)

This will no longer do. Time is also cyclical; it is perhaps mostly a temporalization of memories, as well as duration, aesthetic vision, existential intensity, and political anger. This we are learning from many other contemporary American writers, hyphenated or not, to be sure. *Astoria* is destined to rank among the best and rewarding works of fiction of our time, while installing itself as a milestone in the emerging literary history of Italian America.

CONCLUSIONS

FOR A TOPOLOGICAL CRITIQUE
(WITH REFERENCE TO ITALIAN AMERICAN CULTURE)

Topics has the function of making minds inventive,
as criticism has that of making them exact.

Vico, *New Science*, § 498

The comments that follow are predicated upon an idea of interpretation that can be called topological critique. Of course, I don't mean topological in the sense of the mathematical subdiscipline of topology, but, rather, in terms of the rehabilitation of a critique of the *topos*, the common-place embedded in a culture, the site of occurrence of a recurring exchange. In the tradition of Protagoras, Aristotle, Cicero, Quintilian, Vico, and Chaïm Perelman, these sites of interaction presuppose *ab initio* at least two (but typically more) interlocutors *and* a particular (whether real or imagined) location. Another thinker who inspired me on this path is Ernst Curtius, who studied cultures through specific literary and therefore broadly understood cultural *topoi*, and who is regarded as the initiator of modern *Toposforschung*. I have however reshaped that tradition by expanding it to include insights from authors such as Jean Starobinski and Edward Said, as well as two traditions, one informed by materialism as developed by Marx, Raymond Williams, and Fred Jameson, the other from existential phenomenology through my readings of and writing on such authors as Otto Pöggeler, Paul Ricoeur and Jean-Paul Sartre, strong of the belief that in interpreting a culture one must also be aware of one's own theory and method, and ultimately "for whom does one write?" The result is – I hope – a more contemporary version of a critique of "what people say" over and over within certain communities of speakers until some common denominator can be identified and described as a *topos*, an argument that, though over time degenerated and congealed into cliché, still represents the terrain from which to invent or sketch, by intervening, an outlook, or "a field of inquiry," before analysis can commence. Discourse exists as a relation within a set of agents (speakers, readers, specific contexts), and utterances contain in their very articulation a preferred destination or better yet a purpose (whether achieved or not is a matter of subsequent analysis or reflection).

As the reader learned *strada facendo*, my "Grundmotive" has been Identity, a formation that inevitably compelled awareness of its own articulation (thus requiring meta-critique, auto-critique) as well as, and as importantly, how it related to other constituent agents and "external" factors (thus begging the question of critique-*of,* critique-*for,* whom or what). It follows that critical consciousness or engagement exists as a dynamic tension between the interpreter's own singular take on the world, and the broader view of that same world as canonized or legitimated by a panoply of external forces, *topoi* precisely, whether social, aesthetic, institutional, and so on.

The provisional conclusions tell us that the critique of an ethnic group is no longer tenable or meaningful *if we pretend to conceive the group as a homogeneous whole.* This may seem commonsensical to the academic critic, but does not appear to be so for the intellectual at large, the news anchor, the politician, the neighborhood association, the student. However defined – and the notion of definition itself we have seen has changed considerably over the decades – an ethnic group's identity has experienced and continues to witness varied and often troubled social, political, and artistic developments, such that re-presenting it to a broader society in the name of its immortal uniqueness or exclusive history soon decays into exaggerated stereotype.

"For a Topological Critique"

Identity as the pinnacle of Modernity in both science and philosophy, is no longer a neatly-contoured value in a Postmodern social world. This is not to say that some Postmodern forms of critique have not already been announced *through* Modernism, in the arts as in the sciences: that's not at issue. But it is a fact that the structure and function of the concrete institutions of public discourse (universities included) still employ the same categories, identity foremost, which are departmental and disciplinary, taxonomic even, and which regiment the flow of goods, the action of subjects, the shape of ideas, the tenor of accepted critique. Moreover, fields that employed the notion, such as ethnic, race, and gender studies, have also shown to have such amorphous boundaries as to invite a reconsideration of their principles and objectives. Scholars and thinkers such as Werner Sollors, Richard Alba, Paul Gilroy, Jean Baudrillard, Jean-François Bayart, Immanuel Wallerstein, Jean-Luc Nancy, and Judith Butler, among others, have suggested in their different ways that, when we raise the banner of ethnic identity in a socio-political interaction, *we may be unwittingly cultivating forms of adversarial critiques which in the end perpetuate the structures they were intended to combat*. This is the reason why throughout this book I kept on harping on the necessity to *go beyond dichotomies or binary concepts*. We must constantly allow for at least a triangular relation: me, you, and the world (or language) that contains us both.

If identity legitimates existence, there is no substance with qualities implied, but, rather, as Nancy underscores, "an act of being that qualifies, in a singular manner," at best only *some* of the attributions of relations. We evince from this that identity is a *relational concept*, not a substantive one, destined to re-think itself each and every time the social forces around it change and demand it, and never in an entirely omni-comprehensive manner. At the same time, the act of being compels, by the very gesture of coming out or evidencing it is speaking–*to*, a questioning of the established regulatory or imposed forms of discourse, widely known to be levelling if not outwardly coercive. The critic must seek a dialectical opening, or a site of re-cognition, a space for a participatory interaction within this dynamics. In this vein a topological critique can look at some master tropes from the point of view of their inner evolution and dissolution, or their appearance and concretization in a society, and attempt to reframe the contours of a *contemporary* cultural politics.

To summarize what has been explored in these pages, there is no unitary transcendent identitarian trait to being American. Historically, "we the people" have invented for ourselves and paraded for decades a series of *topoi* -- call them ideologemes or discursive formations if that makes it easier, -- recognizable as, in historical succession, the American Adam, the American Aeneas, the Imperial Self, the Nativist Self, and in more recent times the Great Liberators and the Great Society. As citizens we have also been made participants, willy-nilly, of the claim that for decades we marked world history as being the "American Century" and, approaching the end of second millennium, the presumptuous ideology of imposing a New World Order to some seven billion plus people!

But which America is the "real one?" And is there just "one America"? As noted earlier, just compare a history of America written by Daniel Boorstin with one written by Howard Zinn. Some thirty years ago Benedict Anderson made the point: national identity is a rhetorical invention. Not that this makes it any the less real, quite the contrary: discourse that wins consensus (or submission, or limits on one's freedom) is where our focus should be, as it does not absolve us from confronting what these mega-ideologies perpetrate on the social world. A century earlier, in the hey-day of nationalism, Ernst Renan had made a similar point, implicitly calling for awareness and commitment: a nationality is a daily plebiscite.

The Italian American community, as any community that pins its social-cultural validation if not reason-for-being under a racial or ethnic or national moniker, should understand that whatever they call their identity is an ideology that imposes itself for a certain period of time and then is substituted by another, because each hegemonic discourse lasts just so long as it can muster the production and management of meanings. This applies to sub- or anti-hegemonic discourse as well, which congealed as a documentable *topoi* at specific junctures, were often ignored, then resurfaced. For instance, consider the plight of Italian Americans during World War I and II (those who enlisted and fought *and* those who were interned), the rediscovered filial provenance in the late-sixties/early-seventies ("I'm proud to be Italian" days), then the validating satisfaction accrued through Affirmative Action in the eighties, and finally entry into the literary canon in the nineties.

If, on my theory, and we can't repeat this enough times, we should also go beyond dichotomic, dualistic thinking — employing the neologism "Glocal" is of little help if pronounced and endorsed by mega-corporations — and stop playing the game of saying I am proud of my heritage but I am of course American, or, otherwise stated, I am an American with a difference, which precedes the hyphen (or the slash), because, at some point — say, when you pay your taxes or ask for a passport or are sent to war — you will have to deny the adjective; then Italian Americans should bear in mind that they are constitutively threatened to have to relinquish one part of their selves when certain contingencies arise. But this possibility does not automatically spell out the dissolution of the vaunted double-identity because, at the same time, they also should remember that they have the advantage of being *both*, inside and outside of America, or what America thinks of itself at any given point in time (i.e., during elections, financial crises, or when advocating educational reforms). And there is no contradiction in that: life is *not* logical, *pace* my scientistic colleagues. Rather, we have to contend with *rhetorical strategies*, or what Foucault termed discursive formations, that determine the course of social history. In this perspective, there have been and there are currently a variety of narratives on what would constitute an Italian American identity.

If there is no unitary national discourse that can critically if credibly reveal where the essence (treacherous word!) of this implied half of the identitarian trait resides, then to speak of Italianness is even more perplexing, and rather than citing Antonio Gramsci once again about the failed conjunction between nation and state, or nationhood and people (il popolo), I would suggest consulting an anthropological history of Italy even before a political one. Never really united and constantly traversed and inseminated by countless invaders and abused by all sorts of rulers and, often, and most poignantly, *by their own kind,* the substrate of Italy inscribes an infinite palimpsest of the most diverse cultural forms and linguistic habits. *To claim being Italian is to claim, paradoxically, the right not to absolute identity but rather to perennial differences or worse to pragmatic indifference vis-à-vis the big causes and the grand schemes.* It is conducive to a solipsistic mental anarchy. How many different conceptions of Italy do Italian Americans cultivate, propagandize, and demand respect for? Some know it as tourists, some in nostalgic terms, while others downright concoct themselves a long bygone paradise, a classical, classy, romanticized utopia. Among those who have studied it, there is no quarter either, for the idea and description of a "mother country" or "country of the ancestors" cannot be separated from their ideological and political world-view, as well as from the methods adopted to study the subject in the first place. Nevertheless, my entreat is that Italian Americans must make good on what has revealed itself to be a formidable critical, if privileged, perspectival locus, that is, that of being, to some degree, *both,* inside (symbolically, historically) *and* outside (geo-socially) Italy.

"For a Topological Critique"

One can therefore claim, having the cultural genes, or memes, of both countries, of both Master narratives, to be more complex and therefore critically "superior" to both the Italians and the Americans: for Italian Americans have the advantage of parallax, of constant critical triangulations when looking at issues such as migrations, education, political agendas, and above all the rhetoric of historical discourse. The above translates into the following critical task: take advantage of our *intellectual situatedness* in the mare magnum of both, American and Italian cultural milieus, as practically emarginated and often demonstrably invisible to whatever is the dominant notion of mainstream at a given locus where an exchange occurs. The reason is that to become mainstream (at first a goal of all minorities and hyphenated groups, as they strove to emerge from oblivion and suppression) means ultimately (at a later turn in time) to be leveled, homogenized, made to speak and act in predictable ways because the language to be employed was to be that of the masters, so to speak. In the sixties and the seventies of the past century many hitherto ignored or suppressed groups or constituencies discovered that they could claim to be *both*, staunch Americans *and at the same time* strong critics of its triumphalist and aggressive rhetoric. Thus we witnessed the rise of the "unmeltable ethnics" and a flowering of hyphenated identities that did, in the end, bring about a respectable multicultural sensitivity, political reforms, Supreme Court Decisions that loosened the taboos and the sclerosis that affected democracy in our republic.

But from the end of the Cold War onward, the forces of reaction began to rebuild momentum. Threatened with insurgent nativism and xenophobia, and in order to offer a counter-discourse, perhaps to be hyphenated is not a bad place to be if we rethink its sense and purpose. Scholars recently have proposed the notion of *living the border*, critically and pedagogically inhabiting the fault line, capitalizing on being able to see both sides of a culture or society at the same time, challenging the dominant platitudes, forcing rethinking on any one issue that wishes to be definitive and finite, therefore confining, limiting. These are invitations to critical thinking in a pluralistic society where no absolute solutions to any contested issue exist or can be given. Topological critique is border critique.

The notion of critique at/from the margin is bolstered if we accept a key theoretical premise: *we are all migrants*, as people are constantly on the move: as stated and discussed at the onset of this collection, migrations are not mere epiphenomena suitable for sociological tabulations or economic theses and useful only during political campaigns. *We are always on the move – socially, existentially, educationally.* In terms of class, and in view of the places we live in and communities we deal with, our perspective and our reading of the world and the societies within it, are constantly shifting and requiring recalibrations of all sorts. Some people do not notice, some people do not want to notice, but the world of cultures never stands still. It may be useful to think of island-worlds of culture, not unusually co-existing at the same time and place and often unbeknownst of one another.

Key critical condition to be considered in this topological critique is that of *métissage*, cross-breeding or miscegenation, inspired in part by studies on Mexico and the Indian subcontinent, and to which thinkers such as Serge Gruzinski, Walter Mignolo, Kwane Appiah, Homi Bhabha, Eduard Glissant, Carmen Bernand, Armando Gnisci and others have given a philosophical and political valence. Historically the offspring of invasion, colonization, and exploitation, and formerly tainted by shame -- on the arrogant assumption that there was such a transcendent value (or essence, or substance) as a pure or superior race that must protect and maintain its elective status, -- in post-colonial times the *métisse, el mestizo* has become instead a proud identitarian quality with which to resist or implicitly challenge the universalizing, and imperious Northern European white man's ideal with his science of numbers and taxonomy ready to box everyone in their place.

Along the same lines we find another critical *figura*, that of *hybridity*. In recent decades the hybrid – the person as well as the concept — has witnessed and finally acknowledged that the social actor has gone from an unwanted, or invisible, or instrumentalized subaltern to a self-affirming and defiant multidimensional individual, politically slippery and existentially complex.

Hybrid has several meanings: 1) Technically, it is "the offspring of two animals or plants of different races, breeds, varieties, species or genera." Think of mules or fuchsia flowers. 2) A re-semanticization of the word in specific semiotic environments give us the recently acquired meaning of "something – such as a power plant, vehicle, or electronic circuit – that has two different types of components performing the same function." 3) Figuratively, it means "a person whose background is a blend of two diverse cultures or traditions." 4) Metaphorically, it signifies "something heterogeneous in origin or composition."

Consider now point 3). In terms of descent, every region or province in Italy has been witness to countless invasions and occupations – Calabria alone can document over twenty distinct ethnic groups that have come, settled for a while, then either became absorbed or moved on! Thus culturally, despite diachronically circumscribed periods lasting anywhere from one to three centuries, Italians are a distillation of the most diverse backgrounds: people from Pakistan to Morocco, from Wales to Egypt, from the Normans (in turn from Scandinavia, the Vikings) and Schwabians (southern Germany) to the Carthagenians (ancient Tunisians, in turn from Lebanon, the Phoenicians), from the Tartars to various Slavs, from the Albanians to the Turks to the much revered Greeks, to mention the most easily recognizable, have traveled and dwelled on the peninsula and the islands bordering the Tyrrhenian Sea. And when on Italian soil, they came into contact – or conflict, or exchange – with autochthonous peoples, indeed tribes (the closest thing, by analogy, to American "Indian nations") called Brettii, Lucani, Ausoni, Samnites, Itali, Latini, Oscans, Etruscans, Liguri. When definitions and descriptions of a group or clan or "people" were more circumscribed, just within a day's ride on horseback there were at least ten distinct "peoples" around Rome, in the decades of its founding, if Livy is to be believed. And others further North, in the Padania and Sub-Alpine territories, which had already been settled by Celts, the Huns, and various strands of Goths. Each of these *ethnos* left an indelible mark in any one of the many semiotic fields a culture exhibits at any one point in time. In light of concrete historical facts, considering oneself Italian therefore is reduced to, a) diachronically, which ancestors one *chooses* to be their signal noble forebears and, b) synchronically, one's idea of what Italy is or, better, and more accurately, *wishes* it to be, there being countless counter-examples to prove any claim erroneous or biased. Perhaps the scathing remark made by Prince Metternich of Austria in the XIX century that "Italy is a geographical expression" has still a slight bitter ring of truth? For, ultimately, *to some degree, the way we are existentially all migrants, we are also, genetically, all hybrids*! In the Middle Ages, to refer to a composite allegorical creature they used the word *chimera*: thus the *monstrum* breathes fire (words), thinks it is a lion (power), is basically a sheep (produces nutriment), but sports a serpent's tail (is insidious). When critics say that exponents of a certain group claim, to stave off a levelling and manipulable identity, that we are hybrids, we should ask: how? What part? In what context? For to just state we are all hybrids is akin to saying: we are not a, because we are all $a + n$! This is too vague, bearing no analytical value, nor possessing any ideological or rhetorical incisiveness and specificity. The question should be: what parts of the *monstrum*, which aspects of the hybrid are foregrounded, politicized, allegorized?

A less quirky observation would be to relate the awareness of the stratified composition of Italianness to Vico's notion that "all nations have noble ancestry" and update it with the existential-political idea that *it is we, the actual time-and-place situated human actors, who decide who the noble ancestors are*. A "foreigner" or national of some other far-flung country who studies specific aspects of the Italian cultural heritage, or spends long periods of time in Italy, may legitimately claim an "Italianness" to his/her cultural identity, a point also argued by A. Tamburri. The reason may be attributable to the fact that, if the truth be told, one never identifies with *all* Italians, or *all* Americans for that matter, or *all* of the aspects of the chimera *at once*. Italian history is replete with exclusions, the forgotten, and the "worthless," just as it is chuck-full of great inventors, navigators, saints, artists and entrepreneurs when it comes time to boast and unfurl proudly the national colors, as on Columbus Day parades. *But the historical facts, the data so to speak, lead to the theoretical conclusion that "Italians" (as "nationals" from any country) are all, at bottom, hybrids, creoles, mestizos to some degree.* This is consistent with the notion that *humans are essentially migrants*, argued since the beginning of this book. As well, however, there are different types of migrants, of travelers, of foreigners, as illustrated in the Introduction. Mobility entails transformations, cross-pollination, continuous self-definition. The task of critique is to ask not only what kind of hybrid one is, but, and perhaps more importantly these days, which ones, and why, at some point in time and place, have claimed *not* to be hybrid, vaunting an invented purity or exclusivity, and to whose disadvantage.

And yet, and this is the object of a politically informed topology, multi-tasking, trans-national, post-identitarian hybrid social actors also have been coopted by new-millennium techno-capitalism. Just consider the evolution of advertising strategies over the past quarter of a century: be different, think outside of the box, follow no one, etc. When it comes to merchandising, somehow being different, being of mixed extraction is fine, interesting, in fact constitutive of a certain idea of America! Recall however that scholars have also shown how the techniques of persuasion deployed by the contemporary mega-machine of advertising and consensus-gathering has fine-tuned strategies first developed under authoritarian regimes, with Stalinism, Nazism and Fascism perfecting them to an art. Even the cognate concept of *creolization* is now employed as a marketing tool!

What I submit we should counter foist to this subliminal domestication is rather the idea of *syncretism*. This latter term is another critical *figura* which strengthens topological critique, and is in urgent need of attention and development. Aside from its Greek origins and Humanist reformulation (which implied subjective participation, requiring a *conscious act of judgment* in forging a new content), cultural anthropologists have already studied, identified and posited for analysis,

a) a conscious and an unconscious syncretism,

b) a permanent versus a transitional syncretism, and

c) a subjective versus an objective type.

In all cases we learn that we must re-adapt some idea of what a consciousness is, breaking the lock that neuroscientists have on it: humans have agency and choice. We choose to become whoever we are and we compose a world view from several elements. But we cannot escape the fate of being someone or something *relative to* someone/something else: relativism is not to be brushed aside, rather, as I argued in *The Elusive Hermes*, it must be confronted. Syncretism is one approach to deal with the problem. If we are constitutionally endowed with several possible identities, we must also recognize that society, our specific interlocutors, either prefer or impose one on us, to the exclusion of the others. This is palpable in all encounters. How much of this is psychological, and how much of it is political? And how do we tell the difference?

This reality-based paradigm applies as well to the Americans, whose founding myth was uttered and written by overzealous religious refugees ostracized by even more intolerant monarchies on both side of the Channel. It took a few centuries and much blood spilled to accept, at least before the law of the land, that a certain minoritariam or worse foreign "race" was also entitled to the same national rights and protection under the Law. As we saw in an earlier chapter, in the heyday of the great Amerindian genocide, Americans were simultaneously proud to accept the "wretched of the earth" from all over the globe. Anyone who just stops at seeing this as a "contradiction" in the American collective unconscious is not making a revealing statement. There seem to be at any one point a series or cluster of contending ideologies that strive to be the most representative of what "the nation" is or aspires to. It is well known that the America of Manifest Destiny did in the end succeed in creating a dominant cohesive identity even as two other forms of discourse emerged alongside it, in clear opposition to one another: One was the burgeoning nationalist/imperialist ideology, which grew beyond measure after the second World War; the other, a discourse of the "other," such as the one informing minorities or immigrants who either caved in to coopting assimilation or were ghettoized for maintaining some of form of local and/or limited cultural identity. It did work for some groups, slowly, painfully, but not when the "others" in the amalgam were visibly different (e.g., Africans, Asians, "brown" people). And today still, a look at the breakdown of the recent census reveals that the "true" American is a conceptual invention, a necessary trope, a changeable identifier whose effective "substance" or concrete impact is defined by a relatively small group of individuals (or, better, corporations, since 2010 legally identified as persons with First Amendment rights: cf. *Citizens United vs FEC* and *Speechnow.org vs FEC*), with access and control of the means of production and reproduction of the ideologemes, stereotypes, and media bites that make up public discourse and can now legally impact legislative outcomes. Thus the longest surviving republic in world history has been successful in its meandering parade of self-aggrandizing mythologies to create two hydra-like powerful narratives not always compatible with each other: one well known and ingrained at the micrological level, says: *e pluribus unum*; the other we could call: *peregrinus es non volo*: foreigners beware! A few more remarks are necessary to flesh out the argument.

The first mythology we have heard *ad nauseam*: rehashing the founding ideal of One [country, or people] from the Many, by the end of the XIX century it morphed into the fabled and problematic discourse of the melting pot, "the fires of God round His Crucible." Lofty (and perhaps, why exclude it? well-meaning) ideals notwithstanding, this topos became a banner for a growing conformist social politics: De-racination and forgetting the past were prerequisite to total assimilation into America — i.e., the future. But concurrent with this larger scheme there was a movement to re-launch a particular type of the ideal American, one which, to legitimate its origins, located the prototype in a white North-European Protestant, preferably of Anglo-Saxon stock. But not many looked up where the Anglo-Saxons came from: a marauding hodgepodge from the entrails of medieval North-East Europe who invaded the island of Albion when the Roman Empire collapsed, and were in turn followed by Danes and other Germanic tribes. In any case, as we saw above, a look at the 1911 Dillingham Commission volumes, will be revealing: The America of the post-Civil War era, of the Statue of Liberty era, in other words, is not the America of the World War One years. Or of the aftermath of World War Two. Where are the Brits gone? And the Aryans? It seems that through the last half a century provenance has ceded the spotlight to color, specifically to skin pigment. By the end of the second millennium, cries of "race genocide" were again heard! The *topos* of keeping strangers or those-unlike-me out of the land, and at best selecting these foreigners, like a Viconian recourse, re-inscribes itself back in public discourse. If one believes in education, one must believe we do learn from history.

Which brings us to another crucial point in this national allegory only sketched in an earlier chapter, and that is the thesis that even *before* the melting pot ideal there has always been at work *a process of selection and exclusion* of who might be admitted to the new experiment in democracy, veined as it was with utopian tendencies and biblical mirages (think of all the New Jerusalem utopias launched in the later XIX century, especially in the North-East) concurrent with very strong prejudices toward four-fifths of the world's population. In other words, it was never true that this country readily accepted anyone and everyone, Crevencour and Tocqueville notwithstanding. The claim is that above and beyond actual federal immigration law and other supporting local policies (and often as a result of them), the ruling elites in Washington and the Northeast (not without the strategic support of the Southern landowner elites) have consistently manifested, though most times in tacit ways, a penchant for favoring the arrival and incorporation of the well-bred, the blue-bloods, the mega-capitalists: for there was always an abundance of the "wretched" to do the menial tasks, the dirty jobs. The melting pot ideal — imposed as it was on the later immigrants until they themselves, or at least their children, spontaneously embraced it — turned out to be a useful ideologeme to introduce in public discourse, making it a "concern" in order to regiment locally the seeming unstoppable tides of foreigners arriving on these shores at the beginning of the twentieth-century, then after the Second World War, and now again at the beginning of the twenty-first.

When identity is no longer a case of $A = A$, and its negation is no longer $A = not\text{-}A$, then we might consider what happens when

"For a Topological Critique"

A = B, C, D,...*n*! Plainly stated, we are possessors and merchants of identities, in the plural, each assuming a temporally marked and socially circumscribed form in view of the given interlocutors, as remarked at the outset. Most recently, William McNeill, Clifford Geertz and Chäim Perelman have in different but tightly argued ways enlightened us on this process. Identity is constructed, negotiated time and again in public arenas (whether in the conference hall, on TV networks, at Board of Directors' meetings, etc.). It depends intrinsically on *the rhetoric of the occasion*, in view of a constantly restaged confrontation requiring flexibility, dialogue, new syntheses, reconfigured programmes. Along with this then should go the principle that a *relative* sense of *equality across ethnic, racial, and gender lines* is required solely before the law of the land. But that too is never absolute: that is why we have public debates, law courts, elections and amendments to the Constitution.

In conclusion, a topological critique focuses on strategies of persuasion, leverages other topoi, engages previously unused or underutilized techniques, in order to highlight the locus of a given exchange (a publication, a reading, a performance, a screening and so on) and to what degree it is informed by *power relations.* The same law for the ox and the lion is tyranny, William Blake famously quipped. Recent studies have dumped the linear model of assimilation into a vaguely defined mainstream by immigrants and minorities and have drawn attention to the variety and complexity of *sites of cultural negotiation*, tactics of survival and the creative refashioning of identities more in terms of *flows* than of *structures*. Certain aspects of one's idea of his/her "sense of being" (as opposed to "identity") can be modified, talked about, fashioned into something else in a fluid, experiential manner. Identities and differences being therefore at bottom both malleable and necessarily amorphous, the real battleground that looms ever more menacing is now (as perhaps always was) located in the business and the political worlds, or, rephrasing it, in the *obstinate persis-*

tence of a class struggle paradigm that all nations and peoples have experienced, but seem to have jettisoned for political acceptability or, worse, correctness. In the historically recent discourse of the cross-group, trans-national arena of ecology and the environment, we are reminded of not losing sight of broader concerns, or basic needs like mobility, energy, food production, dignified labor, that impact on the greater society as a whole. As critics, educators, intellectuals at large, we cannot go on doing business as usual when 2, 3, maybe 4 % of the world's population controls the destiny, by and large abusively, of some seven billion individuals, putting more and more controls on the freedom of movement, recording and cataloguing our each and every move, and foisting upon the public consciousness divisive markers of belonging and privilege, access and acceptability.

Knowing that, how many Italian Americans, critics as writers, filmmakers as artists, lawyers as business people are presently engaged in these arenas of contention and *not* be coded by ethnic, national, or linguistic signs that bespeak "identitarian" markers? And is this something that can be done? How much further can the rhetoric of group or "national" identity be pushed as something to be proud of and demand legitimacy for when some of its "representative" spokespersons have made fortunes on self-stereotyping without any irony through cinema, vowed to ban or vote against same-gender marriages, abolish the right for women to choose, show contempt for or worse promote the incarceration or deportation of the newer less fortunate immigrants of different nationalities than their own?

What is left to be done must be conducted in view of the larger dynamics of America as a whole and how its manifold if irrational ideologies stretch their tentacles in ever more insidious ways all over the globe, absorbing and recycling forms of discourse that also and still claim specificity, authenticity, exclusivity, "exceptionalism." Thus even *gender*, *race*, and *identity* politics must be linked again and perhaps primarily *to class struggle*, indeed to the dynamics of capital, drawing attention to the social developments of the last half century, in particular to the demise of the bi-polar world system, and the obvious crises of nationalism and nation-building! If there is going to be a change in how minorities, and immigrants are represented and granted access to the various social and symbolic infrastructures of a society, this cannot come by "resisting" from the outside, as it were (a *topos* that informed critique from the 70s through the 90s), nor by merely pointing the finger as victims or ignored constituencies (a worn-out trope of ethno-politics also from the same decades), nor of course by weaponizing reactions of any sort, but, rather, by striving to occupy legitimate positions where certain decisions are made, where the existing democratic means permit to engage broader concerns, where for once the identity of group means sharing and working with identical or similar concerns that have an impact on the social process as a whole. Think of ecology, weapons of mass-destruction, xenophobia, and the world-wide growing tides of humans fleeing their home regions owing to super-capitalistic exploitation, local warlords, lack of energy, water, intellectuals! And an overstressed physical environment. This is implicitly pleading a case for the cruciality of education and the need to keep it public, not private!

We must learn from our historical past as immigrants and re-fashion ourselves as *perennial political and critical migrants* in the interstices of post-industrial, post-national societies (the recent resurgence of populist-patriotism notwithstanding). We must discard the logic of opposition and antagonism and espouse a rhetoric of *cautiously* engaging the endlessly distorted systems of aggregation and legitimation of power as well as the unavoidable rhetorical tendency of our interlocutors to stage a discourse of self-validation and success. For it has been amply demonstrated that even our "enemies" are being played out: there is no zero-sum conflict, as there exist groups and arrangements where ethnic- and cultural-

"For a Topological Critique"

identities double as weapons at the service of someone/something else.

From the general dustbin of history we need to recover — and modify it to function within this centerless continuously destabilized social continuum — the notion of the self-created *consciousness of relation within delimited horizons*, that is to say, the floating localized fields of interaction. What works for New York may not work for Arizona. We must try to understand ourselves as beings who are constantly reinterpreting who they are, who have at once the humbleness and fearlessness to accept that there is no supratemporal or trans-historical ego or identity, and yet believe that lives make sense primarily on the basis of a positive and encouraging exchange with someone else who is also looking to determine the key values of the *common-place* inhabited. Here, determining an identity is a local necessity that does not require a wholesale reduction to one semiotically framed contour. It is a fact that aspects of this social and political awareness have been the hallmark of forms of critique that sought commonalities within the realm of gender, race, or ethnic studies, and a topological critique can certainly benefits from their findings and programmes.

But there are other unexplored pathways. An even more fundamental context to rethink identity would be the common-place reality that comes into view each time, as locals (in *our* time and place), we meet a "migrant" (an "other," a foreigner, a stranger) or, as migrants (travelers), we meet "locals" (in *their* space or world) and must be aware of and respond to the contextual factors or situation such as they might be. At such interstices – crossroads, bivouacs, staged meetings or chance encounters – we can display the full richness of our many identities in light of an exchange that is both individually empowering and illuminating and socio-politically democratic, positive, and peaceful.

A good deal of this scantily sketched ethic is to be found in Pier Paolo Pasolini's *Lutheran Letters*, a collection of columns published as his last great work, where one can read of an idea of brotherhood which is neither Christian, nor Italian, nor American!, yet predisposed to a world made up ultimately of different "others," those for whom *we* are the other, and who agree on sharing a common humanity, and the same planet, before we even decide to identify ourselves.

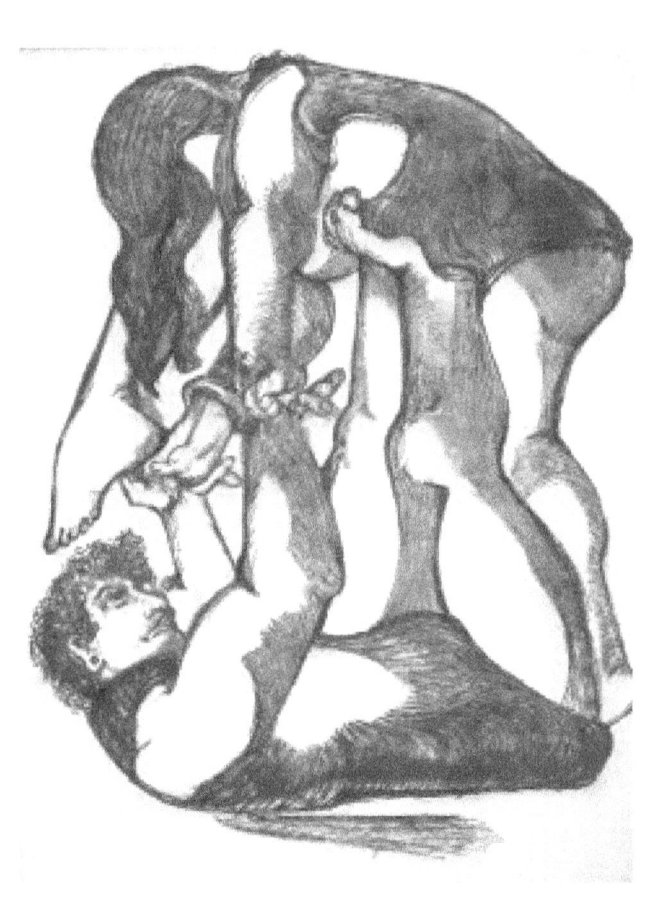

BIBLIOGRAPHY

Abrams, Richard M, ed. *The Issues of the Populist and progressive Eras, 1892-1912.* Columbia (SC): U South Carolina P, 1969.

Abu-Lughod, Janet. "On the Rewriting of History." In Kruger & Mariani, 111-29.

Ahearn, Carol B. "The New Pluralism and Its Implications for Italian American Literary Studies." In Scelsa, La Gumina, Tomasi, eds, 1990:203-08.

Ahmad, Aijaz. *In Theory. Classes, Nations, Literatures.* London: Verso, 1992.

Ahmed, Ali Jimale, ed. *The Invention of Somalia.* Lawrenceville (NJ): The Red Sea P, 1995.

Alba, Richard. *Italian Americans: Into the Twilight of Ethnicity.* New York: Prentice-Hall, 1984.

Al-Bagdadi, Nadia. "Registers of Arabic Literary History." *New Literary History* 39. 3 (2008): 437-461.

Aleandri, Emelise. *The Italian-American Immigrant Theatre of New York City, 1746-1899.* Lewiston: Mellen Press, 2006.

Andersen, Earl R. and Gianfranco Zanetti. "Comparative Semantic Approaches to the Idea of a Literary Canon." *The Journal of Aesthetics and Art Criticism* 58. 4 (2000): 341-360.

Anderson, Benedict. *Imagined Communities; Reflections on the Origin and Spread of Nationalism.* London: Verso, 1983.

Anderson, Quentin. *The Imperial Self.* New York: Vintage, 1971.

Anselmi, William and Kosta Gouliamos. *Elusive Margins. Consuming Media, Ethnicity, and Culture.* Toronto: Guernica, 1998.

Anzaldúa, Gloria. "La Conciencia de la Mestiza." In Fernàndez, 1994: 266-282.

Appadurai, Arjun. "Disjunction and Difference in the Global Cultural Economy." *Public Culture.* Vol. II (Spring 1990), 295-310.

Appignanesi, Richard, ed. *The end of everything: postmodernism and the vanishing of the human.* Cambridge, UK: Icon Books, 2003.

———. *Postmodernism and Big Science.* Cambridge, MA: Totem Books, 1998.

Aprile, Pino. *Terroni.* Transl. I.M Rosiglioni. New York: Bordighera, 2011.

"Bibliography"

Aquarone, Alberto. *Alla ricerca dell'Italia liberale*. Napoli: Guida, 1972.
Arduini, Stefano. *La ragione retorica*. Rimini: Guaraldi, 2004.
_____. *Prolegómenos a una teoría general de las figuras*. Murcia: U Murcia, 2000.
Aristotle. *On Rhetoric*. Ed. and trans. G. A. Kennedy. Oxford: Oxford UP, 1991.
_____. *The Complete Works of Aristotle*. 2 vols. Ed. J. Barnes. Princeton: Princeton UP, 1984.
Arlacchi, Pino. "Perché si emigrava dalla società contadina e non dal latifondo." In Borzomati 157-170.
Artioli, Umberto and Francesco Bartoli, eds. *Il viandante e la sua orma*. Bologna: Cappelli, 1981.
Asor Rosa, Alberto. *Fuori dall'occidente*. Torino: Einaudi, 1992.
_____. *Scrittori e popolo*. Roma: Savelli e Simona', 1966.
Atlan, Henri, et al. *Il pensiero eccentrico*. Milano: Editrice A/Volontà, 1992, N. 4/91-1/92.
Auerbach, Eric. *Figura*. Madison: U Minnesota P, 1984.
Bade, Klaus J. *Europa in Bewegung: Migration von späten 18 Jahrhundert bis zur Gegenwart*. Trans. M. García Garmilla. *Europa en Movimiento*. Barcelona: Critica, 2003.
Bailey, Samuel. "The Future of Italian American Studies: An Historian's Approach to Research in the Coming Decade." In Tomasi, 192-201.
Balibar, Etienne. "Paradoxes of Universality." In Goldberg, 283-94.
Balodimas-Bartolomei, Angelyn. "*Italianità Americana*: A Study of Ethnic Identity Among Second-, Third, and Third-Plus-Generation Italian Americans." In George Guida et al, eds, *What Is Italian America?* New York, IASA, 2015, 156-184.
Banfield, Edward. *The Moral Basis of a Backward Society*. New York: The Free Press, 1958.
Barolini, Helen, ed. *The Dream Book. An Anthology of Writings by Italian American Women*. New York: Schocken Books, 1985.
_____. *Umbertina*. New York: The Feminist Press, 1999 [1979].
_____. *Chiaroscuro: Essays of Identity*. W. Lafayette (IN): Bordighera, 1997.
Barone, Dennis and Stefano Luconi, eds. *Small Towns, Big Cities: The Urban Experience of Italian Americans*. New York: Bordighera P, 2010.

"Bibliography"

Basile Green, Rose. *The Pennsylvania People*. New York: Cornwall Books, 1984.

_____. *Songs of Ourselves*. New York: Cornwall Books, 1982.

Baudrillard, Jean. *The Illusion of the End*. Trans. C. Turner. Cambridge (UK): Polity P, 1994.

_____. *Selected Writings*. Transl. M. Poster. Stanford: Stanford UP, 2001.

Bauman, Zygmunt. *Legislators and Interpreters; On Modernity, Post Modernity, and Intellectuals*. Ithaca: Cornell UP, 1988.

Bayart, Jean-Francois. *The Illusion of Cultural Identity*. Chicago: U Chicago P, 2005.

Bencivenna, Marcella. *Italian Immigrant Radical Culture*. New York: New York UP, 2011.

Ben-Ghiat, Ruth. *Fascist Modernities: Italy, 1922-1945*. Los Angeles: U California P, 2004.

Ben-Ghiat, Ruth and Mia Fuller. *Italian Colonialism*. New York: Palgrave, 2008

Benhabib, Seyla. "The Liberal Imagination and the Four Dogmas of Multiculturalism." *The Yale Journal of Criticism* 12.2 (1999): 401-413.

Bernal, Martin. *Black Athena. The Afro-Asiatic Roots of Classical Civilization*. Rutgers UP, 1987.

Bertellini, Giorgo. *Italy in Early American Cinema*. Bloomington: Indiana University Press, 2009.

Bettin, Cristina. "Italian Jews: From Social Integration to the Construction of a New European Identity," in *The European Legacy: Toward New Paradigms*. London: Routledge, 2013:1-18.

Bezza, Bruno, ed. *Gli italiani fuori d'Italia*. Milan: Franco Angeli, 1983.

Bhabha, Homi K. "Interrogating Identity: The Postcolonial Prerogative." In Goldberg, 183-209.

_____. *The Location of Culture*. New York: Routledge, 1994.

_____. Ed., *Nation and Narration*. London: Verso, 1990.

Biagi, Enzo. *I "come" italiani*. Milano: Rizzoli, 1993.

Boase, Paul, ed. *The Rhetoric of Protest and Reform 1878-1898*. Athens, OH: Ohio UP, 1980.

Bobbio, Norberto. *Ideological Profile of Twentieth-Century Italy*. Trans. L. G. Cochrane. Princeton: Princeton UP, 1995.

_____. *Destra e sinistra*. Roma: Donzelli, 1994.

"Bibliography"

Bodnar, John. *The Transplanted. A History of Immigrants in Urban America.* Bloomington: UP, 1985.

Bolaffi, Angelo and Massimo Ilardi, eds. *Fine della politica?* Roma: Editori Riuniti, 1986.

Bollati, Giulio. *L'italiano. Il carattere nazionale come storia e come invenzione.* Torino: Einaudi, 1996.

Bona, Mary Jo. *Claiming a Tradition. Italian American Women Writers.* Carbondale, IL: Southern Illinois UP, 1999.

———. "Voices of the Silent Ones." *VIA Voices in Italian Americana* 2.1 (Spring 1991): 93-98.

Bona, Mary Jo, ed. *The Voices We Carry. Recent Italian American Women's Writing.* Toronto: Guernica, 1994.

Bona, Mary Jo, and Anthony Tamburri, eds. *Through the Looking Glass: Italian and Italian American Images in the Media.* Staten Island, NY: AIHA, 1996.

Bonaffini, Luigi and Joseph Pericone, eds. *Poets of the Italian Diaspora.* New York: Fordham UP, 2015.

Borzomati, Pietro, ed. *L'emigrazione calabrese dall'Unita' a oggi.* Roma: CSER, 1982.

Boorstin, Daniel. *The Americans.* 3 vols. New York: Vintage Books, 1958, 1965, 1973.

Braudel, Fernand. *On History.* Chicago: U of Chicago P, 1982.

Brenner, Michael, Peter Marsh, & Marylin Brenner, eds. *The Social Contexts of Method.* New York: St. Martin's Press, 1978.

Brettell, Caroline and James Hollifield, eds. *Migration Theory.* New York: Routledge, 2000.

Brodhead, Richard H. "Strangers on a Train: The Double Dream of Italy in the American Gilded Age." *Modernism/modernity* 1.2 (April 1994): 1-19.

Brown, Dee. *Bury My Heart at Wounded Knee.* New York: Holt, Rinehart & Winston, 1970.

Butler, Judith. *Undoing Gender.* New York: Routledge, 2004.

———. *Gender Trouble: Feminism and the Subversion of Identity.* New York: Routledge, 2006.

Caccia, Fulvio. "The Italian Writer and Language." In Pivato, 156-67.

Cafagna, Luciano. *Nord e Sud.* Venezia: Marsilio, 1994.

"Bibliography"

Calderòn, Hector and Saldìvar, José D. eds. *Criticism in the Borderlands. Studies in Chicano Literature, Culture, and Ideology.* Durham: Duke UP, 1991.
Calefato, Patrizia. *Europa fenicia. Identità linguistica, comunità, linguaggio come pratica sociale.* Milano: Franco Angeli, 1994.
Callaro, Marco and Mario Francesconi, *John Baptist Scalabrini, Apostle to Emigrants.* NewYork: Center for Migration Studies, 1977.
Camaiti Hostert, Anna and Anthony J. Tamburri, eds. *Screening Ethnicity: Cinematographic Representations of Italian Americans in the United States.* New York: VIA Folios, 2002.
Candeloro, Giorgio. *Storia dell'Italia moderna.* 8 vols. Milano: Feltrinelli, 1970.
Cannistraro, Philip, ed. *Italian Americans: The Search for a Usable Past.* New York: American Italian Historical Association, 1989.
_____. "Generoso Pope and the Rise of Italian American Politics, 1925-1936." In Tomasi 1985:264-88.
Cannistraro, Philip and Gerald Meyer, eds. *The Lost World of Italian American Radicalism. Politics, Labor, and Culture.* New York: Praeger, 2003.
Carravetta, Peter. *Prefaces to the Diaphora. Rhetorics, Allegory, and the Interpretation of Postmodernity.* W. Lafayette, IN: Purdue UP, 1991.
_____. "Poesaggio." *Paesaggio. Poeti italiani d'America.* A cura di P. Carravetta & P. Valesio. Treviso: Pagus, 1993:9-26.
_____. *Review* of Lydio Tomasi et al, eds. *The Columbus People* (1994), in DIFFERENTIA 6/7 (1994a):369-77.
_____. "Turning in/to the Diaphora." *Romance Languages Annual. Vol. VI.* W. Lafayette, IN: Purdue Foundation, 1994b:v-xv.
_____. "Viaggio." *Segnalibro. Dieci voci contemporanee.* Ed. L. Saviani. Napoli: Liguori, 1995:205-56.
_____. "La questione dell'identità nella formazione dell'Europa," in Franca Sinopoli, ed. *La letteratura europea vista dagli altri.* Roma, Meltemi, 2003:19-66
_____. "Emigrazione, colonizzazione e identità ne *La Rassegna Settimanale* (1878-1881)," in Giuseppe Masi, ed. *Tra Calabria e Mezzogiorno.* Cosenza: Pellegrini, 2007:187-238.
_____. *Del Postmoderno. Critica e cultura in America all'alba del duemila.* Milano: Bompiani, 2009.

_____. *The Elusive Hermes. Method, Discourse, Interpreting.* Aurora, CO: Davies Group Publishers, 2012.

Carrera, Alessandro. "Frail Identities along the Canadian Shield." *DIFFERENTIA* 6.7 (Spring/Autumn 1994): 283-296.

Castles, Stephen and Mark J. Miller, eds. *The Age of Migration. International Population Movements in the Modern World.* New York: Guilford P, 1993.

Castronovo, Valerio. *La stampa italiana dall'Unità al fascismo.* Bari: Laterza, 1973.

Cavaioli, Frank J. "Columbus, Whitman, and the Italian-American Connection." In Krase & DeSena, 127-141.

Cavalli-Sforza, Luca and Francesco Cavalli-Sforza. *The Great Human Diasporas: The History of Diversity and Evolution.* New York: Helix Books, 1995.

Challiand, Gérard and Jean-Pierre Rageau, eds. *The Penguin Atlas of Diasporas.* Transl. A.M. Berret. New York: Penguin, 1995.

_____, Michael Jan, and Jean-Pierre Rageau, eds. *Atlas Historique des Migrations.* Paris: Seuil, 1994.

Chardon, Jean-Marc and Denis Lensel, eds. *La pensée unique: Le vrai procès.* Paris: Economica, 1998.

Charters, Ann, ed. *The Portable Beat Reader.* New York: Penguin, 1992.

Christou, Anastasia. "Geographies of place, culture and identity in the narratives of second-generation Greek-Americans returning 'home'." Unpublished article e-mailed to author.

Cicero, Marcus Tullius. *De inventione, De optimo genere oratorum,Topica.* Trans. H. M. Hubbell. Cambridge: Harvard UP, 1976.

Cinel, Dino. *The National Integration of Italian Return Migration, 1870-1929.* Cambridge: Cambridge UP, 2002.

Cinotto, Simone, ed. *Making Italian America Consumer Culture and the Production of Ethnic Identities.* New York: Fordham UP, 2014.

Cinotto, Simone. "Glocal Italies: un possibile nuovo percorso per lo studio storico delle comunità italoamericane." In *Altreitalie*, Torino, Fondazione Giovanni Agnelli (giugno 2006): 38-51.

Ciuffoletti, Zeffiro and Maurizio Degl'Innocenti, eds. *L'emigrazione nella storia d'Italia 1868/1975.* Firenze: Vallecchi, 1978.

Clifford, James and George Marcus, eds. *Writing Culture: the Poetics and the Politics of Ethnography.* Berkeley: U California P, 1986.

"Bibliography"

Cohen, J. and Federico, G. "Modernization versus tradition: new views and old on agriculture." In *The Growth of the Italian Economy, 1820–1960*. Cambridge: Cambridge University Press, 2001, 30–45.

Cohen, Robin. *Global Diasporas. An Introduction*. Seattle: U Washington P, 1997.

Colajanni, Napoleone. *Storia della banca d'Italia*. Roma: Newton Compton, 1995.

Comberati, Daniele. *"Affrica". Il mito coloniale italiano negli scritti di esploratori e missionari dall'Unita' alla sconfitta di Adua, 1861-1896*. Roma: Cesati, 2013.

Cordasco, Francesco. *Dictionary of American Immigration History*. Metuchen, NJ: Scarecrow P, 1990.

Cordasco, Francesco and Eugene Bucchioni, eds. *The Italians. Social Backgrounds of an American Group*. Clifton, NJ: Augustus M. Kelly Publishers, 1974.

Cortes, Carlos E. "The Hollywood Curriculum on Italian Americans: Evolution of an Icon of Ethnicity," in Lydio F. Tomasi and Piero Gastaldo, eds. *The Columbus People*, pp 90-92

Cosco, James P. *Imagining Italians. The Clash of Romance and Race in American Perceptions, 1880-1910*. New York: SUNY Press, 2003.

Cro, Stelio. *The Noble Savage; Allegory of Freedom*. Waterloo ON: Wilfred Laurier UP, 1990.

Cullen, Jim. *The American Dream. A Short History of an Idea That Shaped a Nation*. New York: Oxford UP, 2003.

Cunsolo, Ronald S. *Italian nationalism*. Malabar, FL: Krieger Publishing Co, 1990.

Curtius, Ernst R. *European Literature and the Latin Middle Ages*. Princeton, NJ: Princeton UP, 1983.

D'Agostino, Peter. "Craniums, Criminals, and the 'cursed Race': Italian Anthropology in American Racial Thought 1861-1924," in *Comparative Studies in Society and History*, Vol. 44, No. 2 (Apr. 2001):319-342.

D'Alfonso, Antonio. *In Italics. In Defense of Ethnicity*. Toronto: Guernica, 1996.

Daniels, Roger. *Not Like Us: Immigrants and Minorities in America, 1890-1924*. Chicago: Ivan R. Dee, 1997.

Davis, John A. *Italy in the Nineteenth Century (1796-1900)*. Oxford: Oxford UP, 2001.
Davis, Kingsley, "The Migrations of Human Populations," *Scientific American*, 1975
DeFatta Barattini, Kathryn. *Academic Perceptions of Italian American Immigration as Seen in Scholarly Journals of the 1880's*. Lewiston: The Edwin Mellen Press, 2004.
De Felice, Renzo. *Le interpretazioni del fascismo*. Bari: Laterza, 1969.
Degl'Innocenti, Maurizio. *See* Ciuffoletti
Del Boca, Angelo. *Gli italiani in Africa orientale. Dall'Unità alla marcia su Roma*. Milano: Mondadori, 1976.
Del Boca, Lorenzo. *Polentoni*. Milano: Piemme, 2011.
Deleuze, Gilles and Felix Guattari. "Geofilosofia." *Millepiani*, Milano: Mimesis, 1993:9-34.
_____. *A Thousand Plateaus. Capitalism and Schizophrenia*. Trans. B. Massumi. Minneapolis: U Minnesota P, 1987.
_____. *Kafka. Toward a Minor Literature*. Trans. R. Bensmaïa. Minneapolis: U Minnesota P, 1986.
Delia Lanza, Carmela. *Long Island Girl*. San Francisco: malafemmina press, 1992.
Del Negro, Giovanna, *Looking Through My Mother's Eyes: Life Stories of Nine Immigrant Women in Canada*. Toronto: Guernica, 1997.
DeMarchi, Vichi and Maria C. Ercolessi. *Terzo mondo e quarto potere*. Roma: Nuova ERI, 1991.
Descombes, Vincent. *Puzzling Identities*. Cambridge, MA: Harvard UP, 2016.
Di Biagi, Flaminio. "A Reconsideration: Italian-American Writers: Notes for a Wider Categorization." *MELUS*. 14. 3-4 (Fall-Winter 1987): 141-151.
Di Cicco, Pier Giorgio. *The Tough Romance*. Montréal: Guernica, 1990.
Di Donato, Pietro. *Christ in Concrete*. New York: Signet, 1993 [1939].
Dieckhoff, Alain. *The Invention of a Nation. Zionist Thought and the Making of Modern Israel*. Transl. by J. Derrick. London: Hurst & Co., 2003.
Dinnerstein, Leonard, Roger L. Nichols and David M. Reimers. *Natives and Strangers. Ethnic Groups and the Building of America*. New York: Oxford UP, 1979.

"Bibliography"

Di Pasquale, Pietro. *Dances With Luigi: A Grandson's Determined Quest to Comprehend Italy and the Italians*. New York: St. Martin's Press, 2005.

Dirlik, Arif. "Culturalism as Hegemonic Ideology and Liberating Practice." In JanMohamed & Lloyd, 394-431.

Di Siena, Giuseppe. "Il problema della razza oggi." In B. Continenza, et al, eds. *I cartografi dell'impero*. Milano: Feltrinelli, 1980, 53-86.

Distasi, Lawrence, ed. *Una storia segreta. The Secret History of Italian American Evacuation and Internment during World War II*. New York: Heyday, 2001

Dore, Grazia. *La democrazio italiana e l'emigrazione in America*. Roma: Morcelliana, 1964.

Drake, Richard. *The Revolutionary Mystique and Terrorism in Contemporary Italy*. Bloomington: Indiana UP, 1989.

Duggan, Christopher. *Francesco Crispi, from nation to nationalism*. Oxford: Oxford UP, 2002.

_____. *The Force of Destiny. History of Italy since 1796*. New York: Houghton Mifflin Harcourt, 2008.

Durante, Francesco, ed. *Italoamericana. The Literature of the Great Migration 1880-1940*. New York: Fordham UP, 2014.

Durišin, Dionyz. *Theory of Literary Comparatistics*. Bratislava: Veda, 1984.

Eco, Umberto. "Rushdie, non c'è più spazio per l'esilio." L'*Espresso* (17 maggio 1992):226.

Ehrmann, Herbert. *The Case That Will Not Die. Commonwealth vs Sacco and Vanzetti*. Boston: Little & Brown, 1969.

Enzensberger, Hans M. *Civil Wars. From L.A. to Bosnia*. New York: New Press Reader, 1994.

Fagiani, Gil. "The Italian Identity of Frank Sinatra." In *VIA Voices in Italian Americana*, Vol. 10, N. 2 (1999), 19-32.

Feldman, Gregory. *We Are All Migrants. Political Action and the Ubiquitous Condition of Migrant-hood*. Stanford: Stanford UP, 2015.

Fernández, Roberta, ed. "Preface." In *In Other Words. Literature by Latinas of the United States*. Houston: Arte Publico P, 1994.

Ferrarelli, Rina. *Dreamsearch*. San Francisco: malafemmina press, 1992.

Finco, Aldo. "The Italian Americans: Their Contribution in the Field of Literature." *Ethnic Literatures since 1776: The Many Voices of America*, 2 vols. Ed. W. Zyla and W. Aycock, Lubbock: Texas Tech Press. 1 (1978): 255-73.

"Bibliography"

Foerster, Robert F. *The Italian Emigration of Our Times*. Cambridge: Harvard UP, 1919.
Fontanella, Luigi. *Migrating Words: Italian Writers in the United States*. New York: Bordighera, 2012.
Forgacs, David and Robert Lumley, eds. *Italian Cultural Studies. An Introduction*. Oxford: Oxford UP, 1996.
Forlenza, Rosario. "'The Next Wave of Italians Has Come to America': Italian Investments and Business in the United States, 1980-2013." In *Journal of Modern Italian Studies*, Vol. 20, Issue 5 (2015): 708-731 (published online: 21 Jan 2016)
Foucault, Michel. *The Order of Things*. New York: Random House, 1994.
_____. *The Archaelogy of Knowledge & The Discourse on Language*. Trans. A.M. Sheridan Smith. New York: Harper & Row, 1976.
Fukuyama, Francis. *The End of History and the Last Man*. New York: Avon, 1992.
Gabaccia, Donna R. *Immigration and American Diversity: A Social and Cultural History*. New York: Wiley-Blackwell, 2002.
_____. *Italy's Many Diasporas*. Seattle. U Washington P, 2000.
_____. "Is Everywhere Nowhere? Nomads, Nations, and the Immigrant Paradigm of United States History," in *The Journal of American History*, Vol. 86, No. 3 (1999): 1115-1134.
Gabaccia, Donna R. and Fraser M. Ottanelli, eds. *Italian Workers of the World: Labor Migration and the Formation of Multi-Ethnic States*. Carbondale: U Illinois P, 2005.
Gadamer, Hans-Georg. *Truth and Method*. New York; Continuum, 1972.
Galasso, Giuseppe. *L'Italia come problema storiografico*. Torino: UTET, 1979.
Gallagher, Shaun. *Hermeneutics and Education*. Albany: SUNY P, 1992.
Galli Della Loggia, Ernesto. *La morte della patria*. Bari: Laterza, 2003.
Gambino, Richard. *Blood of My Blood. The Dilemma of the Italian Americans*. Toronto: Guernica, 1996 [1974].
_____. "Italian Americans, Today's Immigrants, Multiculturalism and the Mark of Cain." *Italian Americana*. XII. 2 (1994): 226-234.
_____. "The Italian-American Teacher." *Attenzione* (Nov. 1979): 57-59.
_____. *Vendetta. The Story of the Worst Lynching in America*. Garden City: Doubleday, 1976.

Ganeri, Margherita. *L'America italiana. Epos e storytelling in Helen Barolini.* Arezzo: Zona Editrice, 2010.
Gardaphé, Fred L. *Leaving Little Italy. Essaying Italian American Culture.* Albany: SUNY P, 2003.
_____. *Italian Signs, American Streets.* Durham: Duke UP, 1996.
_____. *The Italian-American Writer.* Spencertown, NY: Forkroads, 1995.
Garraty, John A., ed. *Labor and Capital in the Gilded Age.* Boston: Little, Brown & Company, 1968.
Garver, Eugene. *For the Sake of Argument. Practical Reasoning, Character, and the Ethics of Belief.* Chicago: U Chicago P, 2004.
Gates, Henry Louis, Jr., ed. *Black Literature and Literary Theory.* New York: Metheun, 1984.
_____. *Loose Cannons.* Oxford: Oxford UP, 1992.
_____. *The Signifying Monkey. A Theory of Afro-American Literary Criticism.* Oxford: Oxford UP, 1988.
Geertz, Clifford. *Interpretation of Cultures.* New York: Basic Books, 1973.
Gellner, Ernest. *Nations and Nationalism.* Ithaca, NY: Cornell UP, 2009.
_____. *Relativism and the Social Sciences.* Cambridge: Cambridge UP, 1987.
Gerstle, Gary. "Liberty, Coercion, and the Making of Americans," in *The Journal of American History*, Vol. 48, No. 2 (Sept, 1997): 524-58.
Ghirelli, Massimo. *Immigrati brava gente. La società italiana tra razzismo e accoglienza.* Milano: Sperling & Kupfer, 1993.
Gibson, Mary. *Born to Crime: Cesare Lombroso and the Origins of Biological Criminology.* New York: Praeger, 2002.
Giddens, Anthony. *Politics, Sociology and Social Theory.* Stanford, CA: Stanford UP, 1995.
Gilroy, Paul. *Against Race. Imagining Political Culture Beyond the Color Line.* Cambridge MA: Harvard UP, 2000.
Gioia, Dana. "What is Italian-American Poetry?" *VIA voices in italian americana* 4.2 (1993): 61-64.
_____. *Can Poetry Matter? Essays on Poetry and American Culture.* St. Paul MN: Graywolf P, 1992.
_____. *The Gods of Winter.* St. Paul MN: Graywolf P, 1991.
Gjerde, Jon, ed. *Major Problems in American Immigration and Ethnic History. Documents and Essays.* New York: Houghton Mifflin, 1998.
Glissant, Eduard. *Poetica del diverso.* Roma: Meltemi, 1998.

"Bibliography"

Gnisci, Armando. *We, the Europeans*. Ed. & transl. M. Rusnak. Aurora CO: Davies Group Publishing, 2014.

Goglia, Luigi, and Grassi, Fabio, eds. *Il colonialismo italiano da Adua all'impero*. Bari: Laterza, 1993.

Goldberg, David, ed. *The Anatomy of Racism*. Minneapolis: U Minnesota P, 1990.

Gòmez-Moriana, Antonio. "Narration and Argumentation in the Chronicles of the New World." In Jara & Spadaccini, 97-120.

Goodman, Nelson. *Ways of Worldmaking*. Indianapolis: Hackett, 1995.

Goodwin, Lawrence. *The Populist Movement. A Short History of the Agrarian Revolt in America*. New York: Oxford UP, 1978.

Gould, Stephen J. *The Mismeasure of Man*. New York: Norton, 1996

Gramsci, Antonio. *Cultural Writings*. Cambridge: Harvard UP, 1975.

Graziano, Manlio. *The Failure of Italian Nationhood. The Geopolitics of a Troubled Identity*. New York: Palgrave-Macmillan, 2010.

Greenblatt, Stephen. *Marvelous Possessions: The Wonder of the New World*. Chicago: U Chicago P, 1992.

Grunwald, Henry. *One Man's America*. New York: Anchor Books, 1997.

Gruzinski, Serge. *La pensée métisse*. Paris: Fayard, 1999.

Gugelberger, Georg M. "Decolonizing the Canon: Considerations of Third World Literature." *New Literary History* 22 (1991): 505-524.

Guglielmo, Jennifer. *Living the Revolution: Italian Women's Resistance and Radicalism in New York City, 1880-1945*. Winston-Salem: U of North Carolina P, 2012.

Guglielmo, Jennifer and Salvatore Salerno, eds. *Are Italians White?* New York: Routledge, 2003.

Guida, George. *Spectacles of Themselves*. New York: Bordighera Press, 2015.

Guillory, John. "Canon." *Critical Terms for Literary Study*. Ed. F. Lentricchia and T. McLaughlin. Chicago: U of Chicago P, 1995.

Habermas, Jürgen. *The Structural Transformation of the Public Sphere*. Cambridge: MIT P, 1991.

Hall, Stuart. *Representation: cultural representations and signifying practices*. London: Thousand Oaks, 1997.

_____. "The question of cultural identity." In Hall, Stuart, David Held and Anthony McGrew, eds. *Modernity and its futures*, Cambridge: Polity P, 1992:274–316

"Bibliography"

Haller, Hermann. *Una lingua perduta e ritrovata*. Firenze: La Nuova Italia, 1993.

Handlin, Oscar. *Race and Nationality in American Life*. Garden City (NY): Doubleday, 1957.

_____. *The Uprooted*. New York: Grosset & Dunlap, 1951.

Harjo, Joy. *She Had Some Horses*. New York: Thunder's Mouth Press, 1983.

Heidegger, Martin. "What Are Poets For." *Poetry, Language, Thought*. Trans. A. Hofstadter. New York: Harper (1971): 89-142.

_____. *Being and Time*. Trans. J. Maquarrie & E. Robinson. New York: Harper & Row, 1969 [1927].

Heller, Agnes. *Renaissance Man*. London: Routledge & Kegan Paul, 1978.

Hendin, Josephine. *The Right Thing To Do*. Boston: David R. Godline, 1998.

_____. "The Uses of Italy" in A. Lombardo and J.W. Tuttleton, eds. *The Sweetest Impression of Life: The James Family in Italy*. New York: New York UP, 1990.

Herbrechter, Stefan. *Posthumanism. A Critical Analysis*. London: Bloomsbury, 2013.

Hess, Robert L. *Italian Colonialism in Somalia*. Chicago: U Chicago P, 1967.

Hinkelammert, Franz, *El nihilismo al desnudo*. Santiago (Chile): Escafandra, 2001.

Hirsch, Eli. *The Concept of Identity*. Oxford: Oxford UP, 1982.

Hirschberg, Stuart, ed. *One World, Many Cultures*. New York: Macmillan, 1992.

Hobsbawm, Eric. *Primitive Rebels*. New York: Norton, 1965

Hobsbawm, Eric and Terence Ranger, eds. *The Invention of Tradition*. Cambridge: Cambridge UP, 1983.

Hodge, John L. "Equality: Beyond Dualism and Oppression." In Goldberg, 89-107.

Holden, Jonathan. *Style and Authenticity in Postmodern Poetry*. Columbia: U of Missouri P, 1986.

Hollinger, David A. *Postethnic America: Beyond Multiculturalism*. New York: Basic Books, 2006.

Hollis, Martin and Steven Lukes, eds. *Rationality and Relativism*. Oxford: Basil Blackwell, 1982.

Holub, Renate. *Antonio Gramsci. Beyond Marxism and Postmodernism*. New York: Routledge, 1992.
Hull Hoffer, Williamjames. *"Plessy v. Ferguson": Race and Inequality in Jim Crow America*. Lawrence: UP of Kansas, 2012.
Ilari, Virgilio. *Inventarsi una patria. Esiste un'identità nazionale?* Roma: Ideazione, 1996.
Irigaray, Luce. *Key Writings*. New York: Continuum, 2004.
Italian Americana. Vol. XII, No. 1 (Fall/Winter 1993):7-37.[Responses to Talese 1993 by Gioia, Mirabelli, DiBartolomeo, Ceresi, De Pietro, Gioseffi, Gambino].
Jameson, Fredric. *Postmodernism, or, The Cultural Logic of Late Capitalism*. Durham: Duke UP, 1992.
JanMohamed, Abdul and David Lloyd, eds. *The Nature and Context of Minority Discourse*. Oxford: Oxford UP, 1990.
Jara, René and Nicholas Spadaccini, eds. *1492/1992: Re/Discovering Colonial Writing*. Minneapolis: U Minnesota P, 1993.
Joxe, Alain. *Empire of Disorder*. New York: Semiotext(e), 2002.
Keridis, Dimitri, et al., eds. *New Approaches to Balkan Studies*. Dulles, VA: Brassey, 2003.
Kennedy, John F. *A nation of immigrants*. New York: Harper Perennial, 2008.
King, Desmond. *Making Americans. Immigration, Race, and the Origins of the Diverse Democracy*. Cambridge: Harvard UP, 2000.
King, Russel, "Generalisations from the History of Return Migration." In *Return Migration: Journey of Hope or Despair?* Ed. B. Ghosh. Geneva: United Nations, 2000:7-55.
Klusmeyer, Douglas. *Membership, Migration, and Identity*. Stanford: Stanford Humanities Review Publishing, 1997.
_____. *Between Consent and Descent: Conceptions of Democratic Citizenship*. Pittsburgh: Carnegie Endowment for International Peace, 1996.
Koselleck, Reinhart. *Futures Past: On the Semantics of Historical Time*. Trans. K. Tribe. Boston: MIT P, 1988.
Krase, Jerome and Judith De Sena, eds. *Italian Americans in a Multicultural Society* [Supplement to *Forum Italicum*]. New York: SUNY/Stony Brook, 1994.

"Bibliography"

Kruger, Barbara and Phil Mariani, eds. *Remaking History*. Seattle: Braille P, 1989.
Larson, Gerald J. and Deutsch, Eliot, eds. *Interpreting across Boundaries. New Essays in Comparative Philosophy*. Princeton: Princeton UP, 1988.
LaGumina, Salvatore. *WOP! A Documentary History of Anti-Italian Discrimination*. Toronto: Guernica, 1999 [1973].
Laplantine, François and Alexis Nouss. *Le métissage*. Paris, Téraèdre, 2011.
Lapolla, Garibaldi. *The Gran Gennaro*. New Brunswick: Rutgers UP, 2009.
Lattimore, Owen. *Silk, Spices, and Empire: Asia seen through the Eyes of its Discoverers*. New York: Delacorte Press, 1968.
Lavie, Smadar, and Ted Swedenburg, eds. *Displacement, Diaspora, and Geographies of Identity*. Durham: Duke UP, 1996.
Lears, Jackson. *Rebirth of a Nation: The Making of Modern America, 1877-1920*. New York: Harper, 2009.
Linos, Katerina. "Understanding Greek Immigration Policy." In Keridis *et al*, 2003:309-344
Livy. *History of Rome*. Oxford: Oxford UP, 2006-2013
Lombardi-Diop, Cristina and Caterina Romeo, eds. *Postcolonial Italy*. New York: Palgrave, 2012.
Luconi, Stefano. *From Paesani to White Ethnics: The Italian Experience in Philadelphia*. Albany, NY: SUNY P, 2001.
_____ "Is Italian-American History an Account of the Immigrant Experience with Politics Left Out? Some Thoughts on the Political Historiography about Italian Americans." In Paolo A. Giordano, and Anthony J. Tamburri, eds. *Italian Americans in the Third Millennium*. New York: AIHA, 2009, 55-74.
Lyotard, Jean-François. *The Postmodern Condition*. Minneapolis: U Minnesota P, 1984.
_____. *Le Différend*. Paris: Seuil, 1984.
Mack Smith, Denis. *Italy and Its Monarchy*. New Haven: Yale UP, 1989.
_____. *Cavour*. New York: Knopf, 1985.
Macioti, Maria and Enrico Pugliese, eds. *Gli immigrati in Italia*. Bari: Laterza, 1991.
Mangano, Antonio, "The Associated Life of the Italians in New York City," in *Charities*, Vol. 12, May 7, 1904, 476-482.

Mangione, Jerre and Ben Morreale. *La Storia. Five Centuries of the Italian American Experience*. New York: Harper, 1992.

Marazzi, Martino. *A occhi aperti: letteratura dell'emigrazione e mito americano*. Milano: Franco Angeli, 2011.

———. *Voices of Italian America*. New York: Fordham UP, 2012.

Marchand, Jean-Jacques, ed. *La letteratura dell'emigrazione. Gli scrittori di lingua italiana nel mondo*. Torino: Fondazione Agnelli, 1991.

Martellone, Anna Maria. "A Plea against the Deconstruction of Ethnicity and in Favor of Political History." *Altreitalie*, (Nov. 1991):106-13.

Martucci, Roberto. *L'invenzione dell'Italia unita. 1855-1864*. Firenze: Sansoni, 1999.

Massey, Douglas S. "To Study Migration Today, Look to a Parallel Era." In *The Chronicle of Higher Education* (8 August, 2000).

Marx, Karl. "The German Ideology." In *The Marx-Engels Reader*. Ed. R.C. Tucker. New York: Norton, 1978: 146-200.

Mazziotti Gillan, Maria. *Where I come from*. Toronto: Guernica, 1995.

———. *The Weather of Old Seasons*. Merrick, NY: Cross-Cultural Communications, 1993.

Mazziotti Gillan, Maria and Jennifer Gillan, eds. *Unsettling America. An Anthology of Contemporary Multicultural Poetry*. New York: Penguin, 1994.

McDonald, Lee Martin. *The Biblical Canon: Its Origins, Transmission, and Authority*. Peabody, MS: Hendrickson Publishers, 2007.

McElderry, Bruce R., Jr., ed. *The Realistic Movement in American Writing*. New York: The Odyssey P, 1965.

McNeill, William H. *Polyethnicity and National Unity in World History*. Toronto: U of Toronto P, 1985.

———. *Plagues and Peoples*. Garden City, NY: Anchor P, 1976.

Mendras, Henri. *L'Europe des Européens*. Paris: Folio, 1997.

Menza, Claudia. *The Lunatics Ball*. Buffalo: Mosaic Press, 1994.

Messina, Anthony, and Gallya Lahav, eds. *The Migration Reader. Exploring Politics and Policies*. London: Lynne Rienner Publishers, 2006.

Mignolo, Walter D. "Literacy and Colonization: The New World Experience." In Jara & Spadaccini, 51-96.

Minni, C.D., ed. *Arrangiarsi. Things Remembered*. Montréal: Guernica, 1989.

Mitrano, John R. "The Garbage Can Model of Ethnic Identity Formation: A Case Study of Generation X Italian Americans." In *The Italian American Review*, Vol. 7, N. 1 (Spring/Summer 1999),83-103

Moe, Nelson. *The View from Vesuvius: Italian Culture and the Southern Question*. Berkeley: U California P, 2002.

Mommsen, Wolfgang. *Theories of Imperialism*. Chicago: U Chicago P, 1982.

Montanelli, Indro and Sergio Romano. *L'Italia dei notabili, 1861-1900*. Milano: RCS, 2013.

Moquin, Wayne and Charles Van Doren, eds. *A Documentary History of the Italian Americans*. New York: Praeger Publishers, 1974.

Moretti, Enrico. "Social Networks and Migrations: Italy 1876-1913." In *International Migration Review*, Vol. 33, No. 13 (Autumn, 1999): 640-57.

Mormino, Gary. *Italians in Florida*. Boca Raton, FL: Center for Interdisciplinary Studies FAU, 2003.

Mudimbe, V. Y. *The Invention of Africa. Gnosis, philosophy, and the order of knowledge*.Bloomington: Indiana UP, 1988.

Mukherjee, Bharati. "Immigrant Writing: Give Us Your Maximalists!" *The New York Times Book Review*, 28 Aug. 1988.

Murphy, Peter. "The Seven Pillars of Nationalism." *Diaspora* 7.3 (1998): 369-415.

Muscio, Giuliana, Joseph Sciorra and Giovanni Spagnoletti, eds., *Mediated Ethnicity: New Italian-American Cinema*. New York: John D. Calandra Italian American Institute, 2010.

Nail, Thomas. *The Figure of the Migrant*. Stanford: Stanford UP, 2015.

Nancy, Jean-Luc. *Identity*. Trans. F. Raffoul. New York: Fordham UP, 2015.

Ngugi, Wa Thiong'o. *Decolonizing the Mind: The Politics of Language in African Literature*. Portsmouth, NH: Heinemann, 2011.

Nocerino, Kathryn. *Death of the Plankton Bar & Grill*. St. Paul, MN: New Rivers P, 1987.

———. *Candles in the Daytime*. West Orange, NJ: The Warthog P, 1985.

———. *Wax Lips*. St. Paul, MN: New Rivers P, 1980.

Norman, Charles, ed. *Poets on Poetry*. New York: Free Press, 1962.

Novak, Michael. *The Rise of the Unmeltable Ethnics*. New York: Macmillan, 1973.

O'Grady, Paul. *Relativism*. Montreal: McGill-Queen's UP, 2002.

"Bibliography"

Ohmae, Kenichi. *The Borderless World. Power and Strategy in the Interlinked Economy*. New York: Harper, 1990.

Orsi, Robert A. *The Madonna of 115h Street. Faith and Community in Italian Harlem, 1880-1950*. New Haven: Yale University Press, 1985.

Ottanelli, Frazer, co-ed. *Italian Workers of the World*, see Gabaccia 2005.

Packard, Vance. *A Nation of Strangers*. New York: Pocket Books, 1974 [1972].

Padget, Ron and David Shapiro, eds. *An Anthology of New York Poets*. New York:Vintage, 1962.

Pakenham, Thomas. *The Scramble for Africa 1876-1912*. New York: Random House, 1991.

Pankurst. E. Sylvia. *Ex-Italian Somaliland*, New York: Greenwood P, 1969 [1951].

Park, Robert. *Race and Culture*. Glencoe (IL): Free Press, 1950.

Pasolini, Pier Paolo. *Poesie*. Milano: Garzanti, 1968.

———. *Scritti corsari*. Milano: Garzanti, 1975.

Pastor, Beatriz. "Silence and Writing: The History of the Conquest." In Jara & Spadaccini, 121-63.

Patea, Viorica and Maria Eugenia Diaz, eds. *Critical Essays on the Myth of the American Adam.* Salamanca: Ediciones Universidad, 2001.

Peirce, Charles S. *Philosophical Writings of Peirce*, New York: Dover, 1955.

Pelc, Jerzy. "Some Methodological Problems in Literary History." *New Literary History* VII.1 (Autumn 1975): 89-96.

Perelman, Chaïm and Lucie Olbrechts-Tyteca. *The New Rhetoric. A Treatise on Argumentation*. Trans. J. Wilkinson & P. Weaver. Notre Dame: Notre Dame UP, 1976 [1958].

Periconi, James. *Strangers in a Strange Land. A Catalogue of an Exhibition on the History of Italian-language American Imprints (1830-1945)*. New York: The Grolier Club, 2012.

Pfaff, William. *The Wrath of Nations. Civilization and the Furies of Nationalism*. New York: Simon & Schuster, 1993.

Pilger, John. *The New Rulers of the World*. London: Verso, 2002.

Pivato, Joseph, ed. *Contrasts. Comparative Essays on Italian-Canadian Writing*. Montreal: Guernica, 1991.

Porcari, Serafino. "Italian American Fiction: A Selected Bibliography: 1950-1993." *Italian Americana*.

Portes, Alejandro, and Rubén G. Rumbaut, *Immigrant America: A Portrait*. Berkeley: U of California P, 1996.
Potolski, Matthew. "Decadence, Nationalism, and the Logic of Canon Formation." *Modern Languages Quarterly* 67.2 (Jun. 2006): 213-244.
Pratt, Mary Louise. "Arts of the Contact Zone." *Profession 91* Vol. IV. New York: MLA, 1991.
Preve, Costanzo. *Ideologia Italiana. Saggio sulla storia delle idee marxiste in Italia*. Milano: Vangelisti, 1993.
Pries, Ludger, ed. *Migration and Transnational Social Spaces*. Aldershot: Ashgate, 1999.
Prigogine, Ilya. *The End of Certainty. Time, Chaos, and the New Laws of Nature*. New York: The Free Press, 1996.
Prigogine, Ilya and Isabelle Stengers. *Order Out of Chaos*. New York: Bantam, 1984.
Procacci, Giuliano. *Storia degli italiani*. 2 vols. Bari: Laterza, 1976.
Pugliese, Stanislao, ed. *Frank Sinatra: History, Identity, and Italian American Culture*. New York: St. Martin's P, 2004.
Pula, James S. "American Immigration Policy and the Dillingham Commission." *Polish American Studies* 37.1 (Spring 1980):5-31.
Quine, Willard V.O. *Ontological Relativity and Other Essays*. New York: Columbia UP, 1969.
Rabasa, José. "Dialogue as Conquest: Mapping Spaces for Counter-Discourse." In JanMohamed & Lloyd, 187-215.
Radhakrishnan, R. "Ethnic Identity and Post-Structuralist Difference." In JanMohamed & Lloyd, 1990: 50-71.
Ranger, Terence, *The Invention of Tradition*. See Hobsbawn.
Ravenstein, E.G. "The Laws of Migration," *Journal of the Statistical Society of London*, Vol. 48, No. 2 (Jun., 1885), 167-235
Reed, Ishmael. "America: The Multicultural Society." *VIA. Voices in Italian Americana* 5.1 (1994): 3-6.
Reich, Steven, ed. *The Great Black Migration: A Historical Encyclopedia of the American Mosaic*. Santa Barbara: ABC/CLIO/Greenwood, 2014.
Reimers, David M. *Still the Golden Door. The Third World Comes to America*. New York: Columbia UP, 1985.
Renan, Ernest. "What is a Nation?" In Bhabha, 1990:8-22.
Ricoeur, Paul. *Oneself as Another*. Trans. K. Blamey. Chicago: U Chicago P, 1992.

"Bibliography"

———. *La Metaphore vive*. Paris: Seuil, 1975.
Riis, Jacob A. *How the Other Half Lives. Studies Among the Tenements of New York*. New York: Dover Publications, 1970.
Robinson, T.M., ed. *Contrasting Arguments: an edition of the 'Dissoi logoi'*. New York: Arno P, 1979.
Rodriguez, Richard. "Mixed Blood. Columbus' legacy: A world made mestizo." *Harper's Magazine* (Nov. 1991):47-56.
Romanelli, Raffaele. *L'Italia liberale (1861-1900)*. Bologna: Il Mulino, 1979.
Romeyn, Esther. "Performing High, Performing Low: Enrico Caruso and Eduardo Migliaccio, *DIFFERENTIA*, Vol. 6-7 (1994): 165-175.
Romano, Rose. *Vendetta*. San Francisco: malafemmina press, 1990.
Romano, Sergio. *Storia d'Italia dal Risorgimento ai nostri giorni*. Milano: Mondadori, 1978.
Romeo, Rosario. *Dal Piemonte sabaudo all'Italia liberale*. Bari: Laterza, 1974.
Rorty, Richard. *Philosophy and the Mirror of Nature*. Princeton: Princeton UP, 1978.
Rosaldo, Renato. *Culture and Truth*. Boston: Beacon P, 1989.
Rosenau, Pauline M. *Post-Modernism and the Social Sciences*. Princeton: Princeton UP, 1992.
Rosoli, Gianfausto. "The Global Picture of the Italian Diaspora to the Americas." In Tomasi, Gastaldo, and Row, eds., 1994:305-321.
———. *Un secolo di emigrazione italiana 1876-1976*. Roma: Centro Studi Emigrazione, 1978.
Rossi, Pietro. "Occidente e società extra-europee in K. Marx e M. Weber." *Rivista di Filosofia* LXXIX.1 (Apr. 1988): 59-95.
Roy, Arundhati. *Power Politics*. Cambridge (MA): South End Press, 2001.
Roth, Paul A. *Meaning and Method in the Social Sciences*. Ithaca: Cornell UP, 1987
Rumbaut, Ruben. "The Crucible Within: Ethnic Identity, Self-esteem, and Segmented Assimilation Among Children of Immigrants." *International Migration Review* 28.4 (1994): 748-94.
Russo, John Paul. *The Future Without a Past: The Humanities in a Technological Age*. St. Louis: U of Missouri P, 2005.
———. "From Italophilia to Italophobia: Representations of Italian Americans in the Early Gilded Age." *DIFFERENTIA* 6.7 (Spring/Autumn 1994): 45-76.

———. "The Poetics of Gilbert Sorrentino." Rivista di Studi Anglo-Americani, 3 (1984-5): 281-303.
Russo, John Paul and Robert Casillo. *The Italian in Modernity*. Toronto: U Toronto P, 2011.
Said, Edward. "Reflections on Exile." In Hirschberg, 422-27.
———. *Orientalism*. New York: Columbia UP, 1980.
———. *The World, The Text, The Critic*. Cambridge: Harvard UP, 1983.
Salmon, Christian. *Storytelling. La machine à fabriquer des histoires et à former les esprits*. Paris: Éditions La Découverte, 2007.
Salvadori, Massimo. *La parabola del comunismo*. Bari: Laterza, 1995.
———. *Storia d'Italia e crisi di regime*. Bologna: Il Mulino, 1994.
Sánchez, Marta Ester. "Setting the Context: Gender, Ethnicity, and Silence in Contemporary Chicana Poetry." In *Contemporary Chicana Poetry. A Critical Approach to an Emerging Literature*. Los Angeles: U of California P, 1986.
Sansalone, Christine. "Issues of Adaptation and Identity in The Lives of Italian-Canadians." In *Italian Canadiana*, Vol. XXIII, 2009:59-67.
Sartre, Jean-Paul. *What is Literature?* Trans. H. Barnes, New York: Colophon, 1972.
Sassen, Saskia. "Why Migration?" *NACLA* XXVI.1 (July 1992): 14-47.
Sautman, Francesca. "Women of the Shadows: Italian American Women, Ethnicity and Racism in American Cinema," in *DIFFERENTIA*, Vol. 6/7 (Spring/Autumn 1994): 219-46.
Showalter, Elaine. *A Literature of Their Own*. Princeton: Princeton UP, 1977.
Schumpeter, Joseph. *Capitalism, Socialism and Democracy*. London: Routledge, 2006.
Scelsa, Joseph, Salvatore La Gumina and Lydio Tomasi, eds., *Italian Americans in Transition*. New York: The American Italian Historical Association, 1990.
Sciorra, Joseph. *Built with Faith: Italian American Imagination and Catholic Material Culture in New York City*. Knoxville, TN: U Tennessee P, 2015.
Serra, Ilaria. *The Imagined Immigrant*. Madison, NJ: Fairleigh Dickinson UP, 2009.
———. *The Value of Worthless Lives*. New York: Fordham UP, 2007.

"Bibliography"

Serres, Michel. *Hermes. Literature, Science, Philosophy*. Baltimore: The Johns Hopkins UP, 1982.
Signorelli-Pappas, Rita. "After immigration." *Women's Review of Books*, July, 1994.
Sinopoli, Franca. "Dalla comparazione intraculturale alla comparazione interculturale." *Manuale storico di letteratura comparata*. Ed. Armando Gnisci and Franca Sinipoli. Roma: Meltemi, 1997: 14-60.
Smith, Anthony D. *Theories of Nationalism*. New York: Holmes & Meier, 1983.
Smith, Susan H. and Melanie Dawson, eds. *The American 1890s. A Cultural Reader*. Durham: Duke UP, 2000.
Sollors, Werner. *Beyond Ethnicity*. New York: Oxford UP, 1986.
Spadolini, Giovanni. *L'opposizione cattolica. Da Porta Pia al '98*. Milano: Mondadori, 1976.
Spalek, John M. and Robert Bell, eds. *Exile: The Writer's Experience*. U North Carolina P, 1982.
Spitzer, Leo. *Critica stilistica e semantica storica*. Bari: Laterza, 1966.
Spivak, Gayatri. "Can the Subaltern Speak," in Nelson, C. and L. Grossberg, eds. *Marxism and the Interpretation of Culture*. Basingstoke: Macmillan Education, 1988:271-313.
Spurr, David. *The Rhetoric of Empire. Colonial Discourse in Journalism, Travel Writing, and Imperial Administration*. Durham: Duke UP, 1993.
Starobinski, Jean. "The Meaning of Literary History." *New Literary History* VII.1 (Autumn 1975):83-88.
_____. *L'oeil vivant II. La relation critique*. Paris: Gallimard, 1970.
Steinberg, Stephen. *The Ethnic Myth. Race, Ethnicity, and Class in America*. Boston: Beacon Press, 1981.
Stepan, Nancy L. "Race and Gender: The Role of Analogy in Science." In Goldberg, 38-58
Stevens, Wallace. "Two or Three Ideas" Norman, 1962 [1951]. 363-375.
Tabori, Paul. *The Anatomy of Exile; A semantic and historical study*. London: Harrap, 1972.
Talese, Gay. "Where Are the Italian American Novelists?" *The New York Times* Book Review, 14 March, 1993.
Tambiah, Stanley H. "Ethnic Conflict in the World Today." *American Ethnologist* 16.2 (1989): 335-50.

Tamburri, Anthony J. *Re-Reading Italian Americana. Specificities and Generalities in Literature and Criticism*. Madison NJ: Fairleigh Dickinson UP, 2014.

_____. *Re-Viewing Italian Americana. Generalities and Specificities on Cinema*. New York: Bordighera P, 2011.

_____. *A Semiotic of Ethnicity. In recognition of the Italian/American Writer*. Albany, NY: SUNY P, 1998.

_____. *To Hyphenate or Not to Hyphenate*. Montréal: Guernica, 1990.

Tamburri, Anthony Julian, Paolo Giordano and Fred Gardaphé, , eds. *From The Margin. Writings in Italian Americana*. W. Lafayette, IN: Purdue UP, 1991.

Tate, Allen. "Tension in Poetry." Norman, 1962 [1938]. 349-362.

Taviani, Paolo E. *Christopher Columbus*. Trans. by L.F. Farina. Rome: Italian Geographical Society, 2000. 3 vols.

Teti, Vito. *La razza maledetta: origini del pregiudizio antimeridionale*. Roma: manifesto libri, 1993.

_____. *Maledetto sud*. Torino: Einaudi, 2013.

Tirabassi, Maddalena. "Making Space for Domesticity. Household Goods in Working-Class Italian American Homes, 1900–1940." In Cinotto, 2014.

Testi, Arnaldo. "L'immagine degli Stati Uniti nella stampa Socialista italiana (1886-1914)." *Nordamericana*, Vol. 1. Venezia: Marsilio (1976): 313-347.

Todorov, Tzvetan. *The Conquest of America*. Trans. R. Howard. New York: Harper & Row, 1982.

Tomasi, Lydio F., Gastaldo, Piero, & Row, Thomas, eds. *The Columbus People*. New York: Center for Migration Studies, 1994.

Tomasi, Lydio, ed. *Italian Americans. New Perspectives in Italian Immigration and Ethnicity*. New York: Center for Migration Studies, 1985.

_____. *The Italian in America: The Progressive View, 1891-1914*. New York: Center for Migration Studies, 1978.

Tomasi, Silvano. "Militantism and Italian-American Unity" in *Power and Class. The Italian American Experience Today*. New York: Center for Migration Studies, 1971, 20-28.

Trager, James, ed. *The New York Chronology* (New York: HarperResource, 2003.

Vacca, Giuseppe. *Vent'anni dopo. La sinistra fra mutamenti e revisioni.* Torino: Einaudi, 1997.
Valesio, Paolo. "I fuochi della tribù." *Poesaggio. Poeti italiani d'America.* P. Carravetta and P. Valesio, eds. Treviso: Pagus, 1994: 255-290.
_____. "The Writer Between Two Worlds." *DIFFERENTIA* 3/4 (Spring/Autumn 1989): 259-276.
Vecoli, Rudolph J. *A Century of European Migrations, 1830-1930.* Urbana: U of Illinois P, 1991.
_____. "The Search for an Italian American Identity. Continuity and Change." In Tomasi 1985: 88-112.
_____. "The Italian Immigrants in the United States' Labor Movement from 1880 to 1920." In Bruno Bezza, ed. *Gli italiani fuori d'Italia* 258-306.
Velikonja, Joseph. "Family and Community: The Periodical Press and Italian Communities," in *The Family and Community Life of Italian American.* New York: American Italian Historical Association, 1983: 47-60.
Vellon, Peter. *A Great Crime Against Our Race.* New York: New York UP, 2014.
Verdicchio, Pasquale. *Bound by Distance. Rethinking Nationalism through the Italian Diaspora.* Madison: Fairleigh Dickinson UP, 1997.
_____. *The Posthumous Poet. A Suite for Pier Paolo Pasolini.* Los Angeles: Jawbone P, 1993.
_____. *Isthmus.* Los Angeles: Littoral Press, 1991.
_____. *Nomadic Trajectory.* Montréal: Guernica, 1990.
Vico, Giambattista. *New Science.* Trans. D. Marsch. New York: Penguin, 1999.
_____. *On the Study Methods of our Time.* Trans. E. Gianturco. London: Cornell UP, 1990.
Villari, Pasquale. *Le lettere meridionali e altri scritti sulla questione sociale in Italia.* Napoli: Guida, 1979.
Villari, Rosario, ed. *Il Sud nella Storia d'Italia. Antologia della questione meridionale.* 2 vols. Bari: Laterza, 1975.
Virilio, Paul. *The information bomb.* Trans. C. Turner. New York: Verso, 2000.
Viscusi, Robert. *Ellis Island.* New York: Bordighera, 2012.

"Bibliography"

———. *Buried Caesars and Other Secrets of Italian American Writing*. Albany NY: SUNY P, 2006.
———. *Astoria*. Toronto: Guernica, 2011.
———. "Gli dei: l'allegoria dell'America italiana." MS, 1990.
———. "Narrative and Nothing: The Enterprise of Italian American Writing." *DIFFERENTIA* 3/4 (Spring/Autumn 1994): 77-98.
———. *An Oration upon the Most Recent Death of Christopher Columbus*. W. Lafayette, IN: Bordighera P, 1993.
———. "The Italian Commonwealth." Unpublished MS, read at NYU on 29 May 1992.
———. "La letteratura dell'emigrazione italiana negli Stati Uniti." In Marchand 1991: 125-138.
———. The Englishman in Italy." In *Brown Institute Studies* (NY), N. 12, 1984:1-27.
———. "The Text in the Dust: Writing Italy across America." *Studi Emigrazione/Etùdes Migrations* (Rome) XIX. 65 (Marzo 1982):123-30.
———. "*De Vulgari Eloquentia*: An Approach to the Language of Italian American Fiction." *Yale Italian Studies* 1. 3 (Winter 1981): 21-38.
Viscusi, Robert and Dana Gioia. "Where to find Italian American Literature." *Italian Americana* XII.2 (Summer 1994): 267-277.
Vitiello, Justin. *Confessions of a Joe Rock*. Franklin Lakes (NJ): Lincoln Spring Press, 1994.
———. *Subway Home*. Franklin Lakes (NJ): Lincoln Springs Press, 1992.
Waldenfels, Bernhard. *Topologie de l'étranger*. Trans. F. Gregorio et al. Paris: Van Dieren Ēditeur, 2009.
Wallerstein, Immanuel. *The Modern World-System*. 2 vols. New York: Academic P, 1974-82.
———. *Utopistics, Or, Historical Choices for the Twenty-first Century*. New York: The New Press, 1998.
Wecter, Dixon. *The Hero in America. A Chronicle of Hero-Worship*. Ann Arbor: U Michigan P, 1942.
Weil, Simone. *The Needs for Roots*. London: Routledge, 1995 [1949].
White Hayden. *The Content of the Form. Narrative Discourse and Historical Representation*. Baltimore: Johns Hopkins UP, 1990.
———. *Metahistory. The Historical Imagination in Nineteenth-Century Europe*. Baltimore: Johns Hopkins UP, 1975.

"Bibliography"

Wilson, Woodrow. *History of the American People*. 5 vols. New York: Harper & brothers Publishers, 1903.
Wirbe, Robert H. *The Search for Order 1977-1920*. New York: Hill and Wang, 1967.
Wolf, Eric. *Europe and the People Without History*. Berkeley: U California P, 1982.
Wulf, Andrea. *The Invention of Nature. Alexander von Humboldt's New World*. New York: Knopf, 2015.
Zangwill, Israel. *The Melting-Pot*. Charleston: Bibliobazaar, 2009.
Zeidel, Robert. *Immigrants, progressives, and exclusion politics: the Dillingham Commission, 1900-1927*. De Kalb IL: Northern Illinois UP, 2004.
Zilioli, Ugo. *Protagoras and the Challenge of Relativism*. Burlington, VT: Ashgate, 2007.
Zinn, Howard. *A People's History of the United States*. New York: HarperCollins, 2003.
Zolberg. Aristide R. *A Nation by Design. Immigration Policy in the Fashioning of America*. New York: Russell Sage Foundation, 2006.

INDEX

Aaron, Daniel, 102
Abbot, Grace, 134
Abrams, Richard M., 116, 120
Abu-Lughod, Janet, 84
Agamben, Giorgio, 207
Ahearn, Carol B., 94, 97, 179, 207, 209
Ahmed, Ali Jimale, 51, 52, 53
Aiello-Gerber, Theresa, 80
Alarcón, Norma., 6
Alba, Richard, 89, 225
Aleandri, Emelise, 112
Anderson, Benedict, 30, 51, 52, 54, 72, 84, 100, 226
Anzaldúa, Gloria 193
Appadurai, Arjun, 86, 116
Appiah, Kwane, 230
Aristotle, 146, 223
Arlacchi, Pino, 76
Asor Rosa, Alberto, 42, 68
Astor, John Jacob, 212
Atwood, Margaret, 94

Backzo, Bronislaw, 41
Bade, Klaus, 5, 6, 10, 22, 26
Badie, Bertrand, 3
Baily, Samuel, 75
Balibar, Etienne, 214
Banfield, Edward, 130
Barolini, Helen, 82, 87, 95, 96, 137, 177, 178, 182, 190, 209

Barr, M.S., 52
Bart, Anna, 147
Barton, Josef, 98
Barzini, Luigi, 42
Basile Green, Rose, 96, 148
Baudrillard, Jean, 86, 106, 225
Bayart, Jean-François, 225
Bell, Daniel, 52
Beltràn, Gonzalo Aguirre, 7
Ben-Ghiat, Ruth, 66
Bencivenna, Marcella, 120, 127
Benhabib, Seyla, 25
Berlusconi, Silvio, 62
Bernal, Martin, 53
Bernand, Carmen, 230
Bertellini, Giorgio, 133
Bezza, Bruno, 110, 247
Bhabha, Homi K., 7, 31, 86, 91, 95, 98, 230
Biagi, Enzo, 41
Black Elk, 117
Blake, William, 238
Boas, Franz, 133
Boase, Paul H., 120
Bobbio Norberto, 41, 69
Bodei, Remo, 41
Bodnar, John, 115, 121
Boelhower, William, 207, 208
Bollati, Giulio, 41, 62
Bona, Mary Jo, 87, 97, 137, 180, 184, 209

"Index"

Boorstin, Daniel, 226
Braudel, Fernand, 52, 71
Brettell, Caroline, 31, 69
Brioni, Simone, 70
Brown, Federal Judge, 119
Bruner, Edward M., 6
Bryant, Dorothy, 178
Bucchioni, Eugene, 126
Butler, Judith, 225

Cacciari, Massimo, 41
Cafagna, Luciano, 72
Calefato, Patrizia, 42
Callaro, Marco, 111
Camaiti Hostert, Anna, 95
Candeloro, Giorgio, 45
Cannistraro, Philip, 44, 110, 120, 127
Capello, Phyllis, 148, 177
Caponegro, Mary, 209
Capotorto, Rosette, 80
Capra, Frank, 135
Carravetta, Peter, 3, 25, 44, 54, 59, 72, 80, 85, 86, 89, 105, 150, 154, 161, 207, 210, 213
Carrera, Alessandro, 96
Caruso, Enrico, 172, 173, 174
Casillo, Robert, 94
Castles, Stephen, 7, 46, 75, 105
Castronovo, Valerio, 45, 63, 64, 67
Cavaioli, Frank J., 207, 218
Cavalli-Sforza, Luca, 23, 26
Cavallo, Diane, 178
Cavour, Count Camillo, 57
Cecchetti, Giocanni, 81
Challiand, Gérard, 14

Charters, Ann, 155
Ciampelli, Bernardino, 137
Ciardi, John, 81, 87, 137, 209
Cicero, Marcus Tullius, 223
Cinel, Dino, 76
Ciresi, Rita, 178
Ciuffoletti, Zeffiro, 60, 61, 63
Clifford, James, 105, 218
Cló, Clarissa, 70
Cohen, Robin, 14, 110
Colajanni, Nicola, 64
Colletti, Lucio, 41
Colombo, Furio, 93,
Columbus, Christopher, 43, 46, 48, 50, 72, 96, 174, 182, 186, 195-202, 205
Comberati, Daniele, 66
Contini, Gianfranco, 99
Cordasco, Francesco, 59, 76, 126
Cordiferro, Riccardo, 137
Corso, Gregory, 87, 102, 149
Cortes, Carlos, 95, 133
Cosco, James P., 123
Crevencour, M.G. Jean de [J. H. St. John], 237
Crialese, Ermanno, 108, 109
Crispi, Francesco, 62, 63, 64, 65
Cuomo, Mario, 168, 174
Curtius, Ernst R., 223

D'Agostino, Peter, 129
D'Alfonso, Antonio, 206, 207, 208, 209
da Vinci, Leonardo, 174
Daniels, Roger, 117, 121
Dante, Alighieri, 43, 57, 72, 69, 171, 180, 213

272

"Index"

Davis, Kingsley, 23
Dawson, Melanie, 120
De Felice, Renzo, 45
De Lillo, Don, 81, 90, 94, 208
De Palchi, Alfredo, 81
De Renziz, Francesco, 63
De Rosa, Tina, 178
De Sanctis, Francesco, 68, 85
De Sena, Judith 44
de Vries, Rachel Guido, 178
Degl'Innocenti, Maurizio, 48, 60, 61, 63
Del Boca, Angelo, 62, 63, 65
Del Negro, Giovanna, 178, 184
Deleuze, Gilles, 51, 69, 106, 193, 207
Delia Lanza, Carmela, 147
Depretis, Agostino, 62
Di Biagi, Flaminio, 207
Di Cicco, Pier Giorgio, 150
Di Donato, Pietro, 87, 95, 137, 215
Di Prima, Diane, 87, 102, 143, 146, 147, 149, 153, 154, 155, 177, 178
Dieckhoff, Alain, 53
Dillingham, William P., 128
Dinwiddie, Emily Wayland, 123
Dore, Grazia, 60, 63
Duggan, Christopher, 64
Durante, Francesco, 112, 137

Ehrmann, Herbert, 127
Enzensberger, Hans Magnus, 131

Fama, Maria, 178

Fanon, Frantz, 91
Fante, John, 87, 94, 137, 215
Farrow, Mia, 173
Feldman, Gregory, 24
Ferlinghetti, Lawrence, 81, 87, 102, 146, 147, 195
Fernández, Roberta, 154, 193
Ferrarelli, Rita, 147
Fiore, Teresa, 70
Fischer, Michael, M.J., 218
Foerster, Robert F., 55, 66, 113
Fontanella, Luigi, 44, 81
Forgacs, David, 86
Foscolo, Ugo, 57, 213
Foucault, Michel, 8, 51, 52, 98, 106, 228
Francesconi, Mario, 111
Frost, Robert, 166
Fukuyama, Francis, 55

Gabaccia, Donna R., 66, 76, 110, 112, 120, 134
Gadamer, Hans-Georg, 99, 174
Galasso, Giuseppe, 41
Galilei, Galileo, 115
Galli Della Loggia, Ernesto, 41
Gambino, Richard, 95, 96, 126, 206, 209, 215
Gardaphé, Fred, 87, 90, 95, 101, 137, 178, 195, 206, 207, 208
Garibaldi, Giuseppe, 57, 174, 213
Garraty, John A., 120,
Garrison, William Lloyd, 118
Gastaldo, Piero, 44, 76, 133
Gates, Jr., Henry Louis, 72, 95, 178

"Index"

Geertz, Clifford, 26, 31, 238
Gellner, Ernest, 6
Gerstle, Gary, 136
Gibson, Mary, 129
Giddens, Anthony, 105
Gilbert, Sandra, 98, 101, 147, 150
Gilroy, Paul, 225
Ginsberg, Allen, 103, 195, 205
Gioberti, Vincenzo, 56
Gioia, Dana, 81, 89, 94, 144, 153, 166
Giordano, Paolo A., 87, 101
Gioseffi, Daniela, 80, 88, 147, 177, 178
Giovannitti, Arturo, 137
Gjerde, Jon, 129
Glissant, Eduard, 230
Gnisci, Armando, 7, 42, 70, 86, 230
Goldberg, David, 84, 100
Goodwyn, Lawrence, 117
Gramsci, Antonio, 62, 67, 68, 72, 92, 104, 112, 213, 214, 228
Grunwald, Henry, 32
Gruzinski, Serge, 6, 7, 230
Guattari, Felix, 69, 193
Gugelberger, George M., 178
Guglielmo, Jennifer, 131
Guglielmo, Thomas, 131
Guida, George, 80

Habermas, Jürgen, 72
Hall, Prescott Farnsworth, 121, 122
Hall, Stephan, 75
Hall, Stuart, 22, 86
Haller, Hermann, 113

Handlin, Oscar, 129, 131, 133, 134
Harjo, Joy, 159
Heidegger, Martin, 146
Heller, Agnes, 68
Hendin, Josephine G., 95
Hess, Robert L., 63
Hill Maher, Kristen, 29
Hinkelammert, Franz, 8
Hirschberg, Stuart, 84, 214
Hobsbawm, Eric, 53, 72, 130
Hodge, John L., 69, 99, 214
Hollifield, James, 31, 69
Homer, 146
Hull Hoffer, Williamjames, 117

Iacocca, Lee, 174
Ilari, Virgilio, 41
Jameson, Frederic, 72, 223
JanMohamed, Abdul, 84
Jara, René, 95
Jones, LeRoi, 103
Joxe, Alain, 7

Kennedy, John F., 47
Keridis, Dimitri, 10, 21
Kerouac, Jack, 103
Khomeini, Ruhollah, 17
King, Desmond, 127, 128, 129, 131, 134
King, Rusell, 5, 26
Klusmeyer, Douglas, 6
Krase, Jerome, 44, 213
Kristeva, Julia, 207
Kusow, Abdi, 52
Kyriakopoulos, Vangelis, 3

274

"Index"

La Barre, Adele, 80, 178
La Gumina, Salvatore, 97
La Polla, Garibaldi, 137
Labriola, Antonio, 68
LaGumina, Salvatore J., 126
Lahav, Gallya, 22
Lanza, Mario, 174
Lapolla, Garibaldi, 95
Lavie, Smadar, 6
Lazarus, Emma, 118
Lears, Jackson, 116
Lecomte, Mia, 70
Lenin, Vladimir, 53
Lentricchia, Frank, 90, 209
Leopardi, Giacomo, 57
Levi, Carlo, 72, 83
Linos, Katerina, 21
Livy, 230
Llyod, David, 84
Lombardi-Diop, Cristina, 70
Lombroso, Cesare, 129
Lualdi, Ercole, 60
Luisi, Carmine, 81
Luperini, Romano, 72
Lyotard, Jean-François, 8, 51, 105, 106

Machiavelli, Niccoló, 57, 72
Mack Smith, Denis, 45, 58, 63
Mangano, Antonio, 111
Mangione, Jerre, 43, 44, 95, 126, 127, 137, 188, 209, 219
Marcus, George, 105, 106, 218
Marcus, James, 105
Markowitz, Leonard, 52,
Marramao, Giacomo, 41
Martucci, Roberto, 53

Marx, Karl, 115, 223
Masini, Donna, 178
Maso, Carol, 209
Massey, Douglas S., 34
Maviglia, Joseph, 150
Mazzini, Giuseppe, 56, 213
Mazziotti Gillan, Jennifer, 179
Mazziotti Gillan, Maria, 80, 81, 88, 98, 147, 151, 177-193
McNeill, William H., 23, 24, 25, 26, 238
Mendras, Henri, 25
Menza, Claudia, 80, 152, 156-161, 178
Messina, Anthony, 22
Metternich, Klemens von, 232
Meyer, Gerald, 110, 120, 127
Meyer, Nicholas, 126
Michelangelo, 72
Micone, Marco, 96
Mignolo, Walter, 98, 230
Milazzo, Richard, 147
Miller, Mark J., 7, 46, 75, 105
Mirabelli, Eugene, 209
Montanelli, Indro, 45
Moore, Michael, 29
Moquin, Wayne, 111, 126
Moretti, Enrico, 110
Morreale, Ben, 43, 44, 126, 188,
Marazzi, Martino, 44, 112
Mudimbe, V.Y., 53
Mukherjee, Bharati, 32
Murphy, Peter, 6
Muscio, Giuliana, 95
Mussolini, Benito, 64

Nail, Thomas, 24

"Index"

Nancy, Jean-Luc, 225
Napoleon Bonaparte, 71, 211, 212, 215, 218, 219
Napolitano, Giorgio, 47
Negri, Antonio, 42
Niceforo, Alfredo, 129
Nietzsche, Friedrich, 8, 51, 146, 180, 205
Nobile, Umberto, 43
Nocerino, Kathryn, 80, 161-166, 178

O'Brien, Flann, 205
O'Hara, Frank, 103
Ohmae, Kenichi, 55
Orsi, Robert A., 111
Ottanelli, Fraser M., 120

Packard, Vance, 31
Paolucci, Ann, 178
Parati, Graziella, 70, 86
Parini, Jay, 98, 151
Pasolini, Pier Paolo, 68, 86, 241
Patriarca, Gianna, 178
Paulicelli, Eugenia, 81
Perelman, Chaïm, 223, 238,
Periconi, James, 90, 123
Pescarella, Cesare, 50
Petrarch, Francis, 57
Pezzarossa, Fulvio, 70
Pfaff, William, 54, 55
Pilger, John, 30
Pinder, David, 5
Pirandello, Luigi, 97
Pirie, Sophia H., 6
Pivato, Joseph, 94, 96, 214, 248
Pöggeler, Otto, 223

Polney, Luciana, 80
Porcari, Serafino, 178
Portes, Alejandro, 10, 20, 21, 34
Powell, Enoch, 5
Preve, Costanzo, 70
Pries, Ludger, 6,
Prigogine, Ilya, 106
Procacci, Giuliano, 45
Protagoras, 223
Puccini, Giacomo, 169
Puzo, Mario, 94, 209

Quintilian, 223

Rabasa, José, 98
Radhakrishnan, R., 79, 86, 98, 214
Rageau, Jean-Pierre, 14
Ranger, Terence, 53
Raptosch, Diane, 101
Ravenstein, E.g., 133
Reagan, Ronald, 196
Reich, Steven, 117
Reimers, David M., 10, 18
Rella, Franco, 207
Renan, Ernst, 55, 226
Repetto, Vittoria, 80, 88, 148, 178
Ricci, Nino, 87
Ricoeur, Paul, 51, 223
Riis, Jacob, 123, 124, 125, 126
Risi, Carmine, 80
Rodriguez, Richard, 179
Romanelli, Raffaele, 45, 58, 59, 61, 63
Romano, Rose, 90, 148, 178
Romano, Sergio, 59
Romeo, Caterina, 70

"Index"

Romeo, Caterina, 70
Romeo, Rosario, 45, 58
Romeyn, Esther, 112
Roosevelt, Theodore, 128
Rosenau, Pauline M., 105
Rossi, Pietro, 98
Row, Thomas, 44, 76
Roy, Arundhati, 30
Rumbaut, Rubén G., 10, 20, 21, 34
Russo, John Paul, 90, 94, 101

Sacco, Nicola, 127
Saggar, John, 75
Said, Edward, 16, 17, 18, 19, 51, 52, 86, 223
Salerno, Salvatore, 131
Salvadori, Massimo, 41, 45, 70
Sánchez, Marta E., 95, 154
Sartre, John-Paul, 31, 223
Sassen, Saskia, 29
Saussure, Ferdinand de, 212
Sautman, Francesca, 95
Scalabrini, Giovanni Battista, 65
Scalapino, Leslie, 147
Scelsa, Joseph, 97
Schumpeter, Joseph, 53
Sciorra, Joseph, 95
Scorsese, Martin, 209
Seferis, George, 17
Serra, Ilaria, 44, 123, 137
Serres, Michel, 8
Severino, Emanuele, 41
Shils, Edward, 105
Signorelli-Pappas, Rita, 184
Silone, Ignazio, 83
Sinatra, Frank, 168, 172, 173

Sinopoli, Franca, 70, 86
Smith, Anthony D., 6, 54
Smith, Susan H., 120
Sollors, Werner, 94, 97, 102, 103, 104, 153, 216, 225
Sonnino, Sydney, 64,
Sorrentino, Gilbert, 81, 87, 90, 94, 101, 102, 146, 147, 208
Spadaccini, Nicholas, 95
Spagnoletti, Giovanni, 95
Speranza, Gino, 130, 136
Spitzer, Leo, 99
Spivak, Gayatri, 111
Starobinski, Jean, 79, 223
Stefanile, Felix, 98, 147, 150
Steinberg, Stephen, 89, 97, 98
Sturino, Frank, 76
Swedenburg, Ted, 6

Talese, Gay, 80, 143, 206, 209, 215
Tambiah, Stanley J., 218
Tamburri, Anthony J., 83, 87, 95, 101, 207, 208, 233
Tarchetti, Emilio, 79, 105
Tate, Allen, 154
Teti, Vito, 130
Tocqueville, Alexis de, 237
Todorov, Tzvetan, 98
Tomasi, Lydio F., 44, 75, 76, 97, 98, 111, 123, 126, 133, 188, 207
Tomasi, Mari, 178
Tomasi, Sylvano, 123
Trager, James, 123
Turati, Filippo, 68
Turner, Fredrick, 94

"Index"

Turner, Lana, 173
Tusiani, Joseph, 81

Vacca, Giuseppe, 41, 69
Valentino, Rudolph, 168,
Valerio, Anthony, 80, 167-175
Valesio, Paolo, 81
Van Doren, Charles, 111, 126
Vangelisti, Paul, 147
Vanzetti, Bartolomeo, 127
Vattimo, Gianni, 209
Veca, Salvatore, 41
Vecoli, Rudolph J., 75, 89, 96, 110, 134
Velikonja, Joseph, 123
Vellon, Peter G., 123, 131, 137
Verdi, Giuseppe, 72
Verdicchio, Pasquale, 149
Verrazzano, Giovanni da, *ix*
Vespucci, Amerigo, 43
Veto, Janine, 147
Vico, Giambattista, 146, 223, 231
Villari, Pasquale, 61
Virgilio, Jacopo, 60, 62
Viscusi, Robert, 80, 81, 83, 84, 95, 96, 143, 148, 187, 195-220

Vitiello, Justin, 149

Walken, Christopher, 126
Wallerstein, Immanuel, 5, 71, 84, 225
Ware, James E., 122
Weil, Simone, 27
Westmoreland, General William, 170
White, Hayden, 51, 52
Whitman, Walt, 195, 218
Williams, Raymond, 223
Wilson, Woodrow, 122, 133
Wolf, Eric, 20, 52, 84
Wulf, Andrea, 53

Zanelli, Francesco, 61
Zangwill, Israel, 135
Zeidel, Robert, 129
Zevin, Jack, 10
Zinn, Howard, 226
Zolberg, Aristide R., 120, 133, 135
Zucconi, Vittorio, 93

www.ingramcontent.com/pod-product-compliance
Lightning Source LLC
Chambersburg PA
CBHW031430160426
43195CB00010BB/682